PRAISE FOR *Orthodox Afterlife*

"In these days of moral relativism when it is assumed that all religions are basically the same and that everyone goes to a happy place when they die, it is salutary to be reminded of the Church's abiding Tradition regarding judgment and the afterlife. John Habib has provided us with just such a reminder, combining Scriptural citations with stories of the saints and selections from their extant writings. The book thus offers a much needed antidote to the lethal error that there is nothing to fear after death for anyone, and that (as it were) 'all dogs go to heaven.' It is a treasure trove of our Tradition."

—Fr. Lawrence Farley
Archpriest, St. Herman of Alaska Orthodox Mission (OCA),
Langley, B.C., Canada; author of several Orthodox titles,
including the *Orthodox Bible Study Companion* series

"Recent years have seen a great deal of speculation about the afterlife, much of it unreliable and not in conformity with the tradition of the ancient Christian Church. John Habib brings us personal accounts of afterlife experiences of Orthodox Christians along with a comprehensible treatment of the Orthodox Church's views on this important but obscure topic. This glimpse into both heaven and hell may surprise and will certainly convict you. Heaven is indeed for real—but not everyone will end up there."

—Katherine Hyde
Editor and author

"Impressive! That's what this book is. It will open your eyes—as it did mine—to a whole new level of understanding of what life after death will be like. This book presents a thorough analysis, based on the actual near death experiences of several individuals and supported by solid Biblical and patristic evidence, of one of the least understood topics in Christianity—the afterlife."

—Fr. Anthony Messeh
Priest, St. Timothy & St. Athanasius Coptic Orthodox Church, Arlington, VA

"In his book *Orthodox Afterlife*, John Habib has done a superb job of illuminating some of the most difficult and mysterious aspects of death and the afterlife. The stories contained within are quite edifying regardless of whether one accepts them to be historical fact or modern-day parables. His treatment of the subject matter is generally thorough and quite faithful to the spirit of the Scriptures and the Church Fathers. John offers us a powerful reminder that we were meant for more than this life."

—Fr. James Guirguis
Priest, St. George Antiochian Orthodox Church, New Hartford, NY;
author, *Ask for the Ancient Paths: Discovering What Church Is Meant to Be*

"John Habib has provided a guide to Orthodox Christian beliefs on the afterlife as viewed especially in the Coptic tradition. It provides biblical grounding, historical treatments, and modern narratives and reflections about the crossing over from this life to the next, whether to light or darkness, depending upon whether one has been by grace ready to receive the guidance of the Holy Spirit. It relates many instances both ancient and modern of Orthodoxy's attestation of the afterlife, including the experiencing of God's Light, and the beauty of Paradise. It will be read by Orthodox believers as a familiar and reassuring teaching for the faithful, and by non-Orthodox as an intriguing and puzzling compendium of hypotheses implausible to some but quite plausible to others."

—Dr. Thomas C. Oden
Former professor of theology and ethics, Drew University; prolific
author; general editor, *Ancient Christian Commentary on Scripture* series

"*Orthodox Afterlife* offers a glimpse—based on various personal accounts—into what happens to us when our spirits leave this physical world and return to God our Creator. John Habib backs up these accounts with references from the Holy Scriptures, sayings from the early Church Fathers, and other historical accounts of saints. Many people wonder what happens after death; this book attempts to answer that question in accordance with various people's near-death experiences and what they each saw. The descriptions of Paradise and Hades are fascinating and should serve as reminders for us all to strive to live holy lives in this world so that we may inherit the kingdom of God, which our Lord is preparing for us."

—Fr. Anastasi St. Antony
Hegumen; steward, St. Antony Monastery, Newberry Springs, CA

"There perhaps is no more important inquiry than that of the afterlife. By its very nature it is elusive: in the words of the Apostle, 'eye has not seen, nor ear heard, nor have entered into the heart of man, the things which God has prepared for those who love Him.' And yet here in this refreshing study we find that a surprising and startling picture emerges: the afterlife or near-death 'experiences' of numerous saintly figures and others are remarkably consistent in their depiction of 'what comes next.' What is more, these experiences are far from speculative—they suggest an underlying and almost overwhelming unity with both Scripture and the Church Fathers. Whether or not one chooses to believe these accounts, what they have to say of the afterlife is in the least fascinating."

—Fr. Daniel Fanous
Priest, St. Peter and St. Paul Coptic Orthodox Church, NSW, Australia; author, *Taught by God* and *The Person of the Christ*; dean and lecturer in theology/New Testament, St. Cyril's Coptic Orthodox Theological College, Sydney, Australia

ORTHODOX AFTERLIFE

2,000 Years of Afterlife Experiences
of Orthodox Christians
and a Biblical and Early Christian View
of Heaven, Hell, and the Hereafter

John Habib

Orthodox Afterlife: 2,000 Years of Afterlife Experiences of Orthodox Christians and a Biblical and Early Christian View of Heaven, Hell, and the Hereafter

Copyright © 2016 by John Habib

All rights reserved.

Designed & Published by:
St. Mary & St. Moses Abbey Press
101 S Vista Dr., Sandia, TX 78383
stmabbeypress.com

All Scripture quotations, unless otherwise indicated, are taken from the New King James Version® Copyright © 1982 by Thomas Nelson, Inc. Used by permission. All rights reserved.

Library of Congress Control Number: 2016911725

10 9 8 7 6 5

ORTHODOX
AFTERLIFE

Contents

Foreword by His Eminence Metropolitan Youssef	15
Preface	17

PART ONE: INTRODUCTION

1. Understanding the Mysteries Herein	23

PART TWO: DEATH AND CROSSING OVER FROM THIS LIFE TO THE NEXT

2. Death	31
3. Crossing Over	57
4. The Terrifying Ordeal	69

PART THREE: THE ABODE OF DARKNESS AND MISERY

5. Hades	101

PART FOUR: THE ABODE OF LIGHT AND JOY

6. Paradise	131
7. The Beauty of Paradise	159
8. Varying Degrees of Reward and Glory	191
9. The Hierarchy of Glory in Paradise (and Heaven)	223
10. Paradise and the Garden of Eden	233

PART FIVE: THE POWER TO DIRECT OUR FATE

11. Second Chance	245

Appendix A: The Life of Father Botros and His Afterlife Story	279
Appendix B: Photos & Images	313
Appendix C: Glossary	321
Endnotes	357
Bibliography	393

Acknowledgements

First and foremost, I must thank God for allowing me the opportunity to complete this work, which is intended for His glory.

I thank my mother for changing my life when she reminded me of my need to prepare for what is to come; and I thank my dad, my sister Maria, and the rest of my family for their continual encouragement. Rafik and Cindy, you are both in many ways the reason my life changed and the initial impetus for this book. Although I have never met you, Samia, thank you for trusting me enough to give me permission to write about your brother, Father Botros, and to include his story. Father Joseph, my beloved friend, thank you for your tremendous efforts and ongoing support. And lastly, but foremost as my spiritual father, a special recognition of gratitude to His Eminence Metropolitan Youssef, to whom I cannot express adequate appreciation and without whom this book would be lacking.

May God bless all of you in this life and, most importantly, in the life to come.

Abbreviations

ANF　　　　　　*The Ante-Nicene Fathers: Translations of the Writings of the Fathers Down to A.D. 325*, Alexander Roberts and James Donaldson, eds. (Buffalo, NY: The Christian Literature Company, 1885–1896).

DECB　　　　　David Bercot, *Dictionary of Early Christian Beliefs* (Peabody, MA: Hendrickson Publishers, Inc., 2010).

NPNF[1]　　　　*Nicene and Post-Nicene Fathers: First Series*, Philip Schaff, ed. (1886–1889; reprinted frequently).

NPNF[2]　　　　*Nicene and Post-Nicene Fathers: Second Series*, Philip Schaff and Henry Wallace, eds. (1890–1900; reprinted frequently).

Coptic Synaxarium　*Coptic Synaxarium*. 4 vols. (Chicago, IL: St. George Coptic Orthodox Church, 1987–1995).

Foreword

By His Eminence Metropolitan Youssef

*Bishop of the Coptic Orthodox Diocese of the
Southern United States of America*

The afterlife is a mystery to all of us. Christianity, in general, tends not to seek answers by mere speculation or guessing, but relies instead on divine revelation to arrive at reliable observations about matters that are beyond our understanding. If God reveals something to us about such mysteries, then that is to be considered true. For the truth about the afterlife, we know what the holy, divinely inspired Bible has already revealed.

Beyond that, however, there are some to whom the afterlife has been exposed in some way and who have shared their experiences with us. The question then becomes: how should we read such accounts? Above all things, we must eliminate whatever contradicts the Holy Scriptures. Anything else which does not contradict Scripture, yet is spiritually beneficial, can be considered for spiritual reflection and meditation. Nevertheless, there is one caveat by which we must abide: we cannot teach anything as Church doctrine which is not derived from the apostles and Scripture, and therefore, the reader is entitled to make his or her own personal assessment about the deductions and conclusions derived from the afterlife accounts in this book. Let me assure you, however, that the author has exerted tremendous effort to ensure the contents of this book are in alignment with biblical teaching and the doctrinal traditions of the Church of God.

But what purpose does this book serve? It is not meant to simply satisfy our human curiosity about the unknown. It has been compiled with the intention of alerting all of us to be ready for Christ's Second Coming, as He warns us: "Watch therefore, for you know neither the day nor the hour in which the Son of Man is coming" (Mt 25:13).

I thank the author for having taken the liberty to write this book from which all of us may benefit. I pray that the Holy Spirit accompanies every word in this book for us to "bear fruits worthy of repentance" (Mt 3:8) and so that, "When He appears, we may have confidence and not be ashamed before Him at His coming" (1 Jn 2:28), through the intercessions of St. Mary, St. Mark, and all the saints. Amen.

Preface

Many who are reading this book might be wary of accepting the idea that the experiences detailed in this book should shed light on their preconceived notions of the hereafter. This is to be expected, for even the Lord Jesus Christ said as much. In the parable of the rich man and Lazarus (Lk 16:19–31), He taught us that even if evidence of the afterlife were to be revealed to us by bringing back someone from the dead to tell us about it, people would still not believe.

> There was a certain rich man who was clothed in purple and fine linen and fared sumptuously every day. But there was a certain beggar named Lazarus, full of sores, who was laid at his gate, desiring to be fed with the crumbs which fell from the rich man's table. Moreover the dogs came and licked his sores. So it was that the beggar died, and was carried by the angels to Abraham's bosom. The rich man also died and was buried. And being in torments in Hades, he lifted up his eyes and saw Abraham afar off, and Lazarus in his bosom.
>
> Then he cried and said, "Father Abraham, have mercy on me, and send Lazarus that he may dip the tip of his finger in water and cool my tongue; for I am tormented in this flame."
>
> But Abraham said, "Son, remember that in your lifetime you received your good things, and likewise Lazarus evil things; but now he is comforted and you are tormented. And besides all this, between us and you there is a great gulf fixed, so that those who want to pass from here to you cannot, nor

can those from there pass to us."

Then he said, "I beg you therefore, father, that you would send him to my father's house, for I have five brothers, that he may testify to them, lest they also come to this place of torment."

Abraham said to him, "They have Moses and the prophets; let them hear them."

And he said, "No, father Abraham; but if one goes to them from the dead, they will repent."

But he said to him, "If they do not hear Moses and the prophets, neither will they be persuaded though one rise from the dead."

The story of Lazarus and the rich man is remarkable, as we have God Himself, the Creator of what awaits us in the afterlife and also the Judge who decides where we go after we die, revealing to us mysteries of the afterlife through a parable.

The apostle Paul saw this reality when he himself was taken up to Paradise and witnessed its indescribable magnificence. Out of humility, though, when he wrote about this, he did not mention his name as being the one blessed with that experience:[1]

> It is doubtless not profitable for me to boast. I will come to visions and revelations of the Lord: I know a man in Christ who fourteen years ago—whether in the body I do not know, or whether out of the body I do not know, God knows—such a one was caught up to the third heaven. And I know such a man—whether in the body or out of the body I do not know, God knows—how he was caught up into Paradise and heard

inexpressible words, which it is not lawful for a man to utter. (2 Cor 12:1–4)

This is not the only place in the Bible that tells of someone experiencing what happens after death and coming back to life. Scripture mentions eight individuals who were raised from the dead: one by Elijah, two attributed to Elisha, three raised by Christ, and two others—one by St. Peter and the other by St. Paul.[2] We also read that at the time of Christ's crucifixion "graves were opened; and many bodies of the saints who had fallen asleep were raised; and coming out of the graves after His resurrection, they went into the holy city and appeared to many" (Mt 27:52–53).

Even during the early Church we find the bishop Irenaeus saying that this kept occurring, whereby some were raised from the dead by the power of the Church's prayers:

> Being able to raise the dead, as the Lord raised them, and the apostles did by means of prayer, . . . [this] has been frequently done in the brotherhood on account of some necessity— the entire church in that particular locality entreating with much fasting and prayer, [that] the spirit of the dead man has returned, and he has been bestowed in answer to the prayers of the saints. . . . [He goes on to criticize detractors who] do not even believe this can possibly be done.[3]

Imagine all the things those who have been raised from the dead could have told us! I hope this book provides you also with the opportunity to take a glance at what may await us after we die, so that Christ's prediction (that people will not be persuaded even "if one goes to them from the dead") will not apply to you. By God's grace, I hope you will be inspired and intrigued by the experiences shared in this book for your own benefit.

Part One

Introduction

Understanding the Mysteries Herein

> To me...this grace was given, that I should preach...the unsearchable riches of Christ, and to make all see what is the fellowship of the mystery, which from the beginning of the ages has been hidden in God who created all things through Jesus Christ; to the intent that now the manifold wisdom of God might be made known by the Church to the principalities and powers in the heavenly places, according to the eternal purpose which He accomplished in Christ Jesus our Lord, in whom we have boldness and access with confidence through faith in Him. (Eph 3:8–12)

Ancient Egyptians have always been fascinated with unraveling the mysteries of death and the afterlife. For thousands of years, they collected their varied beliefs in writings and inscriptions which are collectively known as the *Book of the Dead*. Those beliefs were suddenly discarded about two thousand years ago when a messenger from God known by the name of Mark (the evangelist) taught my ancestors about the true path of salvation, through the Lord Jesus Christ. The Egyptians who worshipped idols eventually were counted among God's people, as was prophesied hundreds of years before Christ was born in a manger. It was none other than the great prophet of Israel Isaiah—who delivered the message:

> Behold, the LORD rides on a swift cloud, and will come into Egypt; the idols of Egypt will totter at His presence, and the heart of Egypt will melt in its midst.

* * *

> In that day there will be an altar to the LORD in the midst of the land of Egypt, and a pillar to the LORD at its border. And it will be for a sign and for a witness to the LORD of hosts in the land of Egypt; for they will cry to the LORD because of the oppressors, and He will send them a Savior and a Mighty One, and He will deliver them. Then the LORD will be known to Egypt, and the Egyptians will know the LORD in that day, and will make sacrifice and offering; yes, they will make a vow to the LORD and perform it. And the LORD will strike Egypt, He will strike and heal it; they will return to the LORD, and He will be entreated by them and heal them. (Is 19:1, 19–22)

Thus, the ancient Egyptian symbol of life—the ankh ☥—was replaced by the true symbol of eternal life—the cross ☦.

I am the proud descendent of that rich history and owe my Christian beliefs to the fulfilled prophecy of God and the efforts of His apostle Mark. Yet, although we Egyptians learned of the true way of salvation, my ancient heritage crept into the present and has led me to wonder about what happens immediately after death and how to prepare for the journey. But that was not always the case. Although I am a Christian, I was not always a devout one. When I was in college, I could not have cared less about life after death, or at least I slowly drifted into passive acceptance that it did not matter. Then one night my mother showed me a copy of a document that altered the course of my life. It has also changed other people's lives and is the catalyst that has led me to write this book some fifteen years later. That document contained an account, written in his own handwriting, of what is touted by many to be the afterlife experience of an Egyptian (i.e., Coptic) Orthodox Christian monk known as Father Botros (whose experience and life story can be found in Appendix A).

After that fateful day, I set out to examine the veracity of what Father Botros wrote, and I challenged my entire belief system as follows: if Orthodoxy is true, then all bona fide Orthodox Christian afterlife accounts and early Christian writings on the subject must be in harmony with one another. Therefore, I limited my search to Orthodox Christians, which includes the shared collective heritage of the Catholic and Orthodox Churches before the Great Schism between east and west, traditionally dated to the eleventh century, as well as those Christians since then who are regarded specifically as Orthodox Christians. Because Orthodox Christians can trace their practices and beliefs all the way back to the time of the apostles, they retain stories of Christian experiences that have since spanned two millennia, including afterlife accounts that have been lost, forgotten, or unintentionally neglected by many in recent times. The truth is (I came to learn) Christians have been relating their afterlife experiences since the time of the apostles.

As you might have guessed, I am an Orthodox Christian—Coptic Orthodox to be specific. I will admit that when I first read Father Botros's writing, there were a few aspects that were quite novel to me. However, as I collected all the reliable writings about the afterlife I could get my hands on, both ancient and contemporary originating from all over the world, I was astonished to find that the most novel aspects of his story were, in fact, the most commonly understood beliefs pronounced by the early Christians, yet which have somehow evaporated, to a great extent, from the collective consciousness of Christians today. Each afterlife experience I came across not only fit within the paradigm of my belief system, but also provided intricate, mystical details about the hereafter that I had not known before. And they all seemed to be saying the same thing.

Instead of just recounting one person's afterlife experience, the several accounts provided will allow you the opportunity to compare and contrast their stories with each other, to assess their homogeneity and determine whether or not that amplifies their cumulative credibility. It is not my intent to impose upon you that you must believe every afterlife experience you will read, but rather it is up to you to determine that for yourself.

Furthermore, in order to set a solid Christian foundation for all of this, you are provided an abundant collection of teachings from the Holy Bible, along with an expansive selection of early historical Christian writings on the subject to further elaborate on the ancient Christian understanding of the afterlife. Those will be provided throughout the book so that you can assess whether or not the afterlife experiences recounted adhere to the tenets of Christianity. (Moreover, as you read you may want to refer to Appendix C, which provides a glossary of Orthodox people and terminology mentioned in this book.)

Now, for those who may feel apprehensive, considering this subject too speculative to be written about, allow me to leave you with one concluding remark made by St. Gregory of Nyssa (*c.* AD

335–395) when he, too, set out to expound upon matters that had no clear answer:

> For my part, in view of the difficulties of the subject proposed, I think the exclamation of the Apostle [Paul] very suitable to the present case, just as he uttered it over unfathomable questions: "Oh, the depth of the riches both of the wisdom and knowledge of God! How unsearchable are His judgments and His ways past finding out! For who has known the mind of the Lord?" [Rom 11:33–34].
>
> But seeing on the other hand that the Apostle [Paul] declares it a peculiarity of him that is spiritual to "judge all things" [1 Cor 2:15], and commends those who have been "enriched" by the divine grace "in all utterance and in all knowledge" [1 Cor 1:5], I venture to assert that it is not right to omit the examination which is within the range of our ability nor to leave the question here raised without making any inquiries, or having any ideas about it.... I assert ... it is ... well ... to introduce a certain order into the discussion and to lead the view on from one point to another.[1]

Part Two

Death and Crossing Over from This Life to the Next

Death

> Therefore, since a promise remains of entering His rest, let us fear lest any of you seem to have come short of it. (Heb 4:1)

What is death? It can be defined as the moment at which a person's spirit is released from the physical body, which has ceased to sustain itself.[1] As one second-century Christian apologist—Athenagoras—put it: "[Upon death] the separation of the soul from the members of the body ... interrupts the continuity of life,"[2] after which "the soul remains by itself, incapable of dissolution, of dispersion, of corruption [i.e., decay], while the body is corrupted and dissolved."[3] That is because the spirit of man is considered to be immortal. Death, then, is "the sequel to a life of want and corruption, and after this we hope for a continuance with immortality."[4]

However, that does not mean the body is to be forgotten. Although at death the spirit leaves the body in the dust, both will eventually reunite together at the end of times, as prophesied by the prophet Ezekiel: "Prophesy to these bones, and say to them, 'O dry bones, hear the word of the LORD! Thus says the Lord GOD to these bones: "Surely I will cause breath to enter into you, and you shall live"'" (Ezek 37:4–5); St. Ambrose (*c.* AD 337–397) remarked on this prophecy saying, "Great is the lovingkindness of the Lord, that the prophet is taken as a witness of the future resurrection, that we, too, might see it with his eyes."[5]

This notion of future bodily resurrection is also substantiated in other passages of the Bible: "Your dead shall live; together with my dead body they shall arise. Awake and sing, you who dwell in dust; for your dew is like the dew of herbs, and the earth shall cast out the dead" (Is 26:19); "Not only that, but we also who have the firstfruits of the Spirit, even we ourselves groan within ourselves, eagerly waiting for the adoption, the redemption of our body"(Rom 8:23). Bishop Augustine of Hippo (*c.* AD 354–430) wrote on this subject as well:

> That final judgment to which they must submit when their bodies are restored to them, and are either tormented or glorified in the very same flesh wherein they once lived here on earth; is it, let me ask you, the case that you were really ignorant of this?[6]

Hence, while some religions diminish the significance of the body, considering it to be merely a means for the spirit to grow and afterward is discarded indefinitely, Orthodox Christians regard the body as a gift from God that will be exalted one day, just as Christ's physical body has forever united to His divinity and has been transformed into a glorious and honored body, "who will [also] transform our lowly body that it may be conformed to His glorious body, according to the working by which He is able even to subdue all things to Himself" (Phil 3:21).

The experiences you are about to read in the next few chapters attest to one simple fact: we continue to live after we die, as spirits. Christ was confronted with the issue of what happens to us after death. In response, He spoke to the Jews about three beloved fathers of Israel who had died—Abraham, Isaac, and Jacob—and said that God is "not the God of the dead, but of the living" (Mt 22:32; Mk 12:27; Lk 20:38). He also explained some features of our existence we can expect after death: "When they rise from the dead, they . . . are like angels in heaven" (Mk 12:25); "Those who are counted worthy to attain that age, and the resurrection from the dead, neither marry nor are given in marriage; nor can they die anymore, for they are equal to the angels and are sons of God, being sons of the resurrection" (Lk 20:35-36).

For this reason we find the Bible characterizes those who have died as having simply "fallen asleep" (Mt 27:52; 1 Cor 15:6, 18, 20; 1 Thess 4:13-15). Even Christ, when raising three different people from the dead, spoke not to the dead bodies but rather to their living spirits. To the son of the widow of Nain He said, "Young man, I say to you, arise!" (Lk 7:14). When He raised the daughter of Jairus, the ruler of the synagogue, Christ "took her by the hand and called, saying, 'Little girl, arise'" (Lk 8:54). To Lazarus He commanded, "Come forth!" (Jn 11:43).

Once a person's spirit is released upon death, as is reflected in the ensuing sources which have been gathered, it has to pass from this limited world to another invisible realm. After that, the spirit is sent temporarily to either of two places—Hades[7] or Paradise—to await God's judgment, after which time "a new heaven" will come into existence while the "first heaven" will have "passed away" (Rev 21:1).[8] Those who are in Paradise will be allowed to live in this new permanent place of bliss, which is appropriately referred to as heaven. Those who have been waiting in Hades, whose names are "not found written in the Book of Life," who are worthy of eternal condemnation, will be "cast into the lake of fire," which is appropriately termed hell, and is regarded as the "second death" (Rev 20:6, 14–15). (Note that I will do my best to distinguish between these terms appropriately. However, since these words are often used indistinctly by many, including most English translations of the Bible, you will find several quoted texts that do not comport with the above; you should, nonetheless, be able to understand the appropriate meaning and term in context.)

At the "last day" (the end of the world), Christ will return for a second visit, at which time He will dispense His judgment upon every person and "will render to each one according to his deeds" (Rom 2:6).

> When the Son of Man comes in His glory, and all the holy angels with Him, then He will sit on the throne of His glory. All the nations will be gathered before Him, and He will separate them one from another, as a shepherd divides his sheep from the goats. (Mt 25:31–32)

"For God will bring every work into judgment, including every secret thing, whether good or evil" (Eccl 12:14). "For we must all appear before the judgment seat of Christ, that each one may receive the things done in the body, according to what he has done, whether good or bad" (2 Cor 5:10).

Everyone who dies before Christ's Second Coming will be "reserved for judgment," "until the day of judgment" comes (2 Pet 2:4, 9; 3:7). Whereas the righteous will be reserved in a temporary place of joy, sinners will be reserved in a temporary place of torment.

> For if God did not spare the angels who sinned, but cast them down to hell[9] and delivered them into chains of darkness... then the Lord knows how to deliver the godly out of temptations and to reserve the unjust under punishment for the day of judgment. (2 Pet 2:4, 9)

Placement into Hades or Paradise is not a judgment per se, but an assignment to one place or another to wait until Christ's Second Coming, when He will formally judge the world. The Coptic Orthodox Church reflects this belief during the Liturgy of the Waters service on Covenant Thursday of Holy Week, in the concluding reading from a homily attributed to St. John Chrysostom (c. AD 350–407) regarding Judas: "He who gave Him up descended into the depths of Hades; there he shall remain unto the end in anticipation of great grief and lament."[10]

That is consistent with what St. Irenaeus (c. AD 130–200), who grew up hearing the teaching of Polycarp (a disciple of the apostle John), understood: "Each class [of those who have died] receives a habitation such as it has deserved, even before the judgment."[11] Bishop Cyprian of Carthage (c. AD 200–258) tells us the same, that the spirits of those who die will "be in suspense [i.e., in a state of uncertainty] until the sentence of God at the day of judgment."[12] Likewise Tertullian (c. AD 160–230) writes: "We maintain that, after life has passed away, you still remain in existence and anticipate a day of judgment. Furthermore, according to what you deserve, you are assigned either to misery or to bliss."[13]

Since, therefore, the Bible speaks of the judgment of God as being a singular event (e.g., "the judgment," "the last day," "the hour of His judgment"), I will refrain, for the sake of clarity, from referring to the temporary allotment of individuals after death as being a particular judgment (as is often the term used). Both sinner and righteous await a permanent judgment and a permanent assignment that will last forever—to either heaven or hell: "And these [the wicked] will go away into everlasting punishment, but the righteous into eternal life" (Mt 25:46).

My goal is not to condemn anyone, but rather to offer motivation to be counted worthy of hearing Christ tell us the following after death: "Come, you blessed of My Father, inherit the kingdom prepared for you from the foundation of the world" (Mt 25:34). Let us now focus on the moment of physical death and the passage of one's spirit from this realm to the next. I will use the term "cross(ing) over" to describe the experience of the spirit from the time it is released from the body until it enters either Paradise or Hades.

From what you are about to read, you will notice two ways in which people experience the afterlife and are able to tell us about it: Some actually die, so that their spirits cross over, but then at some point their spirits are returned to their bodies and they live again. Others, while still in the body, or while in the spirit by some divine power (although they have not actually died yet), are granted the opportunity to observe what comes after death.

The latter phenomenon, referred to by some Church Fathers and other Christians by the term "ecstasy"[14] or "divine vision," is not unheard of in the Bible. St. Paul talks about being "caught up" to Paradise, which he refers to as "the third heaven" (the first being the sky above us, and the second being outer space):

> I know a man in Christ who fourteen years ago—whether in the body I do not know, or whether out of the body I do not know, God knows—such a one was caught up to the third

heaven. And I know such a man—whether in the body or out of the body I do not know, God knows—how he was caught up into Paradise and heard inexpressible words, which it is not lawful for a man to utter.[15] (2 Cor 12:2–4)

St. Irenaeus elaborated on this passage, indicating that it is possible for some to experience some spiritual mysteries without the body, but rather only by one's spirit:

And for this reason he [i.e., St. Paul] added, "Whether in the body, or whether out of the body, God knows," that the body might neither be thought to be a partaker in that vision, as if it could have participated in those things which it had seen and heard; . . . but it is therefore thus far permitted even without the body to behold spiritual mysteries which are the operations of God, who made the heavens and the earth, and formed man, and placed him in Paradise, so that those should be spectators of them who, like the Apostle, have reached a high degree of perfection in the love of God.[16]

The Moment of Death

What is it like to die? Let us consider an extremely detailed account by a Russian Orthodox man named K. Uekskuell. His account was given legitimacy and credence by Archbishop Nikon of Vologda,[17] a member of the Holy Synod of the Russian Orthodox Church. In 1916, the archbishop reprinted Mr. K. Uekskuell's account (which originally appeared in the *Moscow Journal*) in a publication titled *Trinity Pages*, with the following introductory remarks:

In regard to this narrative, in due time, we had correspondence with its author, who, after ascertaining its validity, testified that his subject, after relating his experience, entered into a monastery. In view of the fact that nothing in his narrative is in contradiction to the stand of the Church on the mystery of death and the life beyond death, we feel it beneficial to reprint this article as a separate publication.[18]

The famed Coptic priest, Father Makary Younan Abd El Malak,[19] also regarded this story as being authentic when he recounted it in a notable Arabic sermon from the 1990s about preparing oneself for the afterlife, which has since been titled "Not Ready" (*Gheir Mostaed*).

Mr. Uekskuell was able to recall the moment of his spirit's departure in great detail. He lay in a hospital bed with a serious case of pneumonia, at a point where his illness was becoming very grim with physicians and staff gathered all around him to keep him from dying.

> All my attention was concentrated on myself, but here there also was an astonishing, peculiar quality, a certain state of division within me: I felt and was conscious of myself with complete clarity and certainty, and at the same time I had a feeling of such indifference to myself, that it seemed as if I even had lost the capacity for perceiving physical sensations.
>
> For example, I saw how the doctor extended his hand and felt my pulse—I saw and understood what he was doing, but did not feel his contact with my body. I saw and understood that the doctors, having raised me, continued to do something and were making a fuss over my back, where evidently the

edema had begun, but . . . I felt nothing; and this not because I actually lost the capacity to perceive these sensations, but because . . . having withdrawn somewhere deep within myself, I did not listen to or observe what they were doing to me.

It seemed as if suddenly two beings or essences were manifested in me: one—concealed somewhere deep within, and this was the main part of me; the other—external, and evidently less significant; and now it seemed as if that which had bound these two either burned itself out or melted, and these two essences separated, the stronger of these being felt more vividly and with greater certainty, and the weaker becoming a matter of indifference. This weaker part or being was my body.

I can imagine how, perhaps even only a few days ago, I would have been struck by the manifestation in myself of this hitherto unknown to me internal being and the realization of its superiority over that other part of me, which according to my previous beliefs made up the whole being of [man], but which I now did not even notice.

This state [of being] was most astounding: to live, see, hear, and understand all, and at the same time seemingly not to see or understand anything, to feel such alienation with regard to everything.

Thus, for example, the doctor asks me a question; I hear and understand that which he asks, but I do not reply, I do not give an answer, because I feel there is no reason for me to speak to him. And yet he fusses and worries over me, but he is concerned with that half of me which now has lost all meaning for myself, and with which I feel I have nothing to do.

But suddenly the other half asserted itself, and in so striking and unusual a manner! I suddenly felt myself drawn somewhere downward with irresistible force. During the first minutes this sensation was similar to having heavy, massive weights tied to all the members of my body; but shortly following this such a comparison could not justly describe my state of feeling. This representation of such an attraction now seemed comparatively insignificant.

No, here some kind of law of gravitational attraction of most tremendous power was acting. It seemed to me that . . . not only I as a whole, but every member, every hair, the thinnest tendon, each cell of my body, was separately being drawn somewhere with such irresistibility, as a strong magnet attracts pieces of metal to itself.

And yet, no matter how strong this sensation might have been, it did not hinder me from thinking and being conscious of everything; I was also conscious of the strangeness of this phenomenon. I remembered and was conscious of reality, that is to say, that I lay in bed, that my ward was on the second floor, [and] that below me there was an identical room; but at the same time, according to the strength of the sensation, I was certain that if below me there were not one, but ten rooms piled on top of one another, that this would suddenly give way before me in order to let me pass, . . . [but to] where?

Somewhere further, deeper into the earth.

Yes, namely into the earth, and I wanted to lie on the floor; I exerted myself and began tossing about.

"Agony," I heard this word pronounced over me by the doctor.

Since I did not speak, being completely concentrated

within myself, and [since] my glance expressed a complete absence of affect in relation to the surrounding world, the doctors evidently decided that I was in an unconscious state and spoke about me audibly without restraint. But meanwhile, I not only excellently understood all, but it was impossible for me not to think and observe, to a certain degree.

"Agony, death!" I thought, having heard the words of the doctor. "Am I really dying?" turning to myself, I spoke out loud; but how? Why? I cannot explain this.

I suddenly remembered a learned discourse dealing with the question of whether or not death is painful, which I once read long ago, and, having closed my eyes, I examined myself with regard to what was taking place in me at the time.

No, I felt no physical pain whatsoever, but undoubtedly I was suffering. I felt heavy within and weary. What was this from? I knew of what sickness I was dying; what was the case here? Was the edema choking me, or was it depressing the activity of the heart and this was making me weary? I do not know. Perhaps such was the explanation of my oncoming death according to the ideas of those people, of the world, which now was so alien and remote from me. I, however, only felt an insurmountable striving towards somewhere, an attraction towards something concerning which I already have spoken.

And I felt that this attraction increased with each moment, that I already had just about come very close, almost in contact with, that magnet which was attracting me, which if I should touch, would cause me with my whole body to become fused with it, to grow into one with it in such a manner that no force would then be capable of separating me from it; and the more strongly I felt the proximity of this moment, the more fearful and depressed I became, and this was so because I simultaneously felt a resistance to this with increasing clarity. I felt more clearly that I as a whole could not unite, that something had to separate within me, and that this something was striving away from the unknown object of attraction with the same intensity that the something else in me was striving towards it. It was this struggle that caused me weariness and suffering.

The meaning of the word "agony," which I heard, was entirely understood by me, but now everything in me somehow turned away from my relationships [and] feelings and extended to my conceptions inclusively.

Without doubt, if I had heard this word even at the time when the three doctors were examining me, I would have been frightened to an alarming degree. Likewise, if such a strange turn [of events] had not taken place in my sickness, if I remained in the ordinary state of a sick man, even at the present moment, knowing that death is approaching, I would have understood and explained all that had taken place with me differently; but in the present state the words of the doctor only surprised me, not having aroused that feeling of fear which is characteristic of people who are thinking about death, and I gave an entirely unexpected, in comparison with my previous conceptions, interpretation to that state which I was experiencing.

Mr. Uekskuell is now about to explain his conception of a notion that is sprinkled throughout the Bible regarding the body's connection with the earth. God made us out of dust and pronounced, "In the sweat of your face you shall eat bread till you return to the ground, for out of it you were taken; for dust you are, and to dust you shall return" (Gen 3:19). Elsewhere we find similar remarks: "Then the dust will return to the earth as it was, and the spirit will return to God who gave it" (Eccl 12:7); "All go to one place: all are from the dust, and all return to dust" (Eccl 3:20).

"Well now, so that's what it is! It is the earth that is drawing me so," suddenly it dawned on me. That is to say, not me, but that which belongs to her, that which she let me have for a period of time. "And is the earth drawing it, or is matter itself trying to return to her?"

And that which previously seemed so natural and true, and namely, that after death I should turn completely to dust, now appeared unnatural and impossible. [Fearing that his existence was about to end completely, he thought], "No, I as a whole shall not disappear, I cannot," I almost screamed out loud and made an attempt to free myself, to tear myself from that force which was attracting me; and suddenly I felt a calm within myself.

I opened my eyes, and everything that I saw in the course of that minute, down to the slightest details, registered in my memory with complete clarity.

Having just provided us with an intricate description of what he experienced in his spirit's separation from his body, he goes on to explain the next phenomenon that he experienced: seeing his double. This portion of the narrative also exhibits that a person's spirit is that part of man that retains consciousness and awareness of oneself. It accompanies the body during life, and then lives outside the body after physical death. St. Irenaeus tells us that the soul of a man will "retain the memory of things in this world" after death.[20] Mr. Uekskuell proceeds:

> I saw that I was standing alone within a room; to the right of me, standing about something in a semi-circle, the whole medical staff was crowded together. Having put his hands behind himself and gazing intently at something which I was unable to see due to their figures stood the head physician; behind him, slightly bent forward—the younger physician; the old assistant doctor, holding a bag of oxygen in his hands, with indecision shifted from one leg to the other, evidently not knowing what to do with his apparatus, either to bear it away, or not to do so, since it could still be of use; and the young doctor, having bent down, was supporting something, but due to his shoulder, I was only able to see the pillows.
>
> This group struck me with surprise: at the place where they were standing there was a bed. What was it that drew the attention of these people, what were they looking at, when I already was not there, when I was standing in the midst of the room?
>
> I moved forward and looked where they all were looking.
>
> There on the bed I was lying.
>
> I do not have any recollection of experiencing anything like fear when seeing my double; I only was perplexed: how can this be? I feel myself here, and at the same time I am there also.
>
> I looked at myself standing in the midst of the room. Why this without doubt was me, exactly the same as I always knew myself to be.

I wanted to touch myself, to take the left hand by the right: my hand went right through; I tried to grasp myself at the waist—my hand again went through my body as through empty space.

Struck by such a strange phenomenon, I wanted that someone nearby would help me understand what was happening and, having [taken] several steps, I extended my hand, desiring to touch the shoulder of the doctor; but I felt that I was walking strangely, not feeling contact with the floor; and my hand, no matter how I tried, could not reach the figure of the doctor. Only perhaps a few inches of space remained, but I was not able to touch him.

I made an effort to stand firmly on the floor, but, although my body obeyed my attempts and lowered itself, yet it could not reach the floor just as the figure of the doctor was not able to be reached before. Here also an insignificant amount of space remained, but I could in no way overcome it.

And I vividly remembered how several days ago the nurse of our ward, desiring to guard my medicine from becoming spoiled, lowered a vial containing it into a pitcher of cold water. However, there was much water in the jug and immediately the light vial was buoyed up; but the old nurse, not understanding what had taken place, persistently tried one, two, and three times to lower it down to the bottom of the pitcher and even held it down with her finger in the hope that it eventually would remain there. But hardly had she removed her finger, than it again would be carried upwards to the surface.

Evidently in a similar manner, the surrounding air must have become too dense for me, for present me.

What happened to me?

I called out to the doctor, but the atmosphere in which I was found turned out to be entirely unfit for me; it did not receive and transmit the sounds of my voice, and I understood myself to be in a state of utter dissociation from all that was about me. I understood my strange state of solitude, and a feeling of panic came over me. There really was something inexpressibly horrible in this extraordinary solitude. If a person becomes lost in a forest, is drowning in the depths of the sea, caught in a fire, [or] sitting in solitary confinement, he never loses hope that he will be heard. He knows that he will be understood if his call for help is carried to somebody's hearing; he understands that [if] another living being sees him . . . he will be able to start speaking with him, express what he desires, and the other will understand him.

But to see people about oneself, to hear and understand their conversation, and at the same time know that no matter what happens to you, you have no opportunity whatsoever of informing them of your presence and of expecting help if in need—from such a state of solitude my hairs stood on end, [and my] mind became torpid. It was worse than being on an uninhabited island, because there at least nature would have manifested positive signs of receptivity of one's individuality; but here, in this . . . deprivation of the capacity to associate with the surrounding world, as an unnatural experience for a human being, in it there was so much deathly fear, such a horrible acknowledgment of helplessness, which one is neither able to experience in any other situation nor convey in words.

I, of course, did not give in at once; I attempted in all

possible ways and tried to make my presence known, but these attempts only brought me complete despair. Is it really possible that they don't see me? I thought with despair and repeatedly approached the group of people standing over my bed, but none of them turned around or paid attention to me; and now I looked at myself with perplexity, not understanding how it was possible for them not to see me, when I was the same as I had always been.

Another illustration of seeing one's double can be taken from Father Arseny, a Russian Orthodox priest who was imprisoned in one of the prison camps in Russia, during the days of Stalin. One day he became ill, and his illness grew steadily worse until his fever became so intense that he died. His spiritual son, Alexander, recounts for us what he learned about this priest's experience:

> Everything had disappeared, had faded away. . . . After some time Father Arseny felt an unusual lightness grip him and heard an absolute silence surrounding him. He grew calm. His difficulty in breathing, the mucus that had blocked his throat, the fever that had been burning his body, his weakness and helplessness all disappeared. He felt healthy and energetic.
>
> Now Father Arseny stood by his own bunk, and on it he saw a thin, exhausted, unshaven, almost white-haired man with pinched lips and half open eyes. Near the man he could see . . . a few prisoners whom he . . . especially knew and loved. Father Arseny looked attentively at the man on the bunk and suddenly realized with amazement that the man on the bunk was himself. His friends were gathered near his bunk, the enormous barracks with its numerous population, the

whole vast camp—Father Arseny was suddenly seeing it with absolute clarity. . . . Through the silence that was in him he saw the movements of the prisoners, and although he could not hear them, he could somehow understand clearly what they were saying and thinking. . . . Suddenly he understood that his soul left his body, and he . . . was physically dead.

He understood that . . . he could see not only their physical appearance, but their souls. Through the silence that was in him, he saw the movements of the prisoners. . . . With awe, he realized he could see the state of each of their souls, but he knew that he was no longer with them in this world. An invisible line separated him from this world, and he was unable to cross it. . . . He kneeled, and began to pray, begging God not to leave [those] . . . with whom he had lived in [the] . . . camp. . . .

As he prayed . . . the barracks and the entire camp appeared before his spiritual eyes in a very different way. He saw the whole camp with all its prisoners and its prison guards as if from inside. Each person carried within himself a soul which was now distinctly visible to Father Arseny. The souls of some were afire with faith which kindled the people around them; the souls of others . . . burned with a smaller but ever growing flame; others had only small sparks of faith and only needed the arrival of a shepherd to fan these sparks into a real flame. There were also people whose souls were dark and sad, without even the least spark of light.[21]

The Visual Appearance of One's Spirit

St. Augustine teaches that when the soul is separated from the body, "The man himself who is in such a state, though it be in spirit only, not in body, yet sees himself so like to his own body that he cannot discern any difference."[22] St. Irenaeus likewise tells us:

> The Lord has taught with very great fullness that souls continue to exist. They do not do this by passing from body to body. Rather, they preserve the same form as that of the body to which they were adapted. . . . The Lord states that the rich man recognized Lazarus after death, as well as Abraham. From these things, then, it is plainly declared that souls . . . possess the form of a man (so that they may be recognized).[23]

Mother Erene, a contemporary Coptic nun, tells us of three experiences (more detail given later) that demonstrate this. The first involves a vision where she saw a group of children who were part of a choir that had died in an accident and then proceeded to Paradise. She noticed that each person's "spirit had the form of its body of the flesh, but was shining and more beautiful."[24] Another time, Mother Erene was taken to Paradise to see a departed nun named Mother Ilaria who told her: "I am not in the body. I have abandoned it on earth. It is true that the spirit takes the shape of the body; that is why you can see me now."[25] Moreover, Mother Erene herself had an afterlife experience in which she describes the moment she died as doctors tried to resuscitate her heart, which had suffered cardiac arrest: "In the meantime, I said, 'Lord into

Your hands I commend my spirit.' I beheld myself lying in bed and my spirit took the exact shape of my body."[26]

Mr. Uekskuell was also able to recount for us his impression about his new spiritual form:

> I made an attempt to touch myself, and my hand again only passed through air. "But I am not a ghost. I feel and am conscious of myself, and my body is a real body, and not some kind of delusive 'mirage,'" I thought; and again [I] looked at myself intently and became convinced that my body really was a body, because I could observe it and see its minutest details, even a dot, with complete clarity. Its external appearance remained the same as it had been previously, but evidently its qualities changed.
>
> It became inaccessible to touch, and the surrounding air became too dense for it so that complete contact with objects was not possible.
>
> "An astral body. It seems that is what it is called?" The thought flashed through my mind. "But why, what has happened to me?" I asked myself, trying to remember if I ever had heard descriptions of such states, of strange transfigurations in sickness.
>
> "No, you cannot do anything here! Everything is finished," the young doctor said, waving his hand in a hopeless manner, and went away from the bed on which was lying the other me.
>
> I felt inexpressibly vexed that they continued to reason and fuss over that me which I completely did not feel, which did not exist for me; and [all the while they] were leaving without attention [to] the other real me, which is conscious of everything and being tormented by the fear of obscurity,

seeking and demanding their help.

"Is it possible that they will not find out? Is it possible that they do not understand that I am not there?" With disappointment I thought and, walking up to the bed, I looked at that me, which at the expense of my real me, attracted the attention of the people in the ward.

Not a Cessation of Life

Mr. Uekskuell begins to ponder about the true meaning of "death":

I glanced, and here only for the first time the thought emerged: is it possible that that which has happened to me, in our language, in the language of living people, is defined by the word "death"?

This occurred to me because the body lying on the bed had all the appearances of a corpse: without any movement, not breathing; the face covered with a kind of pallor, with firmly compressed, slightly cyanotic lips, it vividly reminded me of all the deceased that I had ever seen. It may seem strange at first, that only in seeing my lifeless body I comprehended what really had happened to me, but if one carefully considers and thoroughly perceives that which I felt and experienced, such a strange, on first sight, perplexity on my part becomes understandable. With our understanding of the word "death," there is inextricably bound the idea of some kind of destruction—a cessation of life; how could I think that I died when I did not lose self-consciousness for one moment, when I felt myself just as alive, hearing all, seeing all, conscious of all, capable of movement, thought, [and] speech? Of what deterioration could there be any consideration here, when I splendidly saw myself, and at the same time even acknowledged the strangeness of my state? Even the words of the doctor, that "all is over," did not draw my attention and did not call forth a guess concerning that which had taken place—to such a great extent did that which took place with me differ from our conceptions of death!

The dissociation from everything about me, [and] the split in my personality more than anything, could have made me understand that which had taken place, if I should have believed in the existence of a soul, if I were religious; but this was not the case and I was guided solely by that which I felt, and the sensation of life was so clear that I . . . was perplexed with the strange phenomenon, being completely unable to link my [present] feelings with the traditional conception of death; that is to say, while sensing and being conscious of myself, [I could not] . . . think that I do not exist.

Spiritual Cognizance: All Knowing?

Let us briefly turn our attention to another matter. When a person exists in spirit, does he suddenly obtain a sense of increased knowledge and an elevated understanding of things, or does his awareness remain limited just as it was while he was in the flesh? The famed monastic St. John Cassian (*c.* AD 360–435) writes on this subject as follows:

> The souls of the dead not only do not lose their consciousness,

they do not even lose their dispositions—that is, hope and fear, joy and grief. . . . They become yet more alive. . . . [He goes on to say that it makes no sense that our spirits, which are created after the image and likeness of God, should be unconscious after death]. Therefore it follows, and the nature of reason itself demands, that the spirit after casting off this fleshly coarseness by which now it is weakened, should bring its mental powers into a better condition, should restore them as purer and more refined, but should not be deprived of them.[27]

Mr. Uekskuell proceeds to explain his experience on the matter:

Subsequently I often had the opportunity of hearing from religious people—that is to say, those not negating the existence [of] a soul and [the] afterlife—the following opinion or supposition: that as soon as the soul of man has shuffled off its corruptible flesh, it immediately becomes a kind of an all-knowing essence, that for it there is nothing unknown. [This, Mr. Uekskuell explains, is untrue. Yes, although] . . . it is astonishing how in the new [spiritual] realm of reality, in [that] . . . new form of existence, that [the spirit] . . . not only immediately enters into the field of new [spiritual] laws which are revealed to it by the new [spiritual] world and its own changed state of being, but that all this is so akin to it that this transition is like a return to a real homeland [and] a return to its natural state; however, such a supposition, founded mainly on the idea that . . . [cognitive] limitations do not present themselves for the spirit [in the same way as] for the physical part of man, . . . of course, is entirely untrue.

From what has been described above, the reader sees that I arrived in this new world essentially the same as I had left it, that is to say, with practically the very same capacities, conceptions and knowledge which I had while living on earth.

For example, when I wanted somehow to make my presence known, I had recourse to those means which are commonly used in these cases by all living people; that is to say, I called, approached, tried to touch or push someone. Having noticed a new quality of my body, I felt it to be strange. Consequently, my previous conceptions remained in me; otherwise it would not have seemed strange to me. And desiring to become convinced in the existence of my body, I again had recourse to the usual method that I had been accustomed to in these cases as an earthly human.

Body Versus Spirit

Mr. Uekskuell goes on to struggle with the significance of a person's body in relation to their spirit. The Bible teaches us that one's spirit should be led by the Holy Spirit of God, rather than by the whims and desires of the flesh: "For as many as are led by the Spirit of God, these are sons of God" (Rom 8:14). "For you, brethren, have been called to liberty; only do not use liberty as an opportunity for the flesh. . . . I say then: Walk in the Spirit, and you shall not fulfill the lust of the flesh. For the flesh lusts against the Spirit, and the Spirit against the flesh; and these are contrary to one another, so that you do not do the things that you wish" (Gal 5:13, 16–17).

Mr. Uekskuell dwells on this subject:

And this was to be expected. The . . . spirit is created for life with the body; therefore, in what way can the body be anything like a prison for [the spirit] . . . [as if there were] some kind of bonds that chain it to some supposedly unrelated form of existence?

No, the body is a lawful dwelling place that has been, as it were, placed at the disposal of the spirit, and therefore [the spirit] will appear in the other world at that level of its development and perfection which it had attained during its joint existence with the body, in the lawfully established form of its existence. Of course, if during life a person was spiritually developed [and] spiritually disposed, then his soul will feel more related and things will therefore appear more understandable in this new world than [they will to] the soul of the person who lived never thinking of the other world. . . .

Afterwards, in recalling and thinking over my state of being at the time, I noticed that my mental capacities functioned with such striking energy and swiftness, that it seemed not the slightest trace of time remained after I had made the exertion to comprehend, compare, or remember something. Hardly had something appeared before me when my memory, immediately penetrating into the past, would dig up all the slightest bits of knowledge concerning a given subject which were carelessly lying about and forgotten; and that which at another time would doubtlessly have aroused a feeling of perplexity, now appeared as if it were quite apparent. At times, by virtue of some infusion of power, I even guessed beforehand that which was unknown to me;

but this nevertheless not before it actually appeared before my eyes. And it was only this latter condition that turned out to be the outstanding quality of my capacities, besides those other, as it were, expected changes which resulted from my altered state of being.

Having focused closely on the sensation of death and what it feels like to exist in one's spirit, let us now progress further and observe what we may experience as we cross over from this realm to the next.

Crossing Over

> Are You not the One who dried up the sea, the waters of the great deep; that made the depths of the sea a road for the redeemed to cross over? (Is 51:10)

Guardian Angels

Mr. Uekskuell continues to recount his experience, "proceeding with the narration of the further circumstances in [his] unbelievable occurrence":

> Unbelievable! But if up until now it has seemed unbelievable, then these further circumstances will appear as such "naive" stories before the eyes of my learned readers, that it would not be worth relating them; but perhaps for those who should want to view my narration differently, the naiveté itself and scantiness of the material presented will serve as proof of its veracity; because if I were making up this narration—imagining it—then such a wide field opens up for one's fantasia here that, of course, I could have thought up

something more subtle and effective.

Now then, what further took place with me? The doctors walked out of the ward. Both assistant doctors were standing about and trying to explain the stages of my illness and death, and the old nurse turned to [a religious] icon, crossed herself, and audibly expressed the accepted wish in such cases:

"May he inherit the kingdom of heaven, eternal peace to him."

And hardly had she uttered these words when two angels appeared at my side; for some reason in one of them I recognized my guardian angel, but the other was unknown to me. Having taken me by the arms, the angels carried me right through the wall of the ward into the street.

The experience of angels being present at the time of our departure is echoed by a modern-day elder monk from Mount Athos named Father Maximos:

> Our guardian angels will be present . . . during the time when our souls will exit this world and abandon the material body. They will be there at that moment to offer us solace and support during that difficult transition and then help us adjust to the realms of the spirits when our soul will be directed toward God.[1]

Orthodox Christians believe that angels were created to serve God's purposes, one of which is to minister to mankind. "Are they not all ministering spirits sent forth to minister for those who will inherit salvation?" (Heb 1:14). "For He shall give His angels charge over you, to keep you in all your ways" (Ps 91:11). "The angel of the LORD encamps all around those who fear Him, and delivers them" (Ps 34:7).

Although it is not explicitly stated in the Bible, the experiences of Christians in the Orthodox Church have led us to believe that all Christians have guardian angels—a belief which was taught by several of the earliest Church leaders. A writing from around the first or second century and believed by some to be authored by one of the first Christian converts, Hermas, whom St. Paul mentioned in Romans 16:14 ("Greet . . . Hermas"), teaches about "the angel of righteousness" that accompanies us during life:

> The angel of righteousness is gentle and modest, meek and peaceful. When he ascends into your heart, he speaks to you of righteousness, purity, chastity, contentment, and every other righteous deed and glorious virtue. When all of these things come into your heart, know that the angel of righteousness is with you.[2]

St. Ambrose, bishop of Milan in the fourth century, advises that "the angels must be entreated for us, who have been [given] to us as guards."[3] Also, around AD 225, Origen provides even more detail about these personal guardians:

> Every believer—although the humblest in the church—is said to be attended by an angel, who the Savior declares always beholds the face of God the Father [Mt 18:10]. Now this angel has the purpose of being his guardian. So if that person is rendered unworthy by his lack of obedience, the angel of

God is said to be taken from him.[4]

Almost two centuries later (*c.* AD 390) the acclaimed bishop of Nyssa, St. Gregory, informs us that the notion of guardian angels has "credence from its having been handed down from the Fathers," who taught that they are "appointed by [God] to assist in the life of each man."[5] That appointment is believed to be made at the time of each Christian's baptism, as expressed by the famed fourth-century monk of the Egyptian desert, St. Shenouda the Archimandrite:

> Let it be beyond doubt that every one of us, male or female, young or old, who was baptized in the name of the Father, the Son, and the Holy Spirit has been assigned to a designated angel until the day of his death to report to [God] every day what his assigned individual has done by day or by night. Not that God is unaware of what we have done. Heaven forbid! He is more knowledgeable about it. As is written, the eyes of the Lord are watching all the time everywhere on those who commit evil and on those who do good [Prov 15:3]. Rather, the angels are servants [appointed] by the Creator of the universe for those who are going to inherit salvation.[6]

The Bible also teaches us what some of the first converts to Christianity believed about angels. When St. Peter was miraculously released from Herod's imprisonment, he returned to the house of Mary, the mother of John whose surname was Mark, where many new Christians were "gathered together praying":

And as Peter knocked at the door of the gate, a girl named Rhoda came to answer. When she recognized Peter's voice, because of her gladness she did not open the gate, but ran in and announced that Peter stood before the gate. But they said to her, "You are beside yourself!" Yet she kept insisting that it was so. So they said, "It is his angel." (Acts 12:12–15)

From this story we may deduce that those Christians gathered in the house of St. Mark's mother believed St. Peter had his own personal angel who may have come on his behalf—his guardian angel. Moreover, there is implicit evidence of the belief in guardian angels in the book of Judith as well as in the book of Tobit (both accepted as canonical by the early Christians and presently by Orthodox Christians and Roman Catholics although omitted from some Bibles by other Christian denominations). Judith gives praise to God and says, "As the Lord lives, His angel has been my keeper both going here, and abiding there, and returning from there to here" (Jdt 13:20, adapted from the Douay Rheims Bible). The book of Tobit in its entirety also gives an extensive look at how angels can serve as guardians.

Turning to more recent stories related to guardian angels, let us see what the blessed, saintly Mother Erene told her nuns about certain occasions where she actually interacted with and also saw her own guardian angel. Before she became Mother Superior, she used to work long hours in the convent, from four in the morning until ten or eleven at night. She was always concerned that her extreme exhaustion would hinder her from waking up early for prayer. "How will I wake up to pray? Will the time be sufficient? I tell You what, my Lord Jesus Christ, bless my hour of sleep and make it as if it were hours. Make my four or five hours as if they were eight." Each nun had to depend on herself to wake up for prayer, as there was no alarm or bell that would announce the time to pray the Midnight Praises. The Lord heard her prayers and allowed her to hear a voice that would wake her up by calling to her, saying, "Erene . . . Erene . . . Erene . . . get up and pray." Then she tells us:

> When I started waking up and opening my eyes, I used to see an angel standing by my head. He would then turn around and stand in front of me at the end of the bed. When I woke up and sat up in bed, he would disappear. So I used to pray with great joy and I never felt tired. The angel continued to wake me up every night at the same time and in the same way. I would always thank him. Once I asked him, "Who are you?" He said, "I am your guardian angel who accompanies you all the time."[7]

There is one account that one may infer involved the guardian angel assigned to Pope Cyril (Kyrillos) VI, 116th patriarch and archbishop of Alexandria. A woman by the name of Janne Naguib recalls the following:

> One day during the offering of evening incense, His Holiness, holding the holy cross and the censer, walked around the altar three times, and then down into the church. A child, about 5 years old, was walking directly behind the pope, extending his hands to receive a blessing. Some people told him to stop but the child did not listen and continued walking right behind the pope, still extending his hands. His Holiness calmly

told the congregation, "Let him receive the blessing." He continued praying, extending his heart, soul, and existence to heaven, humbling himself in front of the Lord of Hosts. After the prayers ended, we took the child to talk with Father Felobbos. The child amazed us by saying, "I was just walking behind the angel who was walking behind Pope Kyrillos so I could touch his beautiful wings." We glorified God! Although the pope was aware of these heavenly blessings, his humbleness prevented him from ever saying anything.[8]

Ever since I came across this account, I take special notice of what children are looking at or being entertained by during church services, thinking maybe they are seeing things I am unworthy to behold ("Blessed are the pure in heart, for they shall see God" [Mt 5:8]).

I would like to share with you one more story regarding guardian angels. The person who told me about her experience is very dear to me and is someone I would never believe to have fabricated anything like this. My friend told me that when she was a young girl in Egypt, on one particular morning she woke up and noticed something peculiar: while her younger sister lay sleeping next to her, she saw an angel hovering over her body, guarding her. As the angel maintained its gaze at her sister, she could see it continuing to hover over her, with each hand balled into a fist and placed down on the bed on either side about shoulder-width apart, while each arm remained straightened and extended underneath its shoulders. The angel had no legs, but instead its body appeared like a tongue of fire sitting next to her on the bed. Its face emanated light, reminiscent of the appearance of a full moon. On its head was something akin to a crown. Slowly, the angel turned its gaze away from its intended subject and glanced at the girl who was now observing it. Upon realizing it was no longer invisible, the angel turned and ascended until it eventually disappeared.

Angels Accompanying the Spirit after Death

In the funeral prayers of the Coptic Church, the priest implores God about the person's spirit as follows: "Let the angels of light enter it into... life, and let it be in the bosom of our fathers Abraham, Isaac, and Jacob";[9] and also, at the burial site, the priest prays, "Send the angels of mercy, justice, and peace before him, so that they may present him unto You without fear."[10] Also, in the Coptic Synaxarion,[11] you will find numerous accounts of angels present at the time of a person's departure. For example, when the two Roman Christians St. Valerian and St. Tiburtius had their heads cut off at the behest of the infamous emperor Diocletian, we read that the person who ushered them to their demise "saw angels carrying their souls up to heaven and immediately he believed in the Lord Christ."[12]

Another example can be found in the story of St. Paësa (also spelled Paësia).[13] She gave up her originally pious manner of life and turned her home into a brothel. Upon hearing this, a monk, affectionately referred to as St. John the Short (or the Dwarf) (c. AD 339–405), was sent to find her in order to persuade her to return to a righteous manner of life. She repented of her ways and agreed to follow him to a convent. The story continues as follows:

> When they reached the desert, the evening drew on. He, making a little pillow with the sand, and marking it with the sign of the cross, said to her, "Sleep here." Then, a little

further on, he did the same for himself, said his prayers, and lay down. Waking in the middle of the night, he saw a shining path reaching from heaven to her, and he saw the angels of God bearing away her soul. So he got up and went to touch her feet . . . [and] he saw that she was dead.[14]

It is also common among Orthodox Christians to hear about saints and others who, upon death, encountered not only angels, but also the spirits of other saints, oftentimes including St. Mary and on some occasions even the Lord Christ Himself, who would accompany them as they crossed over into Paradise. For example, the Coptic Synaxarion tells us that when St. Anthony the Great "gave up his spirit . . . the angels and the saints took his spirit and carried it to the place of rest."[15] We can also find a similar occurrence at the time that St. John the Short departed:

> The angels and the host of saints came and received his pure soul and took it up to heaven. At that time, his servant came back and saw the soul of the saint surrounded by the host of saints and angels singing before them. Before them all, there was one shining like the sun and singing. The servant marveled at this magnificent sight. An angel came to him and told him the name of each one of the saints. Then the servant asked the angel, "Who is this one in front of them all, who is shining like the sun?" The angel replied, "This is Abba Anthony, the father of all monks."[16]

Another Egyptian desert father, St. Sisoes (d. c. AD 429), experienced a similar event:

When the time came for the great Sisoes to die, his face became illuminated and he said to the fathers who were sitting with him: "Here Abba Anthony has come." After being silent for a little [while] he said: "Here the choir of the prophets has come." Then he became yet brighter and said: "Here the choir of apostles has come." And again, his face became twice as shining; he began to speak with someone. The elders asked him to say with whom he was speaking. He replied: "The angels have come to take me, but I am imploring them to leave me a short time for repentance."

The elders said to him: "Father, you have no need for repentance."

He replied to them: "In truth, I do not know whether I have even placed a beginning of repentance." But everyone knew that he was perfect. Thus spoke and felt a true Christian despite the fact that during his lifetime he had raised the dead at his mere word and was filled with the gifts of the Holy Spirit. And again his face shone yet more: it shone like the sun. All were afraid. He said to them: "Behold, the Lord has come and uttered, 'Bring Me the chosen vessel from the desert.'" With these words he sent forth his spirit. Lightning was seen, and the room was filled with fragrance.[17]

As you read accounts of angels accompanying the departed immediately following death, recall that Christ Himself attested to this fact when He taught, in the parable of Lazarus and the rich man, that when Lazarus "the beggar died," he "was carried by the angels to Abraham's bosom" (Lk 16:22). St. John Chrysostom also taught:

The soul does not go up automatically to that other life, since this is not even possible. If we need a guide when moving from one city to another, much more the soul which has burst out of the flesh and is moving toward the life to come will need guides to lead it.[18]

The Crossover Realm

It is common to think that after death a person will almost immediately find themselves in either a good place or a bad place. However, from what is narrated below, it appears that after the spirit leaves the body, it is taken outside of this visible universe and ventures into an expanse of darkness. I refer to this place as the Crossover Realm because it is here that our spirit enters a transitional locale as it proceeds to cross over into either Hades or Paradise. It is a region unlike anything in the visible world and possesses a few qualities that seem to be commonly experienced: an infinite, limitless space, no sense of time, and as one enters that realm the visible world becomes more and more minuscule and inconsequential.

Mr. Uekskuell describes his encounter with this realm:

It already had grown dark. Snow was silently falling in large flakes. I saw this, but the cold and in general the difference in temperature between the room and outside I did not feel. Evidently these like phenomena lost their significance for my changed body. We began to quickly ascend. And the degree to which we had ascended, the increasingly greater became the expanse of space that was revealed before our eyes. And finally it took on such terrifyingly vast proportions that I was seized with a fear from the realization of my insignificance in comparison to this desert of infinity.

Here also certain peculiarities of my vision became apparent to me. Firstly, it was dark and I saw everything clearly in the dark; consequently, my vision received the capacity of seeing in the dark. Secondly, I was able to include in the field of my vision such a vast expanse of space, which undoubtedly I would not have been able to do with my ordinary vision. And at the time I was not conscious of these peculiarities, but I could not see everything, no matter how broad the field of my vision was; nevertheless a limit existed for it. This I understood very clearly and was terrified by it. Yes, to what a great extent is it characteristic for man to give a permanent kind of value to his individuality; [as for me], I recognized myself to be so very unimportant, a meaningless atom, the appearance and disappearance of which would of course remain unnoticed in this limitless space. But instead of finding some kind of consolation in this, . . . [my sense] of security became [agitated and I became] frightened . . . that I could get lost—that this unbounded vastness would swallow me up like a sorry particle of dust. . . .

The conception of time was absent in my mental state at this time, and I do not know how long we were moving upwards.

The Terrifying Ordeal

Cast the unprofitable servant into the outer darkness. There will be weeping and gnashing of teeth. (Mt 25:30)

Mr. Uekskuell continues recounting for us his experience, describing what he saw after he entered the Crossover Realm:

> Suddenly there was heard at first an indistinct noise. And following this, having emerged from somewhere, with shrieks and rowdy laughter, a throng of some hideous beings began rapidly to approach us.
>
> "Evil spirits!"—I suddenly comprehended and appraised with unusual rapidity that resulted from the horror I experienced at that time, a horror of a special kind and until then never before experienced by me. Evil spirits! O, how much irony, how much of the most sincere kind of laughter this would have aroused in me but a few days ago. Even a few hours ago somebody's report, not... that he saw evil spirits with his own eyes, but only that he believed in their existence as in something fundamentally real, would have aroused

a similar reaction! As was proper for an "educated" man at the close of the nineteenth century, I understood this [idea regarding the existence of evil spirits] to [simply] mean foolish inclinations [and] passions in a human being, and that is why the very word itself had for me not the significance of a name, but a term which defined a certain abstracted conception. And suddenly this "certain abstracted conception" appeared before me as a living personification. Even up to the present time I am not able to say how and why at that time, without the slightest trace of doubt, I recognized evil spirits to be present in that ugly sight. Undoubtedly only because such a designation of it was completely outside of the normal order of things and logic, for if a similar hideous sight appeared before me at another time, undoubtedly I would have said that it was some kind of fiction personified—an abnormal caprice of one's imagination. In short, everything else but in no way, of course, would I have called it a name by which I would have meant something which cannot be seen. But at the time, this designation of its nature took place with such rapidity, that seemingly there was no need to think about it, as if I had seen that which already was well known to me long ago; and since, as I already have explained, at that time my mental capacities functioned with such incomprehensible intensity, I therefore comprehended just as rapidly that the ugly outward appearance of these beings was not their real exterior; that this was some kind of an abominable show which was probably conceived with the purpose of frightening me to a greater degree; and for a moment something similar to pride stirred within me. I then felt ashamed of myself, [and] for man in general, because in order to arouse fear in man, a being who thinks so much of himself, other forms of being have recourse to such methods which we ourselves use with respect to small children.[1]

Having surrounded us on all sides, with shrieks and rowdy sounds, the evil spirits demanded that I be given over to them; they tried somehow to seize and tear me away from the angels, but evidently did not dare to do this. In the midst of their rowdy howling, unimaginable and just as repugnant to one's hearing as their sight was for my eyes, I sometimes caught up words and whole phrases.

"He is ours: he has renounced God," they suddenly cried out almost in unison. And here they lunged at us with such boldness that for a moment fear froze the flow of all thought in my mind.

"That is a lie! That is untrue!" coming to myself I wanted to shout, but an obliging memory bound my tongue. In some way unknown to me, I suddenly recalled such a slight, insignificant occurrence, which in addition was related to so remote a period of my youth that, it seems, I in no way could have been able to recall it to mind.

I recalled how during my years of study, once having gathered at my friend's, after having spoken about school studies, we passed over to discussing various abstract and elevated topics—conversations which often were carried on by us.

"Generally speaking, I don't like abstractions," says one of my comrades, "but here you already have absolute impossibility. I am able to believe in some kind of power of nature which, let us say, has not been investigated. That is to say, I can allow for its existence, even when not seeing its clear cut, definite manifestations, because it may be very insignificant or combined in its effects with other powers, and for this reason difficult to grasp; but to believe in God, as a Being, individual and omnipotent, to believe—when I do not anywhere see clear manifestations of this Individuality—this already becomes absurd. I am told: believe. But why must I believe, when I am equally able to believe that there is no God. Why, is it not true? Is it also not possible that He does not exist?" Now my comrade turned to me for support.

"Maybe not," I let escape from my lips.

This phrase was in the full sense of the word an "idle statement": the unreasonable talk of my friend could not have aroused within me a doubt in the existence of God. I did not particularly listen to his talking; and now it turned out that this idle statement of mine did not disappear without leaving a trace in the air. I had to justify myself, to defend myself from the accusation that was directed against me, and in such a manner the New Testament statement was verified in practice: we really shall have to give an account for all our idle words, if not by the will of God, who sees the secrets of man's heart, then by the anger of the enemy of salvation.

This accusation evidently was the strongest argument that the evil spirits had for my perdition. They seemed to derive new strength in this for the daring of their attacks on me, and now with furious bellowing they spun about us, preventing us from going any further.

I recalled a prayer and began praying, appealing for help to those holy ones [i.e., the saints] whose names I knew and whose names came to mind. But this did not frighten my enemies. A sad ignorant Christian only in name [I was that only then] . . . it seems, almost for the first time in my life, [I] remembered her who is called the intercessor for Christians.

And evidently my appeal to her was intense. Evidently my soul was filled with terror, that hardly had I remembered and pronounced her name, when about us there suddenly appeared a kind of white mist, which soon began to enfold within itself the ugly throng of evil spirits. It concealed them from my eyes before they could withdraw from us. Their bellowing and cackling was still heard for a long while, but according to how it gradually weakened in intensity and became more dull, I was able to judge that the terrible pursuit was gradually being left behind.

The feeling of fear that I experienced took hold of me so completely that I was not even conscious of whether we had been continuing our flight during this terrible meeting or whether it stopped us for a while. I realized that we were moving, that we were continuing to move upward.

Evil Spirits

The terrifying ordeal of seeing evil spirits after death is a notion that is unfamiliar to many, yet it is an experience that has been well understood by early Christians and a belief maintained in the Orthodox Church. For example, the Coptic funeral service includes a prayer requesting that God protect the spirit of the departed from any evil powers that seek to hinder it as it makes its way to Paradise: "O Master, God . . . abolish the resisting power, demolish the dragon's fury, and close up the lion's mouth. Put aside the evil spirits."[2] Likewise in the Eastern Orthodox *Canon on the Departure of the Soul* (or *The Office of the Parting of the Soul from the Body*), the priest prays, "As I depart from earth, vouchsafe me to pass unhindered by the prince of the air, the persecutor, the tormenter, he who stands on the frightful paths and is their unjust interrogator."[3]

It is such a frightening ordeal that the Orthodox Church has certain prayers that specifically incorporate an appeal to St. Mary for help to pass through it. The Coptic Prayer Book of Hours (known as the *Agpeya*) includes a prayer requesting her presence at the time of death:

> O Lady the Virgin . . . to you I appeal, and through you I seek intercession, and upon you I call to help me, lest I might be put to shame. And when my soul departs my body attend to me, and defeat the conspiracy of the enemies, and shut the gates of Hades, lest they might swallow my soul.

Also, the Eastern Orthodox *Canon on the Departure of the Soul* includes the following prayer: "Translate me, O Sovereign Lady, into the sacred and precious hands of the holy angels, that being covered by their wings, I may not see the shameless and foul and dark form of the demons."[4]

Having said that, be assured that by no means does any Orthodox Christian advocate the notion that St. Mary is divine or is on equal footing with God. However, being the Mother of God, she is considered so near and dear to Christ's heart that when she asks something of Him, the request resonates more than from any other person. Who among all women of all time was regarded as worthy to be given the blessing of bearing Christ in their womb? But, "When the fullness of the time had come, God sent forth His

Son" to be "born of a woman," and that woman was St. Mary (Gal 4:4). Elizabeth her relative attested to her high regard, greeting her as follows: "Blessed are you among women, and blessed is the fruit of your womb!" (Lk 1:42). If even the angel of God, Gabriel, greets her in the following manner saying, "Rejoice, highly favored one, the Lord is with you; blessed are you among women" (Lk 1:28), how much more ought we to honor her and expect that God heeds her prayers on our behalf? Mr. Uekskuell understood that, and her intercession paid off, whereby the "terrible pursuit" of evil spirits was thwarted.

Among Orthodox Christians, the belief in the existence of such evil spirits is as irrefutable as believing in angels (and is arguably substantiated outside of Christianity by innumerable stories and legends about experiences with such creatures throughout time). We can surmise from the Bible, as well as from the teachings of the earliest Church leaders, that the devil and his minions used to be angels in heaven. It is believed that all angels, whom we associate with light (cf. 2 Cor 11:14), were created before mankind, possibly as part of the light God created on the first day of all His creation (Gen 1:3). That they were created we learn from the apostle Paul who tells us, "For by Him all things were created that are in heaven and that are on earth, visible and invisible, whether thrones or dominions or principalities or powers. All things were created through Him and for Him" (Col 1:16). The angels were created some time before the "lights in the firmament of the heavens" (i.e., the stars) were made on the fourth day, as is implied from the following verse: "When the stars were made, all My angels praised Me with a loud voice" (Job 38:7, OSB).

At some point in time before the creation of man (which was on the sixth day), or maybe even because of it,[5] many angels, led by

Satan (believed to be a former archangel named Lucifer),[6] opposed God, which led to their banishment from heaven into a new and terrifying abode created specifically for them. There are a few varied opinions regarding what that abode is exactly. Some say the devil and his followers were banished to Hades, the same place the souls of the wicked await the day of judgment; others contend that the proper term for their place of banishment is *Tartarus*.

Tartarus is a Greek word arising out of Greek mythology, and it is used one time in the New Testament,[7] specifically being referred to as the place that fallen angels were sent as punishment. St. Peter tells us: "God did not spare the angels who sinned, but cast them down to hell [i.e., Tartarus] and delivered them into chains of darkness, to be reserved for judgment" (2 Pet 2:4). Some are of the opinion that Tartarus is a place that is distinct from Hades, while others regard Tartarus as a part of Hades. There are also those who regard St. Peter's use of the word Tartarus as simply an allegorical reference, synonymous with Hades. It is important to understand the Greek mythological context of this term to understand better what St. Peter may have meant. Here is what the *Dictionary of Classical Antiquities* has to say on the matter:

> According to the earliest Greek views, [Tartarus was regarded as being] a dark abyss, which lay as far below the surface of the earth as the earth is from the heavens. Above Tartarus were the foundations of the earth and sea. It was surrounded by an iron wall with iron gates set up by Poseidon, and by a . . . thick layer of night, and it served as the prison of the dethroned Cronus, and of the conquered Titans who were guarded by the . . . hundred-armed sons of Uranus. In later times its signification altered, and it came to mean the lower

regions as the place of damnation, in which the wicked who had been condemned by the judges of the world below suffered endless torments.[8]

* * *

According to the belief current among the Greeks, the world of the dead, or the spacious abode of Hades, with its wide doors, was in the dark depths of the earth. . . . The name Tartarus was in later times often applied to the whole of the lower world. . . .[9]

While we can certainly limit our interpretation of St. Peter's mention of Tartarus so as to confine its meaning to an abode separate from Hades, arguably the term can be understood more broadly to refer to or at least incorporate Hades. In support of that proposition one may consider the well-established Orthodox Christian belief that after Christ was crucified, He descended into Hades, to free the worthy captives from the grasp of Satan, who presumably was present there. Also, since Tartarus was believed to signify a kind of prison, then one may deduce that this word was meant to bring to the reader's mind the notion that Satan and his angels were held captive (bound by "chains of darkness");[10] thus, St. Peter can be said to have been simply alluding to the prison imagery invoked by Tartarus, rather than signifying a distinct region. It is this image that St. Jude brings to mind without attributing a specific name to where God cast the devil and his followers: "And the angels who did not keep their proper domain, but left their own abode, He has reserved in everlasting chains under darkness for the judgment of the great day" (Jude 1:6). It is doubtful that St.

Peter meant to give credence to the Greek mythological construct of Tartarus, but likely was instead importing the term's established context into Christian understanding. When we look at the rest of the passage, there is also argument to be made that the place where evil spirits are reserved for judgment is also the same place which St. Peter refers to later, although not by name, where the Lord will similarly "reserve the unjust" as well:

> For if God did not spare the angels who sinned, but cast them down to hell [i.e., Tartarus] and delivered them into chains of darkness, to be reserved for judgment . . . then the Lord knows how . . . to reserve the unjust under punishment for the day of judgment. (2 Pet 2:4, 9)

Some early Christians may be regarded as having assented to this correlation. For example, we find St. Jerome writing to a woman named Marcella, consoling her for the loss of a mutual friend, telling her to rejoice because that mutual friend is enjoying "everlasting felicity," as contrasted with a man who also recently passed away, whom he regarded as wicked and therefore was condemned to Tartarus:

> First, it [i.e., the death of our friend] shows that all must hail with joy the release of a soul which has trampled Satan under foot, and won for itself, at last, a crown of tranquility. Secondly, it gives me an opportunity of briefly describing her life. Thirdly, it enables me to assure you that the consul-elect, that detractor of his age, is now in Tartarus.[11]

We also find Hippolytus of Rome arguably making a similar association in his concluding address to the recipients of his letter:

> By means of this knowledge [i.e., "the true doctrine"], you will escape the approaching threat of the fire of judgment and the sunless scenery of gloomy Tartarus, where there never shines a beam from the irradiating voice of the Word. You will also escape the boiling flood of Gehenna's eternal lake of fire, and the eye ever fixed in menacing glare of the angels chained in Tartarus as punishment for their sins.[12]

Whatever the case may be, we know from Scripture and tradition that the devil and his angels rebelled and were cast out of heaven. Their rebellion seems to have centered around pride and a desire to exalt themselves above God. See what Isaiah writes, which is believed to be about Satan:

> How you are fallen from heaven, O Lucifer, son of the morning! How you are cut down to the ground, you who weakened the nations! For you have said in your heart: "I will ascend into heaven, I will exalt my throne above the stars of God; I will also sit on the mount of the congregation on the farthest sides of the north; I will ascend above the heights of the clouds, I will be like the Most High." Yet you shall be brought down to Sheol, to the lowest depths of the Pit. (Is 14:12–15)

Christ Himself remarks on this incident and says that He, being God Almighty and existing eternally, witnessed Satan's fall: "And

He said to them, 'I saw Satan fall like lightning from heaven'" (Lk 10:18). Origen comments on this verse (*c*. AD 225), teaching that "Satan had at one time been in heaven and had enjoyed a ... portion of that light in which all the saints [presently] participate."[13]

In the Old Testament, God is considered to have spoken about Satan (metaphorically or allegorically under the name of "the king of Tyre") as having been at first "the seal of perfection, full of wisdom and perfect in beauty," who was "in Eden, the garden of God" until he unfortunately fell into "iniquity" and "sinned," and therefore was "cast ... as a profane thing out of the mountain of God" and devoured with fire (Ezek 28:12–13, 15–16).

This is the same Satan who, at the end of times, will empower the antichrist, about whom the apostle Paul tells us, "opposes and exalts himself above all that is called God or that is worshiped," and who will sit "as God in the temple of God, showing himself that he is God ... with all power, signs, and lying wonders" (2 Thess 2:4, 9). St. Paul also tells us that by "being puffed up with pride" we will "fall into the same condemnation as the devil" (1 Tim 3:6).

Origen provides a fair view of the matter:

> Regarding the devil, his angels, and the opposing forces, the teaching of the Church is that these beings do indeed exist.... Most Christians ... hold this opinion: that the devil was an angel and that, having become an apostate, he induced as many of the angels as possible to fall away with him.[14]

Cyprian, bishop of Carthage, provides a plausible impetus for the devil's apostasy:

At the very beginning of the world . . . when he saw man made in the image of God, he broke forth into jealousy with malevolent envy. . . . How great an evil it was, beloved brethren, that caused an angel to fall![15]

That the devil was the head of the rest of the fallen angels can be understood from Christ's remark about the everlasting fire of hell having been "prepared for the devil and his angels" (Mt 25:41). Also, recall that the Pharisees referred to the devil as being the "ruler of the demons," by whom they claimed Christ was casting out demons from the possessed (Mt 9:34). Moreover, in St. John's revelation he saw the following encounter between Satan and Archangel Michael:

War broke out in heaven: Michael and his angels fought with the dragon; and the dragon and his angels fought, but they did not prevail, nor was a place found for them in heaven any longer. So the great dragon was cast out, that serpent of old, called the devil and Satan, who deceives the whole world; he was cast to the earth, and his angels were cast out with him. (Rev 12:7–9)

St. Irenaeus tells us,

Eternal fire was not originally prepared for man, but for him who beguiled man, and caused him to offend. I say, it was prepared for him who is chief of the apostasy, and for those angels who became apostates along with him.[16]

Those fallen angels are always associated with darkness, which is diametrically opposed to all that is good—good being identified with light (note that the Bible refers to God as the "Father of lights"—Jas 1:17). As you have read and will continue to read, when a person enters the Crossover Realm, they usually encounter some sort of struggle between darkness and light, evil and goodness.

This battle is waged and decided on the basis of one pivotal issue: the choices we made during life (including whether we chose to believe in Christ, and then still whether we lived a pure life in accordance with that belief [1 Jn 3:3], for "whoever does not practice righteousness is not of God" [1 Jn 3:10]). Throughout our lives, we engage in a struggle between choosing to do good and choosing to do evil. Unknown to many, invisible influences attempt to induce us to make certain choices. The Holy Spirit, as well as angels it seems (according to some writings and accounts), try to sway us toward what is good: "That good thing which was committed to you, keep by the Holy Spirit who dwells in us" (2 Tim 1:14). In contrast, we have to battle the (usually) invisible intrusions of the devil and his angels: "For we do not wrestle against flesh and blood, but against principalities, against powers, against the rulers of the darkness of this age, against spiritual hosts of wickedness in the heavenly places" (Eph 6:12); that is why Christ told us that every time we pray, we should ask God that He "deliver us from the evil one" (Lk 11:4). The reason for the devil's antagonism is often summed up as "the envy of the devil." He especially envies those who have been baptized and thereby granted access to the place the evil spirits once inhabited, as St. Gregory of Nyssa tells us:

> Therefore . . . it is that after the dignity of adoption the devil

plots more vehemently against us, pining away with envious glance, when he beholds the beauty of the new-born man, earnestly tending towards the heavenly city, from which he fell: and he raises up against us fiery temptations, seeking earnestly to despoil us of that second adornment, as he did of our former array.[17]

The Bible constantly warns us of this struggle and teaches us to stand firmly against evil: "Therefore take up the whole armor of God, that you may be able to withstand in the evil day, and having done all, to stand.... Quench all the fiery darts of the wicked one" (Eph 6:13, 16). "Be sober, be vigilant; because your adversary the devil walks about like a roaring lion, seeking whom he may devour. Resist him, steadfast in the faith, knowing that the same sufferings are experienced by your brotherhood in the world" (1 Pet 5:8–9). St. Paul teaches us not to "give place to the devil" (Eph 4:27). St. James warns us also, "Submit to God. Resist the devil, and he will flee from you" (Jas 4:7).

This invisible struggle between doing what is right, as the "Father of lights" (Jas 1:17) asks us to do, and what is wrong, as the "prince of the power of . . . darkness" (Eph 2:2; 6:12) would prefer, was understood by the early Christian known as Hermas.[18] He tells us that "there are two angels with a man—one of righteousness, and the other of iniquity."[19] We previously saw what he had to say about the angel of righteousness—our guardian angel.

Look now at the works of the angel of iniquity. First, he is wrathful, and bitter, and foolish, and his works are evil, and ruin the servants of God. When, then, he ascends into your heart, know him by his works.... When anger comes upon you, or harshness, . . . a longing after many transactions, and the richest delicacies, and drunken revels, and diverse luxuries, and things improper, and by a hankering after women, and by overreaching, and pride, and blustering, and by whatever is like to these. When these ascend into your heart, know that the angel of iniquity is in you. Now that you know his works, depart from him, and in no respect trust him, because his deeds are evil, and unprofitable to the servants of God. These, then, are the actions of both angels. Understand them, and trust the angel of righteousness; but depart from the angel of iniquity, because his instruction is bad in every deed.[20]

Angels and Devils Struggling Over You

The invisible struggle between angels and devils during our lives takes on a terrifyingly visible spectacle after death. It is consistently manifested in Orthodox Christian afterlife experiences and is a longstanding belief in the Orthodox Church. The notion of this struggle over one's spirit may seem novel to those who have never heard of such an experience awaiting them after death, yet, if anything, it is a very familiar belief found very early on in Christianity. For example, St. Justin Martyr (*c.* AD 100–165) expounds on Psalm 22 and the psalmist's plea to be saved from the sword and the lion's mouth, and affirms that,

> When we arrive at the end of life, we [should] ask the same petition from God, who is able to turn away every shameless evil angel from taking our souls. . . . Hence also God by His Son teaches us . . . always to strive earnestly, and at death to

pray that our souls may not fall into the hands of any such power.[21]

One may also deduce that such an experience is not unfounded when reading St. Jude's reference to the struggle between Satan and Archangel Michael over the body of Moses (cf. Jude 1:9).

Moreover, what makes this experience particularly perturbing is the realization of our sinfulness and how our decisions in life will impact the outcome of it all, as St. John Chrysostom tells us:

> [The soul] often rises and sinks down again toward the abyss, and trembles with fear. . . . For the awareness of our sins always pricks us, especially at that time when we are about to be led away to the examination of accounts in that terrible court. Then, if anyone has been guilty of . . . any . . . wrong, the whole swarm of sins is revived and stands before our eyes to sting our conscience. Just as those who dwell in the prison are in dejection and distress all the time but especially on that day on which they are to be led out to the very doors of the judge, and standing before the courtroom doors, hearing the voice of the judge from inside, are chilled with fear, and are no better off than the dead; so also the soul is in great distress and anxiety at the actual time of its sin, but even more when it is about to be drawn out and led away from this world.[22]

There are a few stories I would like to share that illustrate this ordeal. One story comes from St. Athanasius of Alexandria (*c.* AD 297–373) in his biography of the Father of Monasticism, St. Anthony the Great (*c.* AD 251–356):

Once, for example, when he was about to eat and stood up to pray, about the ninth hour, he felt himself carried off in spirit, and—strange to say—as he stood he saw himself, as it were, outside himself and as though guided aloft by certain beings [i.e., angels]. Then he also saw loathsome and terrible beings standing in the air and bent on preventing him from passing through. As his [angel] guides offered resistance, the others [i.e., evil spirits] demanded to know on what plea he was not accountable to them [i.e., they wanted to know on what basis the angels refused the evil spirits from holding St. Anthony accountable]. Then, when they set themselves to taking an account from his birth, Anthony's guides intervened, saying to them: "As for the things dating from his birth, the Lord has erased them; but as for the time since he became [a] monk and promised himself to God, you can take an account." Then, as they [i.e., the evil spirits] brought accusations but could not prove them, the way opened up to him free and unhindered; and presently he saw himself approaching, so it seemed to him, and halting with himself [i.e., his spirit re-approached his body and entered it again]; and so he was the real Anthony again. Then, forgetting to eat, he spent the rest of the day and all the night sighing and praying. For he was astonished to see against how many we battle and what labors a person has to pass through the air; and he remembered that this is what the Apostle said—"according to the prince of the power of the air" [Eph 2:2]. Here precisely lies the Enemy's power, that he fights and tries to stop those who pass through. Wherefore, too, his special admonition: "Take unto you the armor of God that you may be able to resist in the evil day [Eph 6:13] that having no evil to say of us the Enemy may be put to shame [Titus 2:8]." ... Anthony saw himself entering the air and struggling until he became free.²³

St. Anthony received yet another revelation regarding the plight of our spirits after death as we cross over to the next world:

> Again, he had this favor from God. When he sat alone on the mountain, if ever in his reflections he failed to find a solution, it was revealed to him by Providence in answer to his prayer; the happy man was, in the words of Scripture, "taught of God" [Jn 6:45]. Thus favored, he once had ... a discussion with some visitors about the life of the soul and the kind of place it will have after this life. The following night there came a call from on high saying, "Anthony, rise, go out and look!" He went out, therefore—[since] he knew which calls to heed [from previous experiences with God]—and, looking up, saw a towering figure, unsightly and frightening, standing and reaching to the clouds; further, certain beings ascending as though on wings. The former was stretching out his hands; some of the latter were stopped by him, while others flew over him and, having come through, rose without further trouble. At such as these the monster gnashed his teeth, but exulted over those who fell. Forthwith a voice addressed itself to Anthony, "Understand the vision!" [cf. Dan 8:16; 9:23]. His understanding opened up, and he realized that it was the passing of souls and that the monster standing there was the Enemy, the envier of the faithful. Those answerable to him he lays hold of and keeps them from passing through, but those whom he failed to win over he cannot master as they pass out of his range. Here again, having seen this and taking it as a

reminder, he struggled the more to advance from day to day in the things that lay before him.[24]

St. Anthony's contemporary, St. Macarius the Great, also experienced the presence of evil spirits as he crossed over, until he finally reached Paradise. We know this from a story in which his disciple observed St. Macarius as his spirit ascended to Paradise, as is explained in the Coptic Synaxarion:

> He [i.e., the disciple] heard the devils crying out and calling after him, "You have conquered us O Macarius."
> The saint replied, "I have not conquered you yet."
> When they came to the gates of heaven they cried again saying, "You have conquered us," and he replied [the same] as the first time. When he [finally] entered the gate of heaven they cried, "You have overcome us O Macarius."
> He replied, "Blessed be the Lord Jesus Christ who has delivered me from your hands."[25]

The well-known island missionary and ascetic leader Columba (AD 521–597), the founder of the island monastery of Iona, Scotland, many times in his life saw the battle of demons in the air for the spirits of those who had newly departed. For example, once, calling together his monks, he told them,

> "Now let us help by prayer the monks of the Abbot Comgell, drowning at this hour in the Lough of the Calf; for behold, at this moment they are warring in the air against hostile powers who try to snatch away the soul of a stranger who is drowning

along with them."

[Then after prayer, he said] . . . "Give thanks to Christ, for now the holy angels have met these holy souls, and have delivered that stranger and triumphantly rescued him from the warring demons."[26]

Abba Serapion, an early desert father who dwelled in Egypt, described the death of his fellow monk, Mark of Thrace:

> Looking up, I beheld the soul of the saint already being delivered from the bonds of the body. It was covered by angelic hands with a bright white garment and raised up by them to heaven. I beheld the aerial path to heaven and the opened heavens. Then I saw the hordes of demons standing on this path and heard an angelic voice addressed to the demons: "Sons of darkness! Flee and hide yourselves from the face of the light of righteousness!" The holy soul of Mark was detained in the air for about one hour. Then a voice was heard from heaven saying to the angels: "Take and bring here him who put the demons to shame." When the soul of the saint had passed without any harm to itself through the hordes of demons and had already drawn near to the opened heavens, I saw as it were the likeness of a hand stretched out from heaven receiving the immaculate soul. Then this vision was hidden from my eyes, and I saw nothing more.[27]

Boniface, the eighth-century Anglo-Saxon apostle to the Germans, in one of his letters, gives us the account of a monk from a monastery at Wenlock who died and came back to life after some hours:

> Angels of such pure splendor bore him up as he came forth from the body that he could not bear to gaze upon them. . . . "They carried me up," he said, "high into the air." He reported further that in the space of time while he was out of the body, a greater multitude of souls left their bodies and gathered in the place where he was that he had thought [them to appear] to form the whole race of mankind on earth. He said also that there was a crowd of evil spirits and a glorious choir of the higher angels. And he said that the wretched spirits and the holy angels had a violent dispute concerning the souls that had come forth from their bodies, the demons bringing charges against them and aggravating the burden of their sins, the angels lightening the burden and making excuses for them.
>
> He heard all his own sins, which he had committed from his youth on and had failed to confess or had forgotten or had not recognized as sins, crying out against him, each in its own voice, and accusing him grievously. . . . Everything he had done in all the days of his life and had neglected to confess and many which he had not known to be sinful, all these were now shouted at him in terrifying words. In the same way the evil spirits, chiming in with the vices, accusing and bearing witness, naming the very times and places, brought proofs of his evil deeds. . . . And so, with his sins all piled up and reckoned out, those ancient enemies declared him guilty and unquestionably subject to their jurisdiction.
>
> "On the other hand," he said, "the poor little virtues which I had displayed unworthily and imperfectly spoke out

in my defense.... And those angelic spirits in their boundless love defended and supported me, while the virtues, greatly magnified as they were, seemed to me far greater and more excellent than could ever have been practiced by my own strength."[28]

John of the Ladder (Climacus), a seventh-century Christian monk from a monastery on Mount Sinai, describes an occurrence experienced by a fellow monk before his death:

On the day before his death, he went into an ecstasy of mind and with open eyes he looked to the right and left of his bed and, as if he were being called to account by someone, in the hearing of all the bystanders he said: "Yes indeed, that is true; but that is why I fasted for so many years." And then again, "Yes, it is quite true; but I wept and served the brethren." And again: "No, you are slandering me." And sometimes he would say: "Yes, it is true. Yes, I do not know what to say to this. But in God there is mercy." And it was truly an awful and horrible sight—this invisible and merciless inquisition. And what was most terrible, he was accused of what he had not done. How amazing! Of several of his sins ... [he] said: "I do not know what to say to this," although he had been a monk for nearly forty years and had the gift of [shedding] tears.... And while thus being called to account he was parted from his body, leaving us in uncertainty as to his ... end, or sentence, or how the trial ended.[29]

On a more jovial note, one finds the story of a great desert dweller from the fourth century just before he departed this life:

> It was said of Abba Joseph of Panephysis that when he was at the point of death, while some old men were seated round him, he looked towards the window and saw the devil sitting close to it. Then calling his disciple he said to him, "Bring my stick, for there is one there who thinks I am getting old and have no more strength against him." As he gripped his stick the old men saw that the devil fled through the window like a dog, and disappeared from sight.[30]

Here I want to note that I am familiar with some afterlife experiences that purport to bypass the terrifying ordeal of encountering evil spirits after death. Among many Orthodox Christians, there is the belief that those who partake of the body and blood of the Lord shortly before death will be granted a direct transition to Paradise. See what Archimandrite Tikhon from Russia writes in his book, *Everyday Saints and Other Stories*: "The clergy has long believed that if before a person's death he is able to take Holy Communion, that person's soul immediately goes up to God, without undergoing any ordeals after death."[31]

Regardless of the situation a person may face, a decision will still have to be made. All who neglected to enjoy a life within the loving embrace of Christ, whose life indicated an affinity for works of darkness, will find themselves in Hades. Those who know and love Christ, have followed His commandments, and are righteous will enter into Paradise.

Do not be deceived, God is not mocked; for whatever a man

sows, that he will also reap. For he who sows to his flesh will of the flesh reap corruption, but he who sows to the Spirit will of the Spirit reap everlasting life. (Gal 6:7–8)

As St. Justin Martyr taught: "Each man goes to everlasting punishment or salvation according to the value of his actions."[32]

The actual experience of passing into the Crossover Realm and then to one's final destination may differ for different people. Maybe it is a swift transition. Maybe the transition and struggle between good and evil is felt more than it is seen. What I do know for certain is that we will all end up somewhere—either in Paradise or in Hades.

Before leaving this subject, though, I would like to tell you about an afterlife experience of one particular non-Orthodox Christian that provides another perspective regarding crossing over. On December 12, 2006, I was watching *The Oprah Winfrey Show*, which headlined a story titled, "The woman without a face" (a show that originally aired May 25, 2006). Carolyn Thomas had been shot in the face at point-blank range as a result of a jealous rage by her boyfriend at the time. More than half of her face was shattered. Eventually she recovered enough to appear on *The Oprah Winfrey Show* to tell her story as "the woman who survived." One peculiar part of her story struck me. Oprah asked her, "Do you remember being shot at all?" Carolyn answered that she had an out-of-body experience. Here is what she said, verbatim:

> I remember having an out-of-body experience. And it was kind of like the devil was on one side, God was on one side, and I was falling down this tunnel real, real, real fast. After not getting to the bottom, I just remember this calm feeling

and not feeling any pain and asking God to forgive me for all my sins and if he sees me fit to be here, you know, . . . do something.[33]

Though Ms. Thomas apparently lacked the knowledge to interpret what she was experiencing, the parallels with the stories mentioned above are evident.

Hades or Paradise: A Decision Is Made

At some point, in some manner, the ordeal ends and we will arrive at our due destination. While some will be carried by angels to Paradise, others who are deemed unworthy of heavenly bliss will be led away by devils to Hades. The early Christian, Hippolytus of Rome (*c.* AD 170–235), tells us how he envisions that moment:

> The unrighteous are dragged . . . by angels who are ministers of punishment. These souls no longer go of their own accord. Rather, they are dragged as prisoners by force. And the angels appointed over them hurry them along, reproaching them and threatening with an eye of terror, forcing them down into the lower parts.[34]

St. John Chrysostom also speaks of this when discussing two biblical parables about the demise of two different rich men. One is found in the story of Lazarus (who died and went to a place of comfort) and the rich man (who died and went to Hades). The other is the story of another rich man who kept accumulating material possessions on earth to the point that he said to himself one day, "You have many goods laid up for many years; take your ease; eat, drink, and be merry" (Lk 12:19). St. John Chrysostom tells us:

> Not only the souls of the righteous but also the souls of those who lived in wickedness are led away after death; this is clear from another rich man. For when his harvest was abundant, he said to himself, "What shall I do? I will pull down my barns, and build larger ones" [Lk 12:17–18]. . . . What does God say to him? "Fool! Tonight they require your soul from you" [Lk 12:20]. You see, here [with regard to Lazarus] it says [he] "was carried away by the angels" [Lk 16:22]; [but] there [in the parable of the other rich man], [it says] "they require [your soul]." One was led away as a prisoner, the other was carried on their shoulders as a victor. . . . From that other [rich] man his soul was required by some frightful powers, perhaps sent just for this purpose.[35]

Likewise, St. Ephraim the Syrian (d. AD 373) describes the hour of death:

> When the fearful hosts come, when the divine takers-away command the soul to be translated from the body, when they draw us away by force and lead us away to the unavoidable judgment place—then, seeing them, the poor man . . . comes all into a shaking as if from an earthquake [and] is all in trembling. . . . The divine takers-away, taking the soul, ascend in the air where stand the chiefs, the authorities and world-rulers of the opposing powers. These are our accusers, the fearful publicans, registrars, tax-collectors; they meet

it on the way, register, examine, and count out the sins and debts of this man—the sins of youth and old age, voluntary and involuntary, committed in deed, word, and thought. Great is the fear here, great and trembling of the poor soul, indescribable the want which it suffers then from the incalculable multitudes of its enemies surrounding it there in myriads, slandering it so as not to allow it to ascend to heaven, to dwell in the light of the living, to enter the land of life.[36]

St. Basil the Great (*c.* AD 330–379), in his interpretation of the words of the psalm, "Save me from all those who persecute me, and deliver me, lest they tear me like a lion, rending me in pieces, while there is none to deliver" (Ps 7:1–2), says the following:

> I think that the noble athletes of God who have wrestled considerably with the invisible enemies during the whole of their lives, after they have escaped all of their persecutions and reached the end of their life, are examined by the prince of this world [i.e., Satan—cf. Jn 12:31; 14:30] in order that, if they are found to have wounds from wrestling or any stains or effects of sin, they may be detained. But, if they are found unwounded and sinless, they may be brought by Christ into their rest as being unconquered and free. Therefore, the prophet [i.e., the psalmist, David] prays both for his life here and for his future life. Here he says: "Save me from them that persecute me"; and there, at the time of trial: "Deliver me, lest at any time like a lion he seize my soul." And this you can learn from the Lord Himself, who before His suffering said: "Now the prince of this world comes, and he has nothing in Me" (Jn 14:30).[37]

The Terrifying Ordeal

Abba Theophilus, archbishop of Alexandria (c. AD 385–412), described the terrifying predicament after death in terms that are astonishingly reminiscent of the afterlife experiences in this chapter, almost as if he had some personal knowledge of the reality of the Crossover Realm:

> What fear, what trembling, what uneasiness will there be for us when our soul is separated from the body. Then indeed the force and strength of the adverse powers come against us, the rulers of darkness, those who command the world of evil, the principalities, the powers, the spirits of evil. They accuse our souls as in a lawsuit, bringing before it all the sins it has committed, whether deliberately or through ignorance, from its youth until the time when it has been taken away. So they stand accusing it of all it has done.
>
> Furthermore, what anxiety do you suppose the soul will have at that hour, until sentence is pronounced and it gains its liberty. That is its hour of affliction, until it sees what will happen to it. On the other hand, the divine powers stand on the opposite side, and they present the good deeds of the soul. Consider the fear and trembling of the soul standing between them.... If... worthy, the demons will receive their punishment, and [the soul] will be carried away by the angels. Then thereafter... will the Scripture be fulfilled: "Sorrow and sighing shall flee away" [Is 35:10]. Then your liberated soul will go on to that joy and ineffable glory in which it will be established.
>
> But if it is found to have lived carelessly, it will hear that terrible voice: "Take away the ungodly, that he may not see the glory of the Lord" [cf. Is 26:10]. Then the day of anger,

the day of affliction, the day of darkness and shadow seizes upon it. Abandoned to outer darkness and condemned to everlasting fire, it will be punished through the ages without end.

Where is the vanity of the world? Where is vainglory? Where is carnal life? Where is enjoyment? Where is imagination? Where is ease? Where is boasting? Riches? Nobility? Father, mother, brother? Who could take the soul of its pains when it is burning in the fire, and remove it from bitter torments?

Since this is so, in what manner ought we not to give ourselves to holy and devout works? What love ought we to acquire? What manner of life? What virtues? What speed? What diligence? What prayer? What prudence? Scripture says, "In this waiting, let us make every effort to be found blameless and without reproach in peace" [cf. 1 Cor 1:7–8]. In this way, we shall be worthy to hear it said: "Come, O blessed of my Father, inherit the kingdom prepared for you from the foundation of the world" [Mt 25:34].[38]

Let us now peer into that dreadful and frightful place known as Hades. After that, we will take a peek at some of the wonders that await us in Paradise, by God's grace.

Part Three

The Abode of Darkness and Misery

Hades

> I will show you whom you should fear: Fear Him who, after He has killed, has power to cast into hell; yes, I say to you, fear Him! (Lk 12:5)

As previously explained, the term Hades is used here to refer to the temporary abode where people are reserved for judgment. Hippolytus affirms to us (*c.* AD 205) that Hades is the place "in which all souls are detained until the time that God has determined."[1]

Investigating further into the nature of Hades may seem to be an odd endeavor to some, but it was not uncommon for early Christians to venture upon that inquiry. For example, the Coptic Synaxarion relays that Abba Pachomius (*c.* AD 290–348), regarded as the founder of the cenobitic (communal) life for monastics, "desired once to see Hades, and he saw in a night vision the habitation of the sinners and places of torment."[2]

Note that Hades is not regarded as a place where people simply enter some dormant existence, as if they are sleeping, awaiting the Second Coming of Christ. Rather, as St. Justin Martyr states, "We affirm that the souls of the wicked . . . [are] endowed with sensation even after death."³

Also, be aware that while Hades is temporary, eternal punishment begins there and continues in hell's eternal fire after Christ's Second Coming; moreover, banishment to hell means eternal punishment, not a cessation of life. In the Bible, hell is likened to a "furnace of fire" (Mt 13:42) and a "lake of fire" (Rev 20:14), whose "fire is not quenched" (Mk 9:48) and shall persist as an "everlasting punishment" (Mt 25:46).

The early Christians agree about this. For example, as early as AD 70, a writing attributed to the apostle Barnabas (although recent scholarship regards it as being authored by some other Christian around the first century), indicates that "the way of darkness . . . is the way of eternal death with punishment."[4] Others attest to the same, including Ignatius of Antioch (*c.* AD 110),[5] Justin Martyr (*c.* AD 150),[6] Irenaeus (*c.* AD 180),[7] Cyprian (d. AD 258),[8] and Basil the Great (*c.* AD 370).[9]

Do not think for a moment that God is unfair in the manner in which He dispenses His justice. We know that "God is love" (1 Jn 4:8), while at the same time He is "a just judge" (Ps 7:11): "I will sing of mercy and justice; to You, O LORD, I will sing praises" (Ps 101:1). God confronted those who felt "the way of the Lord is not fair" (Ezek 18:25) in dealing with the fate of sinners and the righteous. He responded by assuring us of His mercy harmonizing with His justice:

> "Do I have any pleasure at all that the wicked should die?" says the Lord God, "and not that he should turn from his ways and live? Yet you say, 'The way of the Lord is not fair.' Hear now, . . . is it not My way which is fair, and your ways which are not fair?" (Ezek 18:23, 25)

"If a wicked man turns from all his sins which he has committed, keeps all My statutes, and does what is lawful and right, he shall surely live; he shall not die. None of the transgressions which he has committed shall be remembered against him; because of the righteousness which he has done, he shall live. . . . But when a righteous man turns away from his righteousness and commits iniquity, and does according to all the abominations that the wicked man does, shall he live? All the righteousness which he has done shall not be remembered; because of the unfaithfulness of which he is guilty and the sin which he has committed, because of them he shall die." (Ezek 18:21–22, 24)

Irenaeus makes the point that one cannot blame God when they have decided to turn away from Him and have of their own choice delivered themselves to darkness; it would be as if a person who shut themselves in a dark room were to blame the sun for the lack of light there:

> For those persons who shun rest shall justly incur punishment, and those who avoid the light shall justly dwell in darkness. For as in the case of this temporal light, those who shun it do deliver themselves over to darkness, so that they do themselves become the cause to themselves that they are destitute of light, and do inhabit darkness; and, as I have already observed, the light is not the cause of such an [unhappy] condition of existence to them; so those who fly from the eternal light of God, which contains in itself all good things, are themselves the cause to themselves of their inhabiting eternal darkness, destitute of all good things, having become to themselves the

cause of [their consignment to] an abode of that nature.[10]

Likewise St. Cyprian taught that "[those] who have done the will of the devil . . . [will] be tormented with the devil himself in unquenchable fire."[11]

Someone may ask though, "How is it just that punishment is going to be forever?" Here is St. John Chrysostom's response to that question:

> "They shall go away into everlasting punishment" [Mt 25:46]; . . . Say not unto me, "Where is the rule of justice preserved entire, if the punishment has no end?" Rather, when God does anything, obey His decisions and submit not what is said to human reasonings. But moreover, how can it be anything else than just for one who has experienced innumerable blessings from the beginning, and then committed deeds worthy of punishment, and neither by threat nor benefit improved at all, to suffer punishment? For if you inquire what is absolute justice, it was meet that we should have perished immediately from the beginning, according to the definition of strict justice.[12]

St. John Chrysostom teaches us about God's fairness by explaining that it is a just God who will give people their fair due in the hereafter relative to how they lived their lives:

> Do you not see how many have departed after a life of virtue and innumerable sufferings without receiving any of the good they deserve? Others, however, have departed after

displaying great wickedness ... enjoying wealth, luxury, and innumerable good things, without suffering even ordinary troubles. So when will these former people receive the reward for their virtue, or these latter people suffer the punishment for their wickedness, if our affairs last only for the present life? ... [Since] God exists, [and] He is just, ... He will repay both the former and the latter as they deserve. But if He would repay both the former and the latter as they deserve, but in this life neither of them have received their deserts, ... obviously there is some time of life in which each of these will have their fitting recompense.[13]

St. John Chrysostom also explains elsewhere that God, in His mercy, allows us each to judge ourselves before He judges us, by means of our conscience: "Why has God set in the mind of every one of us such a continuously watchful and sober judge? I mean the conscience. For there is no judge, no judge at all among men as sleepless as our conscience."[14] He elaborates on this as follows:

When we have committed some wickedness, let us not wait for misfortunes and difficulties. ... Let us cast our vote against ourselves and try in every way to make our defense before God. ... This also is evidence of His love for mankind. Since He is going to demand from us hereafter an account of our transgressions, He has set in us this impartial judge. By judging us here for our sins and making us better, this judge may rescue us from the judgment to come. This is what Paul says also: "If we judged ourselves ... we should not be judged" by the Lord [1 Cor 11:31].[15]

Christ has already shown us His love and mercy in that He suffered for our sake instead of us, "the just for the unjust, that He might bring us to God" (1 Pet 3:18). Bishop Theophilus of Antioch summarizes the Orthodox Christian view on the matter of God's justice as follows (*c.* AD 180):

> He . . . will examine all things, and will judge righteous judgment, rendering merited awards to each. To those who seek immortality by patient endurance in well-doing, He will give life everlasting, joy, peace, rest and an abundance of good things. To the unbelieving and despisers, who do not obey the truth but are obedient to unrighteousness, when they will have been filled with adulteries and fornications, . . . there will be anger and wrath, tribulation and anguish. At the end, everlasting fire will possess such men.[16]

For those who find themselves in Hades, what will they experience? Let us first see what we can glean from Christ's parable about Lazarus and the rich man (Lk 16:19–31). The rich man was "in torments in Hades." He begged Lazarus to "dip the tip of his finger in water and cool" his tongue, being "tormented in this flame." The rich man was then told something that gives us a very significant piece of information: "Between us and you there is a great gulf fixed, so that those who want to pass from here to you cannot, nor can those from there pass to us." This brings to mind the question whether or not there is a third place where departed souls find themselves, other than Hades or Paradise.

The famed Isaac the Syrian (*c.* AD 700) tells us his opinion on this matter:

In the future separation there will be no middle realm between the state that is completely on high and the state that is absolutely below. A person will either belong entirely to those who dwell on high, or entirely to those below. . . . If this is true, which it most certainly is, what is more senseless and more foolish than those who say that "It is enough for me to escape Gehenna [i.e., hell], I do not seek to enter the kingdom!" For to escape Gehenna means precisely to enter the kingdom, even as falling away from the kingdom is entering Gehenna. Scripture has taught us nothing about the existence of three realms, but "When the Son of God will come in His glory, . . . He shall set the sheep on His right hand, but the goats on His left [Mt 25:31, 33]." . . . How have you not understood by these things that falling short of the order on high is in fact, the Gehenna of torment?[17]

The earliest Christian writings are devoid of any mention of the existence of any third realm where people are sent to wait until the Second Coming of Christ, other than Hades or Paradise. Moreover, the belief that such a realm is where spirits exist so that they may be purified or offer repentance and then be elevated to Paradise with the righteous is seriously questionable. The finality of one's plight can be derived from the writings of the fathers when they taught that there is no opportunity for repentance after death. See what one bishop and martyr of the early Church, Victorinus of Syria, says on this matter (*c.* AD 280):

After the death of a man . . . there cannot be added to him anything at all. He cannot be supplemented. Nor can anything avail him in the day of judgment. . . . The wicked . . . cannot be carried across [to the place of rest for the righteous].[18]

St. John Chrysostom also tells us, "When we depart to that place, we have no longer the option of repentance, nor of washing away our misdeeds."[19] This same sentiment is echoed by St. Cyprian of Carthage: "The grief at punishment will then be without the fruit of repentance; weeping will be useless, and prayer ineffectual. . . . When once you have departed this life, there is no longer any place for repentance, no way of making satisfaction. Here life is either lost or kept."[20] St. Basil the Great also taught, "When life is over, there is no longer any opportunity for the improving of piety."[21] His close friend, St. Gregory Nazianzen, urged people to remember that it is "better to be punished and cleansed now than to be sent to the torment to come, when it will be time for punishing only, and not for cleansing."[22]

Prayer for the Departed

Why did the early Christians and, at present, apostolic churches pray for those who have departed? What benefit do such prayers serve? Some think this practice has no biblical support, but even the great apostle Paul prayed for his deceased friend and fellow Christian Onesiphorus; writing to Timothy he prayed, "The Lord grant to him that he may find mercy from the Lord in that Day" (2 Tim 1:18). (In support of the conclusion that he was already deceased, in the same epistle we find that St. Paul did not mention Onesiphorus by name in his concluding greetings, but only his household [2 Tim 4:19].)

The early Christian Church continued this practice. For example, we find St. Cyril, bishop of Jerusalem, teaching his congregation the following (*c.* AD 350):

> We make mention . . . of those who have already fallen asleep . . . for we believe that it will be of . . . benefit to the souls of those for whom the petition is carried up . . . [hoping that God would] grant a remission of their penalties.[23]

Another bishop, known as St. Epiphanius of Salamis, writes the following about two decades later (*c.* AD 374):

> Useful . . . is the prayer fashioned on their behalf, even if it does not force back the whole of guilty charges laid to them. And it is useful also, because in this world we often stumble either voluntarily or involuntarily, and thus it is a reminder to do better.[24]

The Coptic Orthodox archbishop, His Holiness Pope Shenouda III, wrote regarding this matter of prayer for the departed in a similar fashion:

> [We pray for the departed] so that he could at least depart from the world having been absolved by the Church, so that he is no longer bound in any way. That person is then left to the mercy of the One who searches men's hearts and the One who knows all secrets. It is as if the Church is saying to God, "This person has been released from our side by the authority to loose and bind which You gave us [cf. Mt 18:18; Jn 20:23], and so we leave him now to Your mercy and to Your knowledge which is beyond ours."

The Church also prays on behalf of the one who is passing on, for him to be forgiven any sins which he may have committed which were not of the degree that leads to death [cf. 1 Jn 5:16–17]. So what are these sins that do not lead to death? They are uncompleted sins, sins that have not been fully carried out. They [also] may be sins of ignorance, sins committed unintentionally, or sins that are latent, or sins of negligence, for example.

* * *

Let us suppose that a person has died suddenly without having had a chance to confess, or that he has forgotten to confess some sins, and therefore has not received an absolution for them. The Church can give him absolution and asks forgiveness for him, in the *Prayer for the Departed*.[25]

Added to all of that, it is worthy to note that God, who is beyond time, hears our prayers after a person's repose as if they had come before the person departed ("It shall come to pass that before they call, I will answer; and while they are still speaking, I will hear"—Is 65:24).

Father Seraphim Rose, a contemporary American Orthodox monk, summarized his findings from the Church Fathers as follows:

> We have received that even the souls which are held in hell [i.e., Hades] and are already given over to eternal torments, whether in actual fact and experience or in hopeless expectation of

such, can be aided and given a certain small help, although not in the sense of completely loosing them from torment or giving hope for a final deliverance. And this is shown from the words of the great St. Macarius the Egyptian ascetic who, finding a skull in the desert, was instructed by it concerning this by the action of divine power.[26] [That story is from the sayings of the desert fathers where we read Abba Macarius the Great's remarks: "Walking in the desert one day, I found the skull of a dead man, lying on the ground. As I was moving it with a stick, the skull spoke to me. I said to it, 'Who are you?' The skull replied, 'I was a high priest of the idols and of the pagans who dwelt in this place; but you are Macarius, the Spirit-bearer. Whenever you take pity on those who are in torments, and pray for them, they feel a little respite.' The skull further instructed St. Macarius concerning the torments of hell [i.e., Hades], concluding, 'We have received a little mercy since we did not know God, but those who knew God and denied Him are down below us.'"[27]]

Likewise, Catherine P. Roth makes the following assessment of St. John Chrysostom and the Church Fathers in her introduction to the book, *On Wealth and Poverty* (which collects her translation of various sermons by St. John Chrysostom that touch upon the subject of the afterlife, among other things):

> In concluding the third sermon, St. John speaks of the great chasm which separates heaven from hell [cf. Lk 16:26]. This raises the issue of intercessory prayer for the dead. The Fathers of the Orthodox Church generally teach, with the support of Biblical texts like this, that we must make our

choice for or against God in this life, and that once we have passed to the other life we will have no opportunity to escape from hell. Thus, St. John here tells his congregation that, if they have not made their own efforts to acquire virtue during their lives, they must not expect to be saved by the prayers of others, whether of their spiritual father or of any saintly relative. Nevertheless, the Church traditionally prays for the dead, a practice which St. John's discussion assumes. What good do our prayers for the dead accomplish? . . . For those in hell, most of the Fathers say that our prayers are able to lessen their suffering but not actually to release them.[28]

Aside from what has been mentioned above, prayer for the departed is also regarded as an expression of the fellowship of love between us and them. Hence, in certain prayers, we make mention of departed saints whom we are certain are in Paradise, such as St. Mary and St. John the Baptist, not to implore God for mercy on their behalf, but as a pronouncement of our love and affection for them.[29] This, too, is seemingly derived from an early Church tradition, as Bishop Epiphanius tells us that in his time it was customary to "make commemoration of the just."[30] Such prayers align with the Orthodox view of the Church as consisting of all of its members, whether they have already crossed over to the next life or remain striving in this one. The bond of mutual prayer unites the Church as an instrument of communion and solidarity.

Mother Erene, in a conversation with a previously departed nun, Mother Martha, learned something about what it means to pray for the departed. Mother Martha asked her, "Why do you not hold Liturgies for me?" (What is meant here is the practice of attending a Liturgy and providing the name of the departed to be remembered during the pertinent prayers.) Mother Erene asked her what she would gain from such prayers, and Mother Martha responded:

> I won't be given any benefit because everyone will be given according to his or her work. But when I feel that you are thinking about me and praying for me, I come among you during the Liturgy and feel happy. I love being among you and seeing you. And as I pray for you, I like to feel that you remember me in your prayers.[31]

His Eminence Metropolitan Kallistos Ware elaborates further on this matter:

> If, then, as members of a single family we are united by the bond of mutual prayer, and if within this family there is no division between living and departed, then it should surely be considered normal and natural that we pray for the departed, and ask the saints to pray on our behalf. Whether alive or dead, we belong to the same family; therefore, whether alive or dead, we pray for one another.[32]

Irrespective of understanding the exact means and measure by which either the deceased or the living benefit from each other's prayers, the following remarks by Metropolitan Kallistos Ware might prove comforting:

> As regards both our prayer for the departed and the saints' prayer for us, there are obvious limitations to our knowledge.

We can all agree on the need for theological reserve. But such limitations do not constitute a valid reason for refraining from mutual intercession. On any level intercessory prayer remains a mystery. When one living person prays for another living person, we do not understand the manner whereby such prayer proves efficacious. We cannot fathom the precise relationship between the act of prayer, the free will of the other person, and God's grace and foreknowledge. Nevertheless, from our personal experience we know that intercession between the living is effective, and we continue to practice it. The fact, then, that we do not know exactly how our prayers benefit the dead is not a reason for ceasing to pray for them.[33]

Where Is Hades?

St. John Chrysostom gives us his answer regarding the whereabouts of hell, which is applicable likewise to Hades:

You ask where hell is; but why should you know it? You must know that hell exists, not where it is hidden. . . . In my opinion, it is somewhere outside this whole world [i.e., the universe]. . . . Let us attempt to find out not where it is, but how to escape it.[34]

Although it is believed to be in some dimension of existence that is invisible to us who exist in this visible world, yet the Bible always describes hell (or Hades) as being below, as opposed to heaven (or Paradise), which is above. "The way of life winds upward for the wise, that he may turn away from Hades below" (Prov 15:24). "Hades from beneath is excited about you, to meet you at your coming; it stirs up the dead for you" (Is 14:9). "Though they dig into Hades, from there My hand shall take them; though they climb up to heaven, from there I will bring them down" (Am 9:2).[35]

It is also described throughout the book of Revelation (9:1–2, 11; 11:7; 17:8; 20:1, 3) as being a "bottomless pit." Moreover, in the extraordinary story in which King Saul conducts a séance to speak with the deceased prophet Samuel, you find the medium saying she "saw a spirit ascending out of the earth" (1 Sam 28:13). Saul then "stooped with his face to the ground and bowed down" in order to talk with Samuel (1 Sam 28:14). (Recognize that all those who died before Christ's saving act were in Hades, including righteous men like the prophet Samuel.)[36]

St. Irenaeus addressed the question of whether or not Hades exists in some visible realm inside the earth, as some passages of Scripture may suggest. He tells us:

> The Lord observed the law of the dead ... and He waited until the third day "in the lower parts of the earth" [Eph 4:9].... [Accordingly, those] must be put to confusion ... who allege that "the lower parts" refer to this world of ours.... The Lord "went away in the midst of the shadow of death" [cf. Mt 4:16], where the souls of the dead were.... From this, it is clear that the souls ... go away into the invisible place allotted to them by God.[37]

The late Bishop Alexander Mileant of the Russian Orthodox Church (d. 2005) expressed a similar sentiment: "Although, clearly, up and down are relative terms, . . . heaven or hell . . . are two distinct places though they defy geographical description."[38] Moreover, the late Coptic Bishop Youannis of Gharbia, Egypt and its suburbs likewise tells us his opinion regarding the biblical references that imply Hades is literally inside the earth: They are "probably symbolic and pictorial. The reference to the abyss, or Sheol, as being under the earth refers to the fact that it is degraded and ugly, contrary to heaven that is so exalted and sublime."[39]

Experiencing Hades

God often reveals visions of the torments in Hades. Some may be of the impression that such experiences are rare, yet it may be simply that few people want to speak of them. This was suggested by Dr. Maurice Rawlings, a Tennessee physician who specialized in internal medicine and cardiovascular disease and who himself resuscitated many persons who had been "clinically dead." His own interviews of such people yielded the following conclusion:

> Contrary to most published life-after-death cases, not all death experiences are good. Hell also exists! After my own realization of this fact I started collecting accounts of unpleasant cases that other investigators apparently had missed. This has happened, I think, because the investigators, normally psychiatrists, have never resuscitated a patient. They have not had the opportunity to be on the scene. The unpleasant experiences in my study have turned out to be at least as frequent as the pleasant ones. . . .[40] I have found that most of the bad experiences seem to be so painful and disturbing that they are removed from conscious recall so

that only the pleasant experiences—or no experiences at all—are recollected.[41]

Dr. Rawlings goes on to describe how people he interviewed would speak of emerging into a "dark dim environment where they encounter grotesque people who may be lurking in the shadows or along a burning lake of fire. The horrors defy description and are difficult to recall."[42] He also tells us that some who experienced this were "regular church members" who were surprised to find themselves in such a state.[43]

Why does God reveal the torments of Hades to people? According to the sixth-century Roman archbishop, Gregory the Great, the purpose is to deter sinners from continuing in their sinful ways. He states in his notable work, *Dialogues,*

> In His unbounded mercy, the good God allows some souls to return to their bodies shortly after death, so that the sight of hell might at last teach them to fear the eternal punishments in which words alone could not make them believe.[44]

He goes on to describe several experiences and tells of the impression they produced on the beholders. For example, a certain Spanish hermit he knew of by the name of Peter died and saw "hell with all its torments and countless pools of fire." On returning to life, Peter described what he had seen,

> But even had he kept silent, his penitential fasts and night watches would have been eloquent witnesses to his terrifying visit to hell and his deep fear of its dreadful torments. God

had shown Himself most merciful by not allowing him to die in this experience with death.[45]

St. John Chrysostom adds to the discourse the following homily:

> Many persons may be then heard relating horrors, and fearful visions, the spectacle of which the dying are unable to endure, but often shake their very bed with great power, gazing fearfully on the bystanders, the soul urging itself inwards, unwilling to be torn away from the body, and unable to bear the sight of the approaching angels. If human beings that are frightful strike terror into us beholding them, when we see angels threatening, and stern powers among our visitors, what shall we not suffer, the soul being forced from the body, and dragged away, and bewailing much, all in vain?[46]

A young man named Habib Farag, who began his life away from God, died at a young age, but during his short life he grew increasingly closer to God and eventually developed a very strong relationship with St. Mary. The late Bishop Youannis knew him personally, calling him a "saint in St. Anthony's Church in Shobra, Cairo."[47] What follows is what Habib Farag once experienced.

St. Mary took him by the hand to Hades. It appeared as an open cliff filled with fire. The damned there were weeping and wailing. He could not stand to be in that place any longer and became very distressed, so he begged St. Mary to be taken away from there. He was told to make the sign of the cross, and then he found himself taken away from that dreaded place.[48]

The saintly Mother Erene tells another story. A married Coptic man who lived a very sinful life outside the home, and physically abused his wife severely, received a "wake-up call" from the great third-century martyr Philopateer Mercurius (affectionately referred to in Arabic as *Abu Sefein*).[49] After his wife cried out to Mother Erene for help and guidance, one night, Abu Sefein appeared to this man and started talking to him about the afterlife. This is how Mother Erene told the story:

> [After inquiring from the man about the whereabouts of his deceased grandparents, parents, and three dear friends, Abu Sefein says], "Okay, I'm going to tell you the best degree of Hades." Apparently, Hades has degrees.
> So the man says, "Okay, tell me."
> "The best degree of Hades is a place that is pitch black, completely dark, and all that are in it feel extreme despair and guilt. They are miserable and their conscience scolds them. And all of them experience an unbelievable degree of depression and sighing. It is a place of sadness, depression, groaning, darkness, worms that do not die, a bad smell, and a fire that cannot be extinguished." And when [Abu Sefein] says [that this suffering is] "forever," he gestures with his hand and says the word "forever" with a bit of an elongated melody, telling him, "They're going to be there forever, which will never end. Forever. Do you want to be in a place like that or worse? And Hades is really difficult."
> The man replied, "Of course not."[50]

Let us review the key characteristics of Hades that we can glean from the above experiences thus far, and see how Scripture, the

Church Fathers, and other afterlife stories compare with what has already been described:

Extensive Emotional Distress

An intrinsic emotional component is associated with the experience in Hades, described as "extreme despair and guilt," as well as "an unbelievable degree of depression and sighing," which correlates with what was observed by Habib Farag when he saw people "weeping and wailing," so that merely the sight of their plight caused him to suffer intense distress as well. This aligns with St. Paul's indication that "every soul of man who does evil" will, in the afterlife, be subject to "tribulation and anguish" (Rom 2:9). Consider the story of Taxiotes the Soldier, who died and was confronted with evil spirits who took hold of him and brought him to the depths of Hades:

> I saw there the souls of sinners, confined in eternal darkness. Existence there cannot be called life, for it consists of nothing but suffering, tears that find no comfort, and a gnashing of teeth that can find no description. That place is forever full of the desperate cry: "Woe, woe! Alas, Alas!" It is impossible to describe all the suffering which hell contains, all its torments and pains. The departed groan from the depths of their heart, but no one pities them; they weep, but no one comforts them; they beg, but no one listens to them and delivers them. I too was confined in those dark regions, full of terrible sorrows, and wept and bitterly sobbed.[51]

Isaac the Syrian offers his impression of one reason people in

Hades may be afflicted with such emotional misery, telling us their torment arises from realizing they are incapable of participating in the love of God:

> As for me I say that those who are tormented in hell are tormented by the invasion of love. What is there more bitter and violent than the pains of love? Those who feel they have sinned against love bear in themselves a damnation much heavier than the most dreaded punishments. The suffering with which sinning against love afflicts the heart is more keenly felt than any other torment. It is absurd to assume that the sinners in hell are deprived of God's love. Love is offered impartially. But by its very power it acts in two ways. It torments sinners, as happens here on earth when we are tormented by the presence of a friend to whom we have been unfaithful. And it gives joy to those who have been faithful.[52]

Hippolytus of Rome (c. AD 170–235) gives us another perspective on why sinners in Hades experience turmoil:

> Those who are so near [to Hades] hear incessantly its agitation, and they feel the hot smoke. And when the vision is so near, as they see the terrible and excessively glowing spectacle of the fire, they shudder in horror at the expectation of the future judgment, already feeling the power of their punishment.... The fire that is unquenchable and without end awaits these latter ones. So does a certain fiery worm that does not die and that does not consume the body, but continues bursting forth from the body with unending pain.

No sleep will give them rest. No night will soothe them. No death will deliver them from punishment. No voice of interceding friends will profit them.[53]

Origen likewise speaks of the inner turmoil faced by those awaiting the judgment:

When the soul has gathered together a multitude of evil works, and an abundance of sins against itself, at the appropriate time all that assembly of evils boils up to punishment and is set on fire to chastisements. The mind itself . . . will see exposed before its eyes a type of history (as it were) of all the foul, shameful, and unholy deeds it has done. Then will the conscience itself be harassed—pierced by its own goads—and will become an accuser and a witness against itself.[54]

Varying Degrees of Punishment

The story involving Abu Sefein also introduces us to a little-known concept regarding Hades—specifically, that it includes varying degrees of punishment. Notice the juxtaposition of God's mercy and His justice in that even in Hades He does not treat all sinners alike, but instead renders each person "according to his deeds" (Rom 2:6). The notion of degrees in Hades may be implied in the following verses: "For a fire is kindled in My anger, and shall burn to the lowest Hades" (Deut 32:22);[55] if there is a "lowest Hades," there must be some levels of Hades above that.

There are more explicit biblical references to degrees of punishment as well. Christ condemned the Jewish leaders whose way of life proved hypocritical, "who devour widows' houses, and for a pretense make long prayers. These will receive greater condemnation" (Lk 20:47). Additionally, in a parable, Christ tells us of unfaithful servants who will be "beaten with stripes" in accordance with the extent they were unfaithful: "And that servant who knew his master's will, and did not prepare himself or do according to his will, shall be beaten with many stripes. But he who did not know, yet committed things deserving of stripes, shall be beaten with few" (Lk 12:47–48). St. Basil the Great comments on this verse as an indication that there is "a distinction of punishment" in the afterlife.[56]

Isaac the Syrian echoes this belief in varying levels of punishment in Hades as well: "Within both the one state and the other there are diverse degrees of recompense."[57] Origen also tells us that "those here who die . . . in consequence of the deeds done here" are "arranged in a way so as to obtain different places according to the proportion of their sins."[58] Likewise, St. John Chrysostom teaches that some will be given "lighter punishment" whereas others will receive an "unmerciful judgment."[59] An ascetic father of the Syrian Church known as Aphraates the Persian tells us plainly (c. AD 344), "In regard to punishment, I say that not all men are equal. He that sinned much is much tormented. He that offended not so much is less tormented."[60]

Recall also earlier in this chapter the mention of Macarius the Great's experience with the skull that spoke to him: "We have received a little mercy since we did not know God, but those who knew God and denied Him are down below us."[61] This notion, that those who knew God yet strayed from Him are subject to more punishment than those who did not know Him at all, is echoed in the *Shepherd of Hermas*:

Those who have not known God and do evil are condemned to death. However, those who have known God and have seen His mighty works, but still continue in evil, will be chastised doubly and will die forever.[62]

Utter Darkness

The Abu Sefein story mentions Hades as a place that is pitch black and cloaked in utter darkness. The Bible is riddled with the notion that darkness is associated with evil and the abode of sinners in the hereafter. The psalmist tells us, "They dwell in darkness . . . who have long been dead" (Ps 143:3). St. Jude speaks of "ungodly men" who will have a share with "the angels who did not keep their proper domain, but left their own abode" and have been "reserved in everlasting chains under darkness for the judgment of the great day" (Jude 1:4, 6).

St. Jude writes that the ungodly men who are the focus of his epistle are also "wandering stars for whom is reserved the blackness of darkness forever" (Jude 1:13). This phrase, "blackness of darkness," was also used by the apostle Peter to describe the plight of sinners: "These are wells without water, clouds carried by a tempest, for whom is reserved the blackness of darkness forever" (2 Pet 2:17). Recall also the parable in which Christ told us that sinners will be taken and cast "into outer darkness" (Mt 22:13).

Pope Alexander of the Church of Alexandria (early fourth century) spoke of the condition of mankind "because of the fall," explaining that the spirits of the dead were "detained separately from the body in a dark place that is called Hades."[63] Bishop Irenaeus writes on this matter as well: "[God] has prepared darkness suitable to persons who oppose the light, and He has inflicted an appropriate punishment upon those who try to avoid being subject to Him."[64]

To be with God is to be in His light, and the antithesis of that condition is darkness: "God is light and in Him is no darkness at all" (1 Jn 1:5). God "called you out of darkness into His marvelous light" (1 Pet 2:9). "For you were once darkness, but now you are light in the Lord. Walk as children of light . . . and have no fellowship with the unfruitful works of darkness, but rather expose them" (Eph 5:8, 11). Christ Himself tells us, "I have come as a light into the world, that whoever believes in Me should not abide in darkness" (Jn 12:46). Therefore, "Walk while you have the light, lest darkness overtake you; he who walks in darkness does not know where he is going" (Jn 12:35).

In the Coptic Synaxarion we find the story of a boy, a non-Christian, who shared what he was experiencing after death. There was a bishop named Basil (not the famed Basil the Great) who, around the start of the fourth century, was commissioned by the archbishop of Jerusalem to preach Christ in cities where Christianity was not a prevalent religion. As he went from city to city, he would often be beaten and driven out. After arriving at one city in ancient Syria and persuading some to join the faith, he was yet again forced out. Instead of journeying further, he determined to dwell in a nearby cave where he committed himself to supplicate to God that He would bring the rest of the people to the knowledge of Christ. The city's non-Christian governor had only one child, a son, who happened to pass away as Basil was dwelling in the nearby cave. According to the account as recorded in the Coptic Synaxarion, on the day that the governor went to bury his son,

He saw him in a vision at night, standing before him saying: "Call Basil and ask him to pray to the Lord Christ on my behalf because I am in great darkness." The governor woke up from his dream and took the nobles of the city, went to the cave of St. Basil, and asked him to enter the city to pray for his son. The saint agreed to their request and went with them to where the governor's son was buried. He prayed to God with fervent supplication and the son rose up alive with the power of God. The governor, his household, and many of the people of the city believed and were baptized.[65]

Worms and an Awful Stench

Abu Sefein's description of the best degree of Hades included a brief mention of the repulsive smell there as well as another aspect of Hades that Christ Himself mentions when speaking of the torments of hell: worms that do not die. When Christ taught to refrain from sinning by any means necessary, expressing a figurative extent of even plucking one of our eyes out if it causes us to sin, He teaches that sinners will "be cast into hell fire—where 'their worm does not die, and the fire is not quenched'" (Mk 9:47–48, quoting Is 66:24). As repeatedly demonstrated in the writings of the fathers and according to the afterlife experiences in our possession, with regard to the fire and the worms as a means of torment in the afterlife, Christ may have meant what He said, to a large extent, quite literally.

This is what St. Justin Martyr understood, when he wrote, "We know from Isaiah that the members of those who have transgressed will be consumed by the worm and unquenchable fire, remaining immortal. As a result, they become a spectacle to all flesh."⁶⁶ Even the Coptic funeral service includes a prayer by the priest that God save the departed person from "the worm that doesn't rest."⁶⁷

Moreover, we may be able to find more clues regarding this by delving deeper into the meaning of the original word translated as "hell fire," the Greek word *geenna* (γέεννα), which is a transliteration of the Hebrew word *Gehinnom*, which literally means the Valley of Hinnom. The Lord Christ, in His discourse about the abode of sinners in the afterlife, using the term *Gehinnom*, was recalling to people's minds a real location well known to Jews at the time. It was a locale that never contained water, and was recorded in the Bible as the place where children were anciently sacrificed to the idol Molech, in violation of God's prohibition (2 Kg 23:10; 2 Chr 28:3; 33:6; Jer 7:31, 32; 19:2, 6; 32:35). This valley was also given the name Topheth, which means "place of fire." It is claimed that this locale was used as a garbage dump which was burned by continual fires and which drew worms that preyed upon the unconsumed fragments of garbage.⁶⁸

Do note a clear distinction between what Christ speaks of in regards to hell (which is still to come), and Hades (which is the current abode of sinners until judgment day). Scripture, as our primary source of doctrine, does not actually speak of worms also existing in Hades, but according to other sources it appears to be the case nonetheless.

Now let us become acquainted with the following experiences to shed light on the subject of worms and the awful stench in Hades. An eighth-century English chronicler, Venerable Bede, relates how a man from the province of Northumbria returned after being "dead" one whole night. In Hades he found himself in dense darkness:

Frequent masses of dusky flame suddenly appeared before us, rising as though from a great pit and falling back into it again.... Furthermore, an indescribable stench welled up with these vapors, and filled the whole of this gloomy place.... I suddenly heard behind me the sound of a most hideous and desperate lamentation, accompanied by harsh laughter.... I saw a throng of wicked spirits dragging with them five human souls howling and lamenting into the depths of the darkness while the devils laughed and exulted.... Meanwhile, some of the dark spirits emerged from the fiery depths and rushed to surround me, harassing me with their glowing eyes and foul flames issuing from their mouths and nostrils.[69]

Read also the following remarkable account from the Russian Orthodox Church:

Here is the story of two friends. One went to a monastery and led a saintly life and the other remained in the world and lived sinfully. When the sinful friend died, his friend the monk prayed to God for knowledge of his friend's fate. Once, while the monk was in a light sleep, his friend came to him. His friend began to tell him about the intolerable agonies he was experiencing and how a tireless worm was gnawing at him. Having said this, he lifted his clothing over his knee revealing an awful worm, which covered the length of his leg and was consuming it. The lesions on his leg exuded such an odor that the stench woke the monk. He jumped from his cell and the stench from his cell spread through the monastery.[70]

Part Four

The Abode of Light and Joy

Paradise

> To him who overcomes I will give to eat from the tree of life,
> which is in the midst of the Paradise of God. (Rev 2:7)

At the outset, I want to make clear that I cannot possibly give you an exact physical description of Paradise. St. Paul tells us he was "caught up into Paradise[1] and heard inexpressible words, which it is not lawful for a man to utter" (2 Cor 12:4). Referring to Isaiah, St. Paul says, "Eye has not seen, nor ear heard, nor have entered into the heart of man, the things which God has prepared for those who love Him" (1 Cor 2:9).[2] Hence, although people have had opportunities throughout time to observe features of Paradise, no one can truly behold and express in human words the vast glory and wonder of what awaits us. St. Clement of Rome contemplates on this:

> How blessed and wonderful, beloved, are the gifts of God! Life in immortality, splendor in righteousness, truth in perfect confidence, faith in assurance, self-control in holiness! And all these fall under the cognizance of our understandings [now]; what then shall those things be which are prepared for

such as wait for Him? The Creator and Father of the ages, the Most Holy, alone knows their amount and their beauty.[3]

Nonetheless, this chapter is an attempt to relay various aspects of Paradise at a glance, while at the same time keeping in mind that its magnitude and awe can never be truly captured with the inherent limitations of human language. It is an unalterable reality that unlimited beauty cannot be conveyed by a finite mind.

This does not mean we cannot at least make an attempt to give an account in words of what God reveals to us about Paradise. St. John tried describing his revelation from God to us. Likewise, those who have experienced visions of the afterlife can do their best to illustrate what they saw with the words that do exist. The late Bishop Youannis tells us in his book, titled *Heaven*, that "God has revealed to some of the saints on earth a great extent of the majesty and glory of heaven," such as He did with St. Stephen (Acts 7:55–56) and the apostle Paul (2 Cor 12:4).[4]

> Throughout the ages, visions and revelations have been declared to the martyrs, saints, and confessors of the Lord Jesus, confirming the reality of the existence and glory of heaven. These visions and revelations motivated those martyrs in facing their ordeals and hardships, thus they stood firm to the end, until they received their unfading crowns.[5]

Moreover, not only have saints been exposed to visions of Paradise, but (as Bishop Youannis also attests to) many "contemporary people" have taken a glimpse of this mysterious place: "If we come to our present world, we find stories that have actually happened and are worth mention."⁶

Before proceeding, I would like to share with you what the great St. Anthony (or quite possibly his disciple Ammonas)⁷ tells us about why some are given the unique blessing of seeing heavenly visions:

> God dwells in those who have abhorred the world, and even themselves, and who have carried the cross. He feeds their souls with a joy that enriches them and makes them grow noticeably. Among those who accept this celestial joy are a few to whom God reveals His heavenly secrets. He also shows them their celestial positions while they are still in the body. Such people have boldness before Him and He gives them all that they ask for. They are gifted with talents and help people. In every generation, some people have reached that status. And the coming generations will continue to have examples of such people, not only among men, but also among women. Each one of them will be an example to his or her generation and condemn it, because these people struggled until they became perfect.⁸

It is helpful to remember those remarks when examining the sources of the stories that follow.

What Is Heaven?

The Orthodox Church distinguishes mainly among three different "heavens" alluded to in the Holy Bible. The first is the sky—the area comprising the earth's atmosphere, where the "birds of the air" fly (Gen 1:26) and where we see clouds that bring us the "rain from heaven" (Gen 8:2). This area which is directly above the earth was termed "the face of the firmament of the heavens" where "birds fly above the earth" (Gen 1:20) in the story of creation. This is the "face" of the firmament, because it marks the beginning of the second heaven, which is called the "firmament."

The firmament refers to the area beginning at about the edge of the earth's atmosphere and extending into and all throughout the whole material universe in the space beyond earth (outer space). This is regarded as the second heaven. God created stars, the sun, and the moon and placed them in this firmament: "Then God said, 'Let there be lights in the firmament of the heavens to divide the day from the night; and let them be for signs and seasons, and for days and years.' . . . Then God made two great lights: the greater light to rule the day [i.e., the sun] and the lesser light to rule the night [i.e., the moon]. He made the stars also" (Gen 1:14, 16).

The third heaven is what the Church refers to as "Paradise." That is where the Church considers St. Paul to have ascended when he spoke about himself, saying, "Such a one was caught up to the third heaven . . . he was caught up into Paradise" (2 Cor 12:2, 4). The third heaven is what Christ referred to when He told the thief who was being crucified to His right, "Today you will be with Me in Paradise" (Lk 23:43).[9] As mentioned before, Paradise is that level of heaven where the spirits of those who are righteous and deemed worthy of being with God ascend to after death as they await His final judgment.

The Bible seems also to refer to a fourth "heaven," often designated "the heaven of heavens," which seems to be distinct from and greater than the other three heavens mentioned previously. The late Bishop Youannis writes:

Despite the absolute belief that God is present everywhere, the Holy Book constantly describes God to be present in a higher place that is more glorious, which is heaven. . . . The Lord Jesus, glory be to Him, when speaking to Nicodemus, says, "No one has ascended to heaven but He who came down from heaven, that is, the Son of Man who is in heaven" [Jn 3:13]. In this way, despite the belief that God's presence is everywhere, He is always described as being [in that place—the heaven of heavens].¹⁰

His Holiness Pope Shenouda III likewise teaches the following:

The psalmist said about it: "Praise Him, you heavens of heavens" [Ps 148:4]. . . .

All the heavens that humans have reached are nothing compared to the heaven of heavens. For this reason, it was said about our Lord [that He] "has passed through the heavens" [Heb 4:14], "and has become higher than the heavens" [Heb 7:26].

Solomon the Wise mentioned the heaven of heavens on the day he consecrated the temple. He said to the Lord in his prayer: "Behold, heaven and the heaven of heavens cannot contain You" [1 Kg 8:27]. This heaven of heavens, no human has ascended to. The Lord alone came down from it and again ascended to it. Proverbs say[s]: "Who has ascended into heaven, or descended? . . . What is His name, and what is His Son's name, if you know?" [Prov 30:4].

Therefore, the heavens that the Bible mention[s] are [as follows]:

1. The heaven of the birds.

2. The heaven of the stars, the firmament.
3. The third heaven, or Paradise, and
4. The heaven of heavens to which no human has ever ascended.[11]

Having said this, I do not want anyone to be confused and think that God is not present in Paradise. God is omnipresent and is not limited by any place. From the stories that follow, you will see the extent of God's presence in the afterlife as all await Christ's Second Coming. As you read on, join me as I ponder about Paradise and how much it may be different from the "new heaven" and "New Jerusalem" which St. John saw (in Revelation 3:12; 21:1–2) as the final, eternal abode of all the righteous after the end of the world.

Further Clarifying the Distinction Between Paradise and Heaven

In what you are about to read below, you will find a number of verses that describe aspects of what we will observe in heaven (in the future, after the day of judgment) applied to what various sources evince are likewise, to some degree, observable in Paradise now. What are we to make of this? Is there no distinction in what we see and receive in Paradise, and what we await to experience in heaven?

A strictly Orthodox perspective affirms a distinction between the two, and despite all the similarities (which you will read about below), what is allotted to those in Paradise may be regarded as a pledge for a greater and more splendid allotment in heaven, after our physical bodies reunite with our spirits in the second resurrection, on the day of judgment. An exemplary view on this subject can be seen in the following excerpt from St. Augustine:

> All souls have, when they quit this world, their different receptions. The good have joy; the evil, torments. But when the [second] resurrection takes place, both the joy of the good will be fuller and the torments of the wicked heavier, when they shall be tormented in the body. The holy patriarchs, prophets, apostles, martyrs, and good believers, have been received into peace; but all of them have still in the end to receive the fulfillment of the divine promises; for they have been promised also the resurrection of the flesh, the destruction of death, and eternal life with the angels. This we have all to receive together; for the rest, which is given immediately after death, everyone, if worthy of it, receives when he dies. The patriarchs first received it; . . . the prophets afterwards; more recently the apostles; still more lately the holy martyrs, and day by day the good and faithful. Thus some have now been in that rest for long, some not so long; others for fewer years, and others whose entrance therein is still less than recent. But when they shall wake from this sleep, they shall all together receive the fulfillment of the promise.[12]

As you read further, please be sure to remain cognizant of the distinction between heaven and Paradise, even as you observe their apparent similarities.

Progressing to Paradise with the Angels

Let us return to the journey of our spirits after death. First, our spirits leave our bodies, and then a struggle over our fate ensues.

We have already explored one possible outcome of this struggle—Hades. Now we will focus on the Paradise of Joy, prepared for those who are deemed worthy of awaiting Christ's Second Coming there. (Notice that while an abode of punishment was made for the devil [cf. 2 Pet 2:4], an abode of joy was "prepared for you" [Mt 25:34].) It is impossible to predict the exact manner or moment the ordeal in the Crossover Realm will end, revealing that we will be allowed to enter into Paradise by God's grace. However it happens, let us proceed and learn what we can by looking through the eyes of those who have beheld the wonders of Paradise.

Robes, Hymns, and Otherworldly Chants

The stories that follow reveal that the righteous are clad with bright, heavenly robes; some of those stories also seem to manifest that such robes are given to cover ones that our spirits had been clad with during life, and which had been made filthy by our sins over time. This brings to mind the story in the book of Zechariah regarding how he saw the high priest Joshua standing before the Angel of the Lord.

> Now Joshua was clothed with filthy garments, and was standing before the Angel. Then He answered and spoke to those who stood before Him, saying, 'Take away the filthy garments from him." And to him He said, "See, I have removed your iniquity from you, and I will clothe you with rich robes." (Zech 3:3–4)

St. Gregory of Nyssa (c. AD 335–395) refers to this story and gives his impression that it is "teaching us by the figurative illustration that verily in the baptism of Jesus all we, putting off our sins like some poor and patched garment, are clothed in the holy and most fair garment of regeneration [through our own baptism]."[13]

This is reflected in the book of Revelation when the Lord Christ describes the "white garments" which we should keep "white," in which we are to be "clothed" when we stand before Him: "You have a few names even in Sardis who have not defiled their garments; and they shall walk with Me in white, for they are worthy" (Rev 3:4). "I counsel you to buy from Me . . . white garments, that you may be clothed, that the shame of your nakedness may not be revealed" (Rev 3:18). "Behold, I am coming as a thief. Blessed is he who watches, and keeps his garments, lest he walk naked and they see his shame" (Rev 16:15).

Also, in the book of Revelation, St. John saw "one hundred and forty-four thousand of all the tribes of the children of Israel" as well as "a great multitude which no one could number, of all nations, tribes, peoples, and tongues, standing before the throne and before the Lamb" who were all "clothed with white robes, with palm branches in their hands" (Rev 7:4, 9). He writes elsewhere about "twenty-four elders sitting, clothed in white robes" standing "around the throne" of God (Rev 4:4).

Moreover, recall the parable spoken by the Lord regarding the man who was thrown out of the wedding feast for not wearing an appropriate wedding garment (Mt 22:2–14):

> The kingdom of heaven is like a certain king who arranged a marriage for his son, and sent out his servants to call those who were invited to the wedding; and they were not willing to come. . . . Then he said to his servants, "The wedding is

ready, but those who were invited were not worthy. Therefore go into the highways, and as many as you find, invite to the wedding." So those servants went out into the highways and gathered together all whom they found, both bad and good. And the wedding hall was filled with guests.

But when the king came in to see the guests, he saw a man there who did not have on a wedding garment. So he said to him, "Friend, how did you come in here without a wedding garment?" And he was speechless. Then the king said to the servants, "Bind him hand and foot, take him away, and cast him into outer darkness; there will be weeping and gnashing of teeth." For many are called, but few are chosen.

The Bible likens our union in heaven with God as a marriage: "Blessed are those who are called to the marriage supper of the Lamb" (Rev 19:9). Many understand the parable as follows. The king in this parable who held the marriage feast represents God the Father. The king's son is Jesus Christ our Savior. The feast is the world in which He came. The servants are those He commissioned to carry His message: the prophets who preceded Christ, preaching about His imminent coming. People who heard of this, however, neglected the matter and rejected the message. Those invited afterward are the rest of us who were granted the opportunity to participate in the heavenly glories.[14]

What is the meaning of the "wedding garment" in this parable? The Church Fathers and early Christians seem to consistently interpret this to refer to the various virtues of this life that we must be adorned with in order to be fully united with Christ, as the Bible suggests:

Let us be glad and rejoice and give Him glory, for the marriage of the Lamb has come, and His wife has made herself ready. And to her it was granted to be arrayed in fine linen, clean and bright, for the fine linen is the righteous acts of the saints. (Rev 19:7–8)

Tertullian, for example, views the wedding garment as the "sanctity of the flesh."[15] St. Ambrose describes it as the "wedding garment of faith, . . . the vestment of charity and the veil of grace."[16] St. Cyril of Jerusalem considers it to signify purity, teaching that we should "put on the brightest robe of chastity."[17] St. John Chrysostom considers the garment to be "the life and practice"[18] of the heavenly life in Christ, as well as the garment which "belonged to the king"[19] that "signifies virtue."[20] St. Augustine interprets the wedding garment as an indication of righteousness, explaining how necessary it is for us to be clothed in virtue in order to meet Christ, the beloved Bridegroom, and to honor His bride, the Church:

> The garment that was looked for is in the heart, not on the body; for had it been put on externally, it could not have been concealed even from the servants. Where that wedding garment must be put on, hear in the words, "Let your priests be clothed with righteousness" [Ps 132:9]. Of that garment the Apostle speaks: "Having been clothed, we shall not be found naked" [2 Cor 5:3]. . . . Surely this garment is worn only by the good, who remain in the feast, and are brought safely by the grace of the Lord to that other feast which no bad man can approach [i.e., heaven]. . . .
>
> What is that wedding garment then? This is the wedding garment: "Now the purpose of the commandment," says the

Apostle, "is love out of a pure heart, from a good conscience, and sincere faith" [1 Tim 1:5]. This is the wedding garment. Not love of any kind whatever; for very often they who are partakers together of an evil conscience seem to love one another.

For the wedding garment is taken in honor of the union, that is, of the Bridegroom to the Bride. You know the Bridegroom; it is Christ. You know the Bride; it is the Church. Pay honor to the Bride, pay honor to the Bridegroom. If you pay due honor to them both, you will be their children. Therefore, make progress in this. Love the Lord, and so learn to love yourselves; that when by loving the Lord you shall have loved yourselves, and you may securely love your neighbor as yourselves.[21]

Thus we find the sixth-century bishop, Andrew of Caesarea (Cappadocia) remark:

Let us be zealous... fulfilling at all times the word of Solomon, "Let your garments be always white" [Eccl 9:8], not making them filthy through evil deeds. For in this way, having decorated our souls in a way fit for marriage, we shall present ourselves lovely for union with the King, and we shall receive the eternal blessings in Christ, our God.[22]

Let me now share a story that may help reveal more on this subject.[23] His Holiness Pope Shenouda III had a close friend from his youth named Fayez. Fayez's daughter, Layla, was therefore also close to His Holiness throughout her life, whom she knew as Uncle

Nazer when he was still a layman (and often unwittingly referred to him by that same name even after he was ordained a bishop). There was a time when Layla stopped going to church as often as she should, and therefore stopped partaking of Communion due to her job at the time.

She tells a story about a dream she experienced one morning. She saw His Holiness at the door of St. Mark's church in Alexandria. He was there to give the sermon he typically would give on Sundays. Layla met him at the door of the church before he entered and asked him to pray for her. His Holiness responded, "Okay, Layla. Come, and I'll pray for you." So he prayed for her and said, "Look Layla, I'm going to give the sermon, and [in the meantime] I want you to cry earnestly from your heart and say 'O Lord' three times. And when I come back, . . . tell me what you saw."

Layla said, "Okay." She followed the pope's advice and fervently cried out "O Lord" three times. Suddenly she saw the martyr St. George on his horse, and although she was dreaming, she heard the pattering of his horse's hooves almost as if she were awake. St. George was holding a large sword with which he began to swat at innumerable flies and mosquitoes that were hovering all around her until all of them were killed.

Then St. George looked at her and said, "It is done," and disappeared. His Holiness had completed his sermon and, returning to Layla, asked her about what she had seen.

She explained everything. Then His Holiness asked her what seemed to Layla like a peculiar question: "Would you like to see your image as God sees you right now?"

Perplexed, she responded, "Yes, of course. Is there anyone who would not want to see that?" Suddenly she found herself wearing a dress that was torn up and not very clean. She was surprised at how unappealing her attire was. So she asked His Holiness, "Is this really how I look?"

"Yes, this is your image as God sees you."

Layla also could see patches that looked new, so she inquired, "What are these new patches that have been put into my robe?"

His Holiness told her, "These are the good things you have done in your life."

So then she asked, "Well, how do I make this robe white and clean?" She truly did not like the way she looked at all, having thought all this time that God saw her with utmost beauty and glamour.

His Holiness chuckled and told her, "Layla, by Communion, by the blood of the Lamb, this robe will become white."

As you read the stories that follow, notice how often you hear of some white attire covering the spirits of those in Paradise.

Now let us turn to another aspect of the afterlife: the praising of God. We know from the Holy Bible that in heaven angels praise God incessantly, with praises in which we will participate as well. We read in the book of Psalms, "Blessed are those who dwell in Your house; they will still be praising You" (Ps 84:4), and "Praise Him, all His angels . . . all His hosts" (Ps 148:2). Isaiah the Prophet, in a heavenly vision,

> saw the Lord sitting on a throne, high and lifted up, and the train of His robe filled the temple. Above it stood seraphim; each one had six wings: with two he covered his face, with two he covered his feet, and with two he flew. And one cried to another and said: "Holy, holy, holy is the LORD of hosts; the whole earth is full of His glory!" (Is 6:1–3)[24]

In the book of Revelation, St. John says he "looked, and . . . heard the voice of many angels around the throne, the living creatures, and the elders; and the number of them was ten thousand times ten thousand, and thousands of thousands" (Rev 5:11). St. John also saw "the four living creatures" and said "they do not rest day or night, saying: 'Holy, holy, holy, Lord God Almighty, who was and is and is to come!'" (Rev 4:8). Elsewhere he tells us about how he "heard a voice from heaven, like the voice of many waters, and like the voice of loud thunder . . . [and] heard the sound of harpists playing their harps. They sang as it were a new song before the throne, before the four living creatures, and the elders" (Rev 14:2–3; also cf. 15:2–4).

Moreover, you may also notice in Revelation 7:9–12 that the "great multitude" of people "of all nations" cry out to the Lord, "Salvation belongs to our God who sits on the throne, and to the Lamb," after which (in a coordinated, participatory response to the people) "the angels [that] stood around the throne" said, "Amen! Blessing and glory and wisdom, thanksgiving and honor and power and might, be to our God forever and ever. Amen." Hippolytus of Rome envisioned that not only will Paradise itself be full of the sounds of chanting, but that as we pass to there we will be "hymned by angels."[25]

The following stories will give you another perspective on the above-mentioned aspects of the afterlife experience.

Regarding the white robes it seems we will don, there is the early Christian account of Troy's famous martyr, Perpetua, whose brother apparently visited Paradise in a vision or by some other means. Her brother Saturus narrates his dream:

The angels said to us, "Come . . . enter and greet your Lord."

> And we came near to a place, the walls of which were such as if they were built of light; and before the gate of that place stood four angels, who clothed those who entered with white robes. And being clothed, we entered and saw the boundless light, and heard the united voice of some who said without ceasing, "Holy! Holy! Holy!"[26]

Mother Erene once saw a vision which she revealed during a vigil for the Coptic New Year's Day (*Nayrouz*) feast in her convent with families who had suffered the untimely departure of their loved ones. A vehicle accident had killed most of the young members of a choir called the Children of the Apostles from St. George's church in Heliopolis, Egypt. They had been taking a trip together to provide assistance to the poor in the outskirts of Egypt.

Out of humility, so as not to receive any earthly glory, Mother Erene did not plan to tell this story to anyone. However, out of obedience, she complied with her father confessor's command to share the story in order to console and comfort those who were in need of it.

> While I was praying in my cell at the time of the incident, I felt that I was out of my flesh and in my spirit looking at the incident.... I saw the accident and suffered emotionally. I made the sign of the cross and wondered, "Where am I? What do I see? Who are they?" Then suddenly I heard a sound answering my questions saying, "They are with the trip of the choir of the church of *Mari-Girgis* [i.e., St. George] from Heliopolis [in Cairo, Egypt]."
>
> Then I looked and I saw a pillar of light between heaven and earth above the bus. The pillar had a . . . beautiful,

strong, radiant light. Two rows of angels were around the pillar arrayed in white garments. Their faces were emanating luminous light. The angels were beautiful and were singing beautiful praises. Every one of our youth that gave up his or her spirit was given a shining white garment. Their spirits had the form of their former bodies of flesh, but were shining and more beautiful. Every one of the youth had a shining face like the pillar of light. The angels gave to every one of our children, to each youth, a cross of light in their right hand, a candle in their left hand, and a crown on his or her head. The angels ascended while singing beautiful praises. Our children sang the same praises along with the angels. Their sounds mixed with the praises of the angels as they went upward in a beautiful procession. St. Mary was at the front of the procession. She was very beautiful in appearance and emanated bright light; and she was wearing a garment of light just like the pillar of light [in its color, glow, and intensity]. Her dress had small golden crosses although St. Mary usually has appeared in the past wearing sky-blue colored clothing....

Then I heard a sound [from heaven] that was full of love and compassion saying aloud, "Come unto Paradise." The procession was disappearing, beginning with St. Mary the Virgin, then the angels, then the righteous saints, then the heavenly choir. Everyone disappeared, and then eventually the pillar of light also disappeared and was taken up to heaven.[27]

Mother Erene went on to affirm that it was through the grace of the divine mysteries that the children were able to receive their reward: they had confessed and taken Communion, and they departed this life while they were practicing works of love to serve the poor.

Mother Erene shared another story about a person she called "the man with the *galabeya* [a long tunic worn by Egyptians, particularly by villagers] and *takia* [a conical head covering]."[28] His name was Rushdy and he lived a good, Christian life in one of the villages of Qena, Egypt. He was devout and very simple. His life revolved around three activities: work, prayer, and reading the Bible. During the times of the year when the Coptic Church had no pre-assigned fast, he would eat just bread and cheese. During church fasting periods, he would break his fast with simple food, eating fried ground beans (*falafel*) or fava cooked beans (*ful mudammas*).

Although this man was extremely poor, he was satisfied, fulfilling St. Paul's advice that "having food and clothing, with these we shall be content" (1 Tim 6:8). Moreover, despite his poverty, he would always give alms to the poor. His mercy extended even to the galabeya and takia he owned, which he would freely give to those in need. After such occasions, he would come home and ask his wife to sew him a new galabeya and takia—a request met with resistance, strife, and bickering. She would try to persuade him to simply give fabric to the poor person instead of forcing her to sew a new galabeya to replace the one he had given away. However, he would just help his wife sew the new garment, praying constantly.

Life went on in this monotonous way until he departed to Paradise. Mother Erene tells us the following:

> They called the villagers from the neighboring villages ... and placed him in a casket as they waited for his relatives to arrive. Just when they were about to close the casket, they noticed some movement coming from within the coffin. Then slowly

Rushdy rose up out of the coffin and all the people who were present were frightened.

He told them not to be afraid. He explained that he will stay alive for three days with them, then he will go back to Paradise.

He explained to them what he experienced after his death: "When I died, I saw a very beautiful angel. He took me in a procession to Paradise. I knelt down in front of the Lord of Glory. He told me that I did many works of mercy by giving my clothes and hats to my poor brothers and that I was pure and simple. The Lord asked the angel to teach me a new song. I found myself saying praises like the angels. I have never said praises like that before. The Lord asked the angel to take me to visit the fathers [i.e., the saintly monks and clergy who had previously departed], the saints, the martyrs, and my mother and father. I saw St. Mary the Virgin sitting next to the Lord of Glory. I visited the martyrs, the saints, my relatives, and my acquaintances. The Lord of Glory told me that I should return back to the earth. I told the Lord that it is good for me to be with Him. Heaven is beautiful and is full of joy and peace. He told me to go back for three days to tell people to do works of mercy, and then I will return to Paradise. The Lord said that I should tell everyone that when people perform works of mercy, He would give them mercy in heaven; He also wanted me to tell people to live in His fear and carry out His commandments to inherit the glory of . . . heaven." Rushdy departed again after three days as he said.[29]

From the stories mentioned thus far, we are able to glean

some beautiful elements regarding Paradise. These features are mentioned to some degree in the funeral prayers of the Coptic Church, when the priest prays as follows: "This soul that we are gathered for, ... open for it, O Lord, the doors of Paradise ... so it may chant with all the angels";[30] and also, if the deceased is a child, the priest prays, "Let Your servant be among the children that preceded him/her, that are gathered at the peaceful places in Your kingdom.... Clothe him/her with them in the pure garment" (cf. Rev 7:9).[31]

Now let us turn our attention to some other aspects of the afterlife.

God's Presence & Heaven's Light

As discussed in previous chapters, darkness is associated with evil, while the antithesis of darkness—light—is associated with God. We have already seen the pillar of light and the bright white robes that were given to the choir in the story above, for truly "unto the upright there arises light in the darkness" (Ps 112:4). The Bible teaches us that God is "the true Light which gives light to every man coming into the world" (Jn 1:9). Christ Himself, in His frequent discourse as recorded in the Gospel of John, tells us this: "I am the light of the world. He who follows Me shall not walk in darkness, but have the light of life" (Jn 8:12).

Those who have believed in Christ are called to abide in His light. To abide in God's light is to follow His commandments, reflecting His light in our lives, which is a condition to receive the grace of salvation: "If we walk in the light as He is in the light, ... the blood of Jesus Christ His Son cleanses us from all sin" (1 Jn 1:7). If we do not act in a manner that conforms to

God's calling for us to be holy (cf. Lev 11:44; 19:2; 1 Pet 1:15), then we will suffer condemnation: "And this is the condemnation, that the light has come into the world, and men loved darkness rather than light, because their deeds were evil" (Jn 3:19).[32] A true Christian will therefore do well to heed Christ's calling for each of us to be "the light of the world" (Mt 5:14), "for it is the God who commanded light to shine out of darkness, who has shone in our hearts to give the light of the knowledge of the glory of God in the face of Jesus Christ" (2 Cor 4:6).

It is not by some happenstance or coincidence that God calls Himself the true Light, while at the same time fills Paradise with light that emanates from Himself. In the following afterlife experiences, you will see that Paradise is full of light, and the source of light is not the sun or some star, but extends from God and carries with it His divine presence in some mysterious manner. This light is not something a person will merely see, but it also imparts feelings of exceeding peace, joy, and comfort as it pervades the inhabitants of Paradise.

The Bible attests to Christ emitting indescribable light, as is evident when Saul (who later became known as the apostle Paul) saw Christ after His resurrection: "Suddenly a great light from heaven shone around me" (Acts 22:6), which was "brighter than the sun" (Acts 26:13),

> and I fell to the ground... and those who were with me indeed saw the light and were afraid... and since I could not see for the glory of that light, being led by the hand of those who were with me, I came into Damascus. (Acts 22:7, 9, 11)

Ezekiel the prophet also saw "the appearance of the likeness of the glory of the Lord," describing "the appearance of fire with brightness all around" (Ezek 1:27–28).

Isaiah prophesies about the day all the Gentiles (non-Jews) turn to God, when "the Redeemer will come to Zion" (Is 59:20):

> Arise, shine; for your light has come! And the glory of the Lord is risen upon you.... The Gentiles shall come to your light, and kings to the brightness of your rising.... You shall call your walls Salvation, and your gates Praise. The sun shall no longer be your light by day, nor for brightness shall the moon give light to you; but the Lord will be to you an everlasting light, and your God your glory. Your sun shall no longer go down, nor shall your moon withdraw itself; for the Lord will be your everlasting light. (Is 60:1, 3, 18–20)

Also, St. John tells us in his vision of the future that in heaven, at the end of time, he saw a new city, "New Jerusalem," and that "city had no need of the sun or of the moon to shine in it, for the glory of God illuminated it. The Lamb [Christ] is its light" (Rev 21:2, 23). "There shall be no night there: They need no lamp nor light of the sun, for the Lord God gives them light" (Rev 22:5).

Hippolytus of Rome (*c.* AD 170–235) tells us of heaven's light enjoyed by those who will reach there:

> When those who are conducted by the angels who are appointed unto the souls have passed... the righteous are... brought to a locality full of light. And there all the righteous persons from the beginning dwell. They are not ruled by any necessity. Rather, they perpetually enjoy the

contemplation of the blessings that are in their view. Also, they delight themselves with the expectation of other blessings, ever new. . . . The faces of the fathers and the righteous are seen to be always smiling, as they wait for the rest and eternal revival in heaven that follow this location [i.e., Paradise].[33]

In the funeral services of the Coptic Church you will find mention of the "unending joy" felt "in the sovereignty of light . . . prepared for those who please Him [God],"[34] as well as a prayer that God will allow the spirit of the deceased to "find rest in the bosom of Abraham, Isaac, and Jacob, in the light of [the] living, in the region of repose and rest" (cf. Ps 56:13).[35]

Let us return now to the story of Mr. Uekskuell. When we last left his story, he was in the midst of a struggle between angels of light and angels of darkness over his spirit. Then suddenly, after he appealed to the Mother of God for her intercession, everything subsided and he continued his flight upward toward Paradise.

> The infinite expanse of space again spread itself before me. Having passed through some of its distance, I saw a bright light above me: it resembled, as it seemed to me, our sunlight, but was much more intense. There, evidently, is some kind of kingdom of light.
>
> "Yes, namely a kingdom, full of the power of light," guessing by means of a special kind of feeling yet not understood by me, I thought, because there was no shade with this light. "But how can there be light without shade?" Immediately my perplexed conceptions made their appearance.
>
> And suddenly we were quickly carried into the field of this light, and it literally blinded me. I shut my eyes, brought

my hands up to my face, but this did not help since my hands did not give shade. . . .

"My God, what is this, what kind of light is this? Why for me it is like regular darkness! I cannot look, and as in darkness, can see nothing," I implored, comparing my earthly vision to that of my present state, and forgetting, or perhaps even not realizing, that now such a comparison was of no use here, that now I could see even in the dark.

This incapacity to see, to look, increased in me the fear before the unknown, natural in this state of being found in a world unknown to me, and with alarm I thought: "What will come next? Shall we soon pass this sphere of light, and is there a limit to it, an end?"

Mother Erene tells us about a glimpse of Paradise and its light which she observed when God allowed her as a consolation to see her recently departed mother's place there:

One day an angel took me up to heaven where I saw what eye has not seen, as our teacher St. Paul says. I cannot describe what I saw because honestly it is far above my abilities. I saw my mother and there was another woman like her with her. She told the lady, "This is my daughter, the nun I told you about." I walked with my mother in Paradise and saw beautiful greenery, pools of water which were similar to rivers, very beautiful flowers, and an amazing light that fills the heart with an unutterable celestial joy. I asked my mother if they beheld God in Paradise and she answered, "Yes, God is with us, we see Him, we enjoy His presence and He fills everywhere."[36]

Allow me to briefly mention a little story I heard involving the miracle-working saint, Pope Cyril VI, the 116th patriarch of Alexandria. Once, when he was in church attending to the evening offering of incense, a deacon overheard him saying "good morning" toward the icon of St. Mary as he censed it. The deacon was taken aback and thought to remind the pope that night had already fallen and that they were well into the evening. The patriarch told him that he meant what he said, because in Paradise, where St. Mary is, there is never any night and the light of God persists without end.

Another story comes from a hieromonk (priest-monk) I met from the famed St. Anthony Monastery in Egypt, Father Bishoy El-Antony, who graciously allowed me to share a number of afterlife accounts that he was witness to in some way or another. One story involved a friend and fellow monk—Fr. Shenouda—whom he knew at the monastery in which they both resided.[37]

Fr. Bishoy was away from the monastery for a short time, and upon his return he was told a monk had passed away. In the world, even though a person who has died is enjoying the sights and splendor of Paradise, people on earth tend to ignore that and simply bemoan their death. For monastics, however, death is not treated in the usual manner; they regard it as simply leaving the monastery and returning home to Paradise. Hence, upon hearing that his friend had died, Fr. Bishoy simply said, "Oh what a shame, I wish I could have said goodbye before he left." But that was it: no tears, no big deal.

After a week or so, Fr. Bishoy was preparing the bread for the liturgical service—referred to as the *corban* (cf. Mk 7:11). Fr. Bishoy had forgotten that this monk had passed away when, as if he were still alive, that same monk walked into the room. He greeted Fr. Bishoy, and when Fr. Bishoy looked up at him, he noticed that although the monk had looked very sick before, he now seemed so much healthier and stronger. "Your health is quite good now!" he said.

Fr. Shenouda responded, "Yes, because Christ takes care of our health, my son."

Fr. Bishoy agreed, and then he noticed something else that was different. The monk had some physical illness that caused tears to drip often from his eyes, but they were not there anymore. "Have your tears stopped, or what?"

Fr. Shenouda responded, "Christ wipes away all our tears, my son" (cf. Rev 7:17).

Fr. Bishoy looked at the subtle smile on the monk's face and was impressed with his improved health and demeanor, but then continued with preparing the corban. Then he inquired of the monk about something else he noticed: "When I passed by your cell, I found it dark."

Fr. Shenouda responded: "We are living in light all the time, my son. We do not need light." Fr. Bishoy was quite impressed with such a spiritually elevated response and asked Fr. Shenouda to pray for him. Fr. Shenouda assured Fr. Bishoy that he does. "I am. I am praying for you, my son." Fr. Bishoy noticed that he was very serious when he told him that, and so he asked him why that was so. The monk said, "It is because I am always busy praising the Lord."

The conversation continued for a while longer with the monk responding in similar ways, and then after blessing Fr. Bishoy and praying for him, he left. Then, to his alarm, Fr. Bishoy remembered he had been told this monk had already passed away. He was confused: the other monks had told him he died, and they would not joke about something like that. So Fr. Bishoy left the corban room with an urgent desire to understand what had just happened. He went to the cell of one of the monks and insistently knocked on his door, at an odd time to do so—about an hour after midnight (the monks were set to wake up just a couple of hours later to join in praises and begin their day). The monk in the cell opened his door in bewilderment and asked, "What, is there a fire or something?"

This may seem like an odd question to ask, but apparently Fr. Bishoy (as he tells me with a humorous undertone) had a reputation of accidentally starting fires in the monastery. "No," Fr. Bishoy responded, "there's no fire."

"Then what?"

"Did Father Shenouda die?" asked Fr. Bishoy.

"You came knocking on my door at one in the morning, and you know the Midnight Praises are in just two hours, just to ask me that question?"

Fr. Bishoy maintained his steady and intent look as he explained, "This is a serious matter, Father."

The monk responded, "Yes, of course he passed away."

"Did you bury him yourself?" Fr. Bishoy asked.

"Yes, of course I did."

Fr. Bishoy then offered, "Can I give you a piece of information?" The monk asked what it was. Fr. Bishoy then continued, with all seriousness: "You buried him alive and he escaped from his burial place."

The monk was taken aback and said, "What is this you are saying? What do you mean he escaped from his burial place?"

"I saw him just now," Fr. Bishoy explained.

"Father, what do you mean? The doctors at the monastery told me he was dead, and I buried him myself. Let's go there now."

The monk and Fr. Bishoy hurried to the place of Fr. Shenouda's burial and saw it was secure and there was no way the monk could have escaped. Then Fr. Bishoy explained to the monk about his encounter with Fr. Shenouda. After hearing everything, the monk understood what was going on. "You woke me up for no reason. Did you not pay attention to what he was saying? All the things he told you were about heaven. He is living in heaven, not on earth, and since you never got the chance to say goodbye to him, he came to visit you." Fr. Shenouda was living in comfort and peace, delighting in the light of Paradise in continuous praise with Christ, who told us He "will wipe away every tear" (Rev 7:17), where there is "no more pain, for the former things have passed away" (Rev 21:4).

We will continue to see God's light and presence in many of the stories in the next chapter.

The Beauty of Paradise

> But as it is written: "Eye has not seen, nor ear heard, nor have entered into the heart of man the things which God has prepared for those who love Him." (1 Cor 2:9)

In the previous chapter, Mother Erene, in her vision of her own deceased mother's place in Paradise, described some of the beauty she saw around her: "I walked with my mother in Paradise and saw beautiful greenery, pools of water which were similar to rivers, [and] very beautiful flowers."

It is truly amazing to think that Paradise is visually reminiscent of the beauty on earth, yet at the same time retains an indescribable, ineffable quality, so that when we think of the most beautiful places on earth and the awe and exhilaration they inspire in us, we know that Paradise is infinitely more beautiful to a mysterious and inexplicable extent! In other words, if you think it is beautiful here, you literally cannot imagine exactly how beautiful it is there.

The Bible gives us an idea of some of the visual spectacle that awaits us in the afterlife, particularly in reference to descriptions of heaven. Christ tells us about "many mansions" (Jn 14:2) that we will find there. St. John tells us in his revelation of heaven about the "sea of glass, like crystal" that is before the throne of God (Rev 4:6), and also about the "pure river of water of life, clear as crystal, proceeding from the throne of God" (Rev 22:1) in the new city in heaven—"holy Jerusalem" (Rev 21:10). About this city, St. John says, "having the glory of God, her light was like a most precious stone, like a jasper stone, clear as crystal" (Rev 21:11). That light emanates from God Himself, "for the glory of God illuminated it" (Rev 21:23), "and the nations of those who are saved shall walk in its light" (Rev 21:24).

We are told we will be able to see "the tree of life" which has visible "fruits" and "leaves" (Rev 22:2). St. John reveals to us that in heaven we will see (and presumably smell) incense: "the twenty-four elders" are seen with "golden bowls full of incense, which are the prayers of the saints" (Rev 5:8), and also an "angel, having a golden censer . . . was given much incense . . . and the smoke of the incense, with the prayers of the saints, ascended before God from the angel's hand" (Rev 8:3–4).

Some may wonder to what extent we will see God in the afterlife. St. John tells us, on the one hand, that "no one has seen God at any time," yet he continues by explaining, on the other hand, that "the only begotten Son, who is in the bosom of the Father, He has declared Him" (Jn 1:18). Some may say, as Christ's disciple Philip said, "Show us the Father" (Jn 14:8). To that Christ responded, "Have I been with you so long, and yet you have not known Me, Philip? He who has seen Me has seen the Father. . . . Believe Me that I am in the Father and the Father in Me" (Jn 14:9, 11). The stories you are about to read consistently evince that in Paradise, we will see the Lord Jesus Christ, "the image of the invisible God" (Col 1:15), in whom "dwells all the fullness of the Godhead" (Col 2:9). Notice how in the preceding verse St. Paul seems to delineate a distinction between the invisible Father and the visible Christ. The early Church Fathers repeatedly demonstrate a similar belief, often attesting to it quite stringently. For example, St. Irenaeus writes, "concerning the Creator . . . He is the invisible God [as] shall be shown as we proceed"; "[That the Scriptural passages which say] 'No man shall see God and live' . . . and 'No man shall see God' are spoken concerning the invisible Father, the Maker of the universe, is evident to us all."[1] Elsewhere he elaborates that Christ "became the dispenser of the paternal grace for the benefit of men . . . revealing God indeed to men, but presenting men to God, and preserving at the same time the invisibility of the Father."[2] The earlier Church Fathers particularly seemed much more resilient in their adherence to maintaining that the Father is invisible than did later Fathers who provided some caveats to elaborate on this notion.

Does this mean that the Father is not visible and will never be visible in any capacity whatsoever in the afterlife? Exploring a similar question may provide some insight, which is: has the Father ever been seen, to any extent? There is a divide among Orthodox Christians regarding how to answer. Many believe that all visions of God throughout time, whether in the Bible or elsewhere, are visions of the Son, the Lord Jesus Christ, rather than the Father. Others are of the opinion that the Father has been seen to some extent by certain individuals, such as in Daniel's vision of "the Ancient of Days" (Dan 7:9–28) and John's vision of "Him who sat on the throne" from whom the Lamb "took the scroll" (Rev 5:1–6). The former argument can be said to rely predominantly on the Bible's express indication that "no one has seen God at any time," but "the only begotten Son, who is in the bosom of the Father, He has declared Him" (Jn 1:18); in conjunction with St. Paul's declaration that Christ is "the image of the invisible God" (Col 1:15), it is therefore presumed that the Father is invisible to us, while Christ is visible.

In spite of this, those who argue that the Father has been and can be seen indicate that such a notion is not inconsistent with the above-referenced verses, because what *is* seen of the Father is not His *fullness*, but rather some minute glimpse of the Father that in no way captures His full essence. As the prolific Coptic author, Fr. Tadros Yacoub Malaty, puts it: "If I cannot drink the whole river, would that mean that I couldn't drink of it in moderation and as much as it is convenient for me?"[3] Likewise, St. John Chrysostom marks a distinction between seeing the Father in His full nature, and seeing just some manifestation of God that can be consumed by the beholder. After providing examples from the Bible (Is 6:1; Jn 12:41; Ezek 1, 10; Dan 7:9; Ex 33:13) where the Father has, in his view, been seen in some regard, St. John says, "And others have seen Him. How then says John, 'No man has seen God at any time?' It is to declare, that all these were instances of His condescension, not the vision of the essence itself unveiled."[4] St. John even extends this to the Lord Jesus Christ, saying that since He is the "image of the invisible God," He is likewise invisible, in the sense that His full essence is invisible, and what has been seen of Him was merely His manifestation in the flesh:

> Does then this special attribute [of being invisible] belong to the Father only, [and] not to the Son? Away with the thought. It belongs also to the Son; and to show that it does so, hear Paul declaring this point, and saying, that He "is the Image of the invisible God" [Col 1:15]. Now if He be the Image of the Invisible, He must be invisible Himself, for otherwise

He would not be an image. And wonder not that Paul says in another place, God was manifested in the flesh [1 Tim 3:16]; because the manifestation took place by means of the flesh, not according to His essence. Besides, Paul shows that He is invisible, not only to men, but also to the powers above, for after saying, was manifested in the flesh, he adds, was seen of angels. So that even to angels He then became visible, when He put on the flesh; but before that time they did not so behold Him, because even to them His essence was invisible.[5]

One may consider then that what St. John Chrysostom is saying proves contrary to what Christ said of the angels, that they see the Father in heaven (Mt 18:10). St. John refutes this point by describing what the angels see as an "intellectual vision which is possible [even] to us, and having God in our thoughts,"[6] but that only Christ has seen the full essence of the Father:

None knows Him as the Son knows Him. As then many have seen Him [they have been granted this] in the mode of vision permitted to them, but no one has beheld His essence; so, many of us know God, but what His substance [is] cannot be known, except only by He who was begotten of Him.... "As the Father knows Me, even so I know the Father" [John 10:15].[7]

In contrast, we find Archbishop Theophilus of Antioch (d. c. AD 183–185), who considers that when mankind becomes immortal, the invisible God can then be perceived:

As the soul in man is not seen, being invisible to men, but is perceived through the motion of the body, so God [and here the context seems to refer to the unbegotten Father] cannot indeed be seen by human eyes, but is beheld and perceived through His providence and works.... [But] when you shall have put off the mortal and put on incorruption, then shall you see God worthily. For God will raise your flesh immortal with your soul; and then, having become immortal, you shall see the Immortal.[8]

In the afterlife experiences surveyed in this book, no one describes seeing the full essence of God, or seeing a manifestation of the Father in some form, but rather only seeing the image of the invisible God as was made manifest in the Lord Jesus Christ. The Bible tells us that, at the least, this is what we can expect. For example, Christ told the thief on the cross, "Today you will be with Me in Paradise" (Lk 23:43). He also told His disciples that He would depart this life in order to prepare a place for them in the next: "And if I go and prepare a place for you, I will come again and receive you to Myself; that where I am, there you may be also" (Jn 14:3). St. Paul also understood that to depart to Paradise means to be with Christ in His presence, as he wrote to the Corinthians: "We are confident, yes, well pleased rather to be absent from the body and to be present with the Lord" (2 Cor 5:8).

The Church Fathers express the same sentiment as well: St. Hilary of Poitiers (*c.* AD 300–368) remarks that the "glory of God is invisible to carnal eyes," but this is simply the case "at the present time" when one is still alive in the carnal body.[9] St. Cyprian of Carthage (*c.* AD 200–258) tells us about the eventual "joy of being admitted to the sight of God . . . to be so honored as to receive the joy of eternal light and salvation in the presence of Christ the Lord, your God."[10] We also have the letter of St. John's pupil, St. Polycarp (c. AD 69–155), who encouraged the church of the Philippians to "yield obedience to the word of righteousness, and to exercise all patience" by reminding them of the examples set by recent Christian martyrs "and in Paul himself, and the rest of the apostles. This do in the assurance that all these have not run in vain, but in faith and righteousness, and that they are now in their due place in the presence of the Lord."[11]

Abba Silvanus, a Palestinian who moved to Sinai in AD 380 and is counted among the desert fathers, had an experience that further attests to God's presence in Paradise:

> His disciple Zacharias entered [Abba Silvanus's cell] and found him in ecstasy with his hands stretched towards heaven. Closing the door, he went away. Coming at the sixth and ninth hours he found him in the same state. At the tenth hour he knocked, entered, and found him at peace and said to him, "What has happened today, father?" The latter replied, "I was ill today, my child." But the disciple seized his feet and said to him, "I will not let you go until you have told me what you have seen." The old man said, "I was taken up to heaven and I saw the glory of God and I stayed there till now, and now I have been sent away."[12]

It is fair to assume that God's presence in the afterlife will endow us with a sense of exceeding peace, just as when Christ appeared to the disciples after His resurrection and said to them, "Peace be with you" (Jn 20:19). Such peace will be unlike anything the world can give us, as Christ tells us, "Peace I leave with you,

My peace I give to you; not as the world gives do I give to you" (Jn 14:27). Heaven will thus be a place of joy where a person will be "comforted" (Lk 16:25), and where "there shall be no more death, nor sorrow, nor crying. There shall be no more pain, for the former things have passed away" (Rev 21:4). Think of the preceding collection of verses as you read the following accounts.

In a previous chapter, I introduced you to the experience of a young Coptic Christian who, while married, lived a life of sin outside the home, and inside the home consistently mistreated his wife. Then one day the great martyr Abu Sefein appeared to him (in an effort to revive his spiritual life) and told him about Hades. Afterward, he also described Paradise. Mother Erene recounts the story:

> Abu Sefein told him his life story, and [among other things] said, "My parents baptized me when I was young, and then I got older and started to pray, confess, and take Communion. . . . And when I would sit and pray with God, I would have a very amazing feeling of peace and joy. I used to say, 'Oh Christ, if the time with you on earth and in the world is so good like this and gives joy in this way, then what is heaven going to be like?'" The story [about his life] went on about going to war and then the part about the emperor who asked him to offer incense to the idols and how Abu Sefein told him, "No," at which time the emperor threatened torture, to which he responded, "Then torture me."
>
> Then Abu Sefein told the man, "Notice, from what year was I martyred? From [AD] 250. From [AD] 250 I have been in Paradise." And when [Abu Sefein] says [that the afterlife is] "forever," he gestures with his hand and says the word

"forever" with a bit of an elongated melody. "The people that follow the commandments [of God] go to Paradise where peace and joy abound, and you are present with the Lord."

Abu Sefein said, "I'll tell you about Paradise."

The man replied, "Okay, tell me."

He said, "Paradise is extremely beautiful. The plants and trees are beautiful (they're not like what you have on earth, but look like it), and the rivers look like crystal. And the most beautiful aspect of it is the Lord of Glory. His light fills Paradise, giving joy and peace, and all are happy and singing and praising and glorifying with the angels. So which one do you want? This or that [i.e., Paradise or Hades]?"

The man replied, "Of course, Paradise."

[Abu Sefein said], "So repent."

[The man replied], "Well, if I repent, will God accept me?"

[Abu Sefein exclaimed], "Ah! Of course, He has His arms open wide for you! Go into His embrace!"[13]

Mother Erene goes on to talk about how this man dedicated his life to serve the youth who are spiritually lost and how he has exhibited great success in his efforts.

An Egyptian Muslim woman, formerly named Nahed, tells us of a vision of Christ she beheld. Her conversion story is encapsulated in a book titled, *Islam Encounters Christ: A Fanatical Muslim's Encounter with Christ in the Coptic Orthodox Church*.[14] We might be able to gather more clues about the appearance of Paradise by reading her story.

At one point in the book, she tells us about an experience where she suddenly noticed that she was "dressed in a long gown that stretched to the ground," with long sleeves, and which was gray in color, covered with silver. Her head was covered with a scarf of the same color. When she looked at the ground, although the dress covered her feet, she was able to notice that she was barefoot. Then she was surprised by the appearance of the ground below her:

> What a beautiful color! It was deep green. I had never seen such a beautiful color before, nor experienced such a soft texture. I kept rubbing it with my feet to get a feel in order to understand what this soft lawn [might] be.

Afterward, she lifted her gaze and noticed "a marvel that words can never describe"—mansions in Paradise.

> It was like the castles we envision in our imagination. No, it was more marvelous than that. It was something that no imagination could grasp. A very big place that had tall columns, so high the eyes could not see their capitals, lined with lustrous silk reflecting beautiful lights.

Then she noticed something else about this new heavenly habitation: the pleasant aroma. "The place was filled with incense. I knew this scent; it was similar to that which I associated with Samiah, but a lot sweeter." (Samiah was a Coptic woman who taught at the same school where Nahed was a professor. In the subtle process of Nahed's conversion, Samiah provided an outlet and a means to discuss Christianity in her private office. On such occasions, Nahed usually smelled incense.)

At some point she tells us she was granted permission to take a brief stroll around. She felt something akin to "a breeze of refreshing cool air" that swept over her and provided her with "wonderful comfort." She conjectured that it seemed like birds were flapping their wings above her head, although she could see nothing to corroborate her intuition. In this place she felt imbued with a sense of "peace, joy, and comfort." She was granted an opportunity to look around and saw beautiful scenery, which her eyes could not totally encompass, nor did she sense any limit to what she was observing.

Then, suddenly, Christ appeared. Some old men with "very white" clothes and long white beards knelt down as Christ walked towards His "great throne." She tells us, "He did not walk on the ground in steps, [but instead] . . . walked as if He was [being] carried on a cloud or as [if He was] a shadow, until He reached the throne and sat on it."

The sight of Christ caused her to feel a sense of incomparable love, kindness, gentleness, comfort, peace, and happiness. This is how she described her vision:

> How wonderful! I found myself following Him without thinking and without intention. I followed Him and knelt at His feet. A mysterious feeling swept across me, a mixture of joy, fear, happiness and peace, and I felt a strong tremble throughout my body as if it were an electric jolt. I could not control my body; it quivered out of control. I asked myself, what is this mysterious feeling? Who is He I am kneeling to with all these men? I must raise my head and look at Him to know who He is. I collected my strength and looked at Him. O Lord! What am I seeing! I cannot describe it. I

cannot find the appropriate words to describe Him. What is this shining face and what is this crystal complexion! What is this beauty.... He wore a light colored garb, had a crimson shawl on His left shoulder, and His golden hair cascaded to His shoulders like velvet....

I kept staring at His brightly shining face and at His neck. It looked like a pillar of pure crystal. I looked again at His shining face and at His very fair complexion. The more I looked at Him, the more I got attached to Him, and the more and more I wanted to know about Him, and who He was.

Suddenly, He opened His eyes and looked at me. I could not take the look in His eyes and fell on my face. Oh my God, what do I see! And what are these eyes! I felt as if I was going to die or faint from what I saw. His eyes were big, emitting powerful rays as if they were rays of the sun. The irises of His eyes were so wide that they could contain the whole globe. Their color was clear blue like... clear skies or like pure water with a tinge of green. What were these rays that fell on me and swept my body like electricity? I could not look at Him for a moment. I wanted to know Him. I loved Him. I wanted to look at Him. I gathered my strength; I must look at Him one more time. Yes, I raised my head and looked at Him. Oh! What a wonder! He is looking at me. His face is coming closer to me. And what a look on His face: loving, kind and gentle....

I love Him because I feel His incomparable love to me. And for the third time I gathered my strength and lifted my head up to look at Him despite the fear that gripped me, and despite the fact that my body was shaking so hard, beyond control. I was awash in comfort, peace and happiness. I looked at Him, and what a wonder!

(Her vision was mixed with a tinge of fear because Christ was confronting her for persecuting, in various ways, Coptic Christians.)

Notice that Nahed's vision of Paradise was accompanied by a certain aroma of incense, which she experienced, to a more subtle degree, every time her Coptic friend Samiah talked to her about Christ. Suspecting that this odor was somehow linked to the location of their meeting, she tells us how she "began to change the meeting place to other areas in the school. Sometimes it was the school balcony and sometimes it was in the school garden. To my surprise, the aroma was always there."

Mention of pleasurable smells is commonly found in stories related to heavenly experiences or miraculous wonders. Miracles often occur in which oil seeps mysteriously out of various icons (one such miracle I have personally witnessed), and this oil always retains a certain pleasant, heavenly scent.

Such an aroma was present in the afterlife experience of Salvius of Albi, a sixth-century hierarch of Gaul, who returned to life after having been dead for about half the day. He gave the following account to his friend, Gregory of Tours:

> When my cell shook four days ago, and you saw me lying dead, I was raised by two angels and carried to the highest peak of heaven until I seemed to have beneath my feet not only this miserable earth but also the sun and moon, the clouds and stars. Then I was conducted through a gate that shone more brightly than the light of the sun and entered a building where the whole floor shone with gold and silver.

The light was impossible to describe. The place was filled with a multitude of people . . . stretching so far in all directions that one could not see where it ended. The angels made a way for me through the crowd of people in front of me, and we came to the place towards which our gaze had been directed even when we had been far away. Over this place hung a cloud more brilliant than any light, and yet no sun or moon or star could be seen; indeed, the cloud shone more brightly than any of these with its own brilliance. A voice came out of the cloud, as the voice of many waters. Sinner that I am, I was greeted with great respect by a number of beings, some dressed in priestly vestments and others in ordinary dress; my guides told me these were the martyrs and other holy men whom we honor on earth. . . .

As I stood here there was wafted over me a fragrance of such sweetness that, nourished by it I have felt no need of food or drink until this very moment. Then I heard a voice which said: "Let this man go back into the world, for our churches have need of him."

I heard the voice but I could not see who was speaking. Then I prostrated myself on the ground and wept. "Alas, alas, O Lord!" I said. "Why hast Thou shown me these things only to take them away from me again? . . ."

The voice which had spoken to me said: "Go in peace. I will watch over you until I bring you back once more to this place." Then my guides left me and I turned back through the gate by which I had entered, weeping as I went.[15]

Thereafter, "Salvius was so nourished by the fragrance that he needed no food or drink for over three days; the fragrance vanished and his tongue became sore and swollen only the moment that he revealed his experience."[16]

Boniface tells us how a monk from Wenlock (mentioned previously in Chapter 4) eventually passed through the terrifying ordeal of evil spirits and then "saw also a place of wondrous beauty" where "a fragrance of wonderful sweetness came to him from the breath of the blessed souls rejoicing together. The holy angels told him that this was the famed Paradise of God." Later this monk

> beheld shining walls of gleaming splendor of amazing length and enormous height. And the holy angels said: "This is the sacred and famous city, the heavenly Jerusalem, where holy souls live in joy forever." He said that those souls and the walls of that glorious city . . . were of such dazzling brilliance that his eyes were utterly unable to look upon them.[17]

Gregory the Great (sixth-century archbishop of Rome) in his *Dialogues* tells us also of a person named Romula:

> While they stood around Romula's bed at midnight, a light suddenly shone down from heaven flooding the entire room. Its splendor and brilliance struck fear and dread into their hearts. . . . Then they heard the sound of an immense throng. The door of the room was thrown wide open, as if a great number of persons were pushing their way in. Those who stood round the bed had the impression that the room was being crowded with people, but because of their excessive fear and [the] extreme brightness they were unable to see. Fear paralyzed them and the brilliant light dazzled their eyes. Just

then a delightful odor filled the air and with its fragrance calmed their souls which were still terrified by the sudden light. . . .

Looking at her spiritual mother Redempta, she said in a pleasant voice, "Do not fear, mother, I shall not die yet." [For three days the fragrance remained and on] the fourth night Romula again called her mistress and asked to receive Holy Communion. Scarcely had Redempta and her other disciple left the bedside when they saw two choirs of singers standing in the square in front of the convent. . . . The soul of Romula was set free from the body to be conducted directly to heaven. And as the choirs escorted her soul, rising higher and higher, the sound of their singing gradually diminished until finally the music of the psalms and the sweetness of the odor vanished altogether.[18]

Moving on now to an extraordinary experience that captures for us an extensive glimpse of Paradise, we have a story about a nun named Mother Ilaria (also spelled Hilaria), as recounted to us by Mother Erene:

Our Mother Ilaria was a holy nun. She was nominated to preside over the convent of Abu Sefein and was well qualified to lead the nuns. She loved . . . prayer very much. . . . One day, a nun that was a physician came to me and told me that she saw our mother Ilaria kneeling in her cell. In front of her was a manuscript of the Psalmody prayers, and she looked very tired. I told that nun to check on her. She did so and found that our mother Ilaria had departed to the Lord while she was kneeling and praying.

The Beauty of Paradise

There was a nun[19] that loved her tremendously and so she was grieving intensely. That nun was praying in tears one night . . . when suddenly she saw appear before her a nice, handsome man who asked her to make the sign of the cross. She made the sign of the cross and then asked him about his identity. He told her that he was an angel that came to take her to . . . Paradise and to show her Ilaria. She thought that this meant her time of departure to heaven came. He told her that a divine power would lift them up. She stood next to him and sure enough a divine power lifted them up toward . . . heaven vertically, and then they moved in a horizontal line. She saw vast places. Every section had green pasture and was very beautiful. The places were separated by long corridors. The Lord of Glory appeared sitting on His throne at the end of each hallway. All the souls could see the Lord of Glory. She saw a pure crystal river. She could not describe the beauty of what she saw, as St. Paul said: things that "eye has not seen." The angel left her with our mother Ilaria.

Mother Ilaria asked her why she was weeping; and to console her, she told her that she is in a place of great glory, rest, and peace. Mother Ilaria talked to her about the beauty of . . . heaven. There is a difference between one [person's place] . . . and the other regarding the amount of greenery and flowers: one can have more of them than the other. It is as the Scripture says, "One star differs from another star in glory" [1 Cor. 15:41]. But our Lord Jesus Christ is seen by all. Mother Ilaria told the nun, "Come and see my place."

She found it beautiful and bringing joy; it was in a desert and around it there was no greenery or flowers. The nun asked her, "Mother Ilaria, why do you have your place here while you were a nun and an exemplary person?"

She said, "Because my hands were tight."

So the nun asked her, "And what did you have to offer?"

She replied, "I was a miser and I would never give my things to any nun. In the past, the book of *The Paradise of the Fathers* was not available to every nun. I used to have one. However, if a nun asked me to lend it to her, I would not as I feared that she would tear it. And if I ever gave it to one, I would keep telling her, 'Look after it and don't tear it.'"

The nun asked, "And why is this a big deal?"

She said, "It implies the love of possessions. Besides, I had other things which I would not lend to the nuns to keep them in good condition. When the nuns used to collect money for the poor families, I used to refuse to share."

She asked our mother Ilaria if she could... meet the Lord of Glory to thank Him and worship Him. Our mother Ilaria told her that she would be burned because she still had the flesh that could not endure the fire of His divinity. She said, "You cannot stand going there."

"Why?" the nun asked.

She answered, "You would not be able to put up with His strong light."

So the nun asked her, "Then how do you see Him?"

She replied, "I am not in the body. I have abandoned it on earth."

So the nun told her, "I would like to give it a try and go as far as I can." The nun walked with her a long way, and the angel was with them. At the end of the way, the Lord Jesus Christ was [seen] sitting on the throne. They kept going closer and closer to Him. The closer they got, the more she felt His splendor, and His light started burning her like fire. She then said, "No Mother Ilaria, I cannot get any closer."

But she would reply, "It is all right, give it a try."

The angel too was encouraging the nun and telling her, "Try." She did try to get closer but felt that her face was burning.

So she finally said, "That is it. I cannot come any closer." And the angel told her, "Yes, that is enough, as you are still in the body."

When the nun saw the Lord of Glory, she saw . . . His eyes . . . full of love, compassion, kindness, and exceeding fatherhood. She wanted . . . to throw herself in His bosom and she was filled with great joy. "No matter what I say or describe," the nun said, "I can never find words that express and reveal the love, kindness, and tenderness that emanated out of Him."

The angel came back to her and told her that the Lord of Glory commanded the angel to show her the places of the fathers the saints, her father, and her mother. Her parents had beautiful places, but the place of her mother was more beautiful because her mother was simple and pure.

She told the Lord that she was willing to stay in Paradise, remaining with the Lord and not returning to her life on earth. The Lord of Glory told her that she should go back because she came with her bodily flesh and that she still has to fulfill her mission and calling. The angel took her hand and they walked horizontally and then vertically downward. Then she found herself in her cell. She went to meet the nuns and they found that her face was reddish and radiant. Her skin stayed like that for two months; then the light faded gradually.[20]

No Sense of Time or Boredom

A question people often ponder is whether they can withstand being in Paradise for an extensive amount of time, regarding it as a place where they will surely suffer tremendous boredom. "All you do is praise God? Won't it get boring?" Those are the concerns that people often express. They probably think of standing in church or alone praying, and how quickly they become restless, looking forward to something other than prayer for entertainment.

We spend our lives on earth seeking ways to make ourselves happy, engrossed in a never-ending search for fulfillment. In Paradise, however, as appears from the experiences provided herein, and as expressed in Scripture, we no longer need to look for joy; it is something freely given to us in abundance. To grasp a sense of the joy a person has in Paradise, let me tell you of a woman who was willing to accept death for the sake of that joy even though she was leaving a lot behind on earth.[21] Father Bishoy El-Antony prefaces the story by saying, "I've been with many people during the time of their death. I could not believe it myself."

At 27 years old, that woman was suffering from cancer. She had a daughter who was about 5 years old, named Mariam, whom she loved very much. The woman knew an untimely death was likely, and so she felt deep sorrow at the thought of leaving her daughter behind. This was a continual source of grief and anguish which she persistently expressed for years. Although she was undergoing chemotherapy treatment, those who loved her felt a miracle might be the only cure. Fr. Bishoy accompanied her to many monasteries to ask for the prayers of the saints, but it was not God's will to heal her.

Eventually she was faced with the moment she dreaded—the moment of death. She was lying on a hospital bed about to die, which was a predicament her husband could not bear to watch or be present for, so he took their young daughter and left. Until her last conscious breath, she kept pleading with desperate tears, "Father, I do not want to die, please! I want to take care of my daughter! I love her so much, please Father!" She refused to accept death.

Fr. Bishoy and some servants of the church stood by her side as she lay there in a coma. A physician informed them that her death was just a few minutes away. All present in the room kept praying for her. What happened next, Fr. Bishoy says, "I cannot ever forget."

All of a sudden, as her eyes remained closed, she grasped Fr. Bishoy's hand and squeezed it tightly as she shrieked in terror, "Stop them! Help me! They want to take me; they are so close! I do not want to go [with them]! They have terrible faces! They look like they are wearing black and red; they are trying to take my soul!" She kept repeating such things and caused a frenzy in the hospital.

Fr. Bishoy himself was flustered as he tried to figure out how he could help her. Immediately he told the servants around him, "Pray, pray, just read the psalms, read the psalms!"

As Fr. Bishoy recounts the story, he says, "We kept praying, all of us; and her scream is still in my ear."

After a few minutes and a great deal of wholehearted prayer, she finally became very calm. Then she began to speak again with the utmost serenity as she smiled and described what she was seeing and experiencing: "Thank God, they have left, and angels have come to take my spirit." She described the appearance of the angels she saw and then said, "I will go with them. Look at what they are showing me! Wow! They showed me Christ, there He is; He is very far away but I see Him very well!" She continued to describe features of Paradise. Then she went into what appeared to be a coma for ten minutes. Afterward, something very strange happened.

Unexpectedly she sat up and opened her eyes (Fr. Bishoy remembers her blue eyes—a feature uncommon for an Egyptian). She had the most pleasant smile on her face and told those present, "Why am I so worried about Mariam? I am sure God is going to take care of her. Jesus will take care of her. I went to heaven, I have seen everything, and I want to go there. I want to stay there. It is fantastic, Father. You cannot imagine how lovely it is. If you saw it, you would insist on coming with me."

At that Fr. Bishoy responded, "I wish."

He asked her to tell him about heaven, but she answered, "No. You pray for me; give me absolution." Afterward she departed in peace. Clearly, Paradise was so delightful that even the most pressing of concerns on earth cannot compare to the joy one feels there.

Now, I want you to think of the notion of boredom: ingrained within it is the idea that time is passing while you are not occupied with a sufficiently interesting activity. However, you have already read about the utter happiness one feels in Paradise. How about the concept of time, though? As has been explained previously, beginning once a person enters the Crossover Realm, the concept of time seems to disappear, and you enter an existence that is not bound by it. As in Hades, likewise in Paradise, it seems that time does not exist, and thus the feeling that time is passing so "slowly" that you get bored would not be an issue.

Time was created by God for the visible world, as Pope Alexander—the nineteenth archbishop of Alexandria (d. *c.* AD 326)—mentions: "It is established that both . . . time and all space . . . [were] made by Him."[22] St. Justin Martyr likewise writes, "Time was created, . . . [for] the creation of time had received its original constitution from days and months and years."[23] St. Augustine says of God, "You are the Author and Creator of all ages, . . . You have made all time; and before all times You are, . . . You made time itself."[24] It appears that the invisible realms, however, were never limited in such a way, and continue to exist outside the laws of time. After death, as there is "neither sleep, nor pain, nor corruption, nor worry," says Hippolytus of Rome, there is also no "night, nor day measured by time."[25] When we die and join God, we will become "partakers of the divine nature" (2 Pet 1:4); it seems then that, as St. Gregory the Theologian (*c.* AD 328–390) writes, "the Sources of time are not subject to time,"[26] and therefore, neither will we be. Metropolitan Kallistos likewise indicates that afterlife experiences have expressed "truths about a state that is no longer subject to the categories of time and space, in the form at present known to us, and which it is thus impossible to describe directly."[27] Read the following experience from Mother Erene to help you understand.

After her father confessor, Bishop Makarious (a saintly Coptic Orthodox Bishop of the city of Qena, Egypt) departed, Mother Erene wept fervently over her loss. She used to pray, "Lord, You have too many saints in heaven; we wish You would have kept Bishop Makarious here on earth, because in him we saw a manifestation of Your image, love, and holy life." One day Mother

Erene became sick with a fever, which required her to take an antibiotic every six hours. Despite all her pain, she stood up to pray, and then, suddenly, found herself in a beautiful place that was exceedingly vast, peaceful, and full of joy—Paradise. The entire locale was illuminated with a heavenly light that instilled in the soul a yearning for praise and thanksgiving for the Lord Christ. And then came Bishop Makarious arrayed in a beautiful, heavenly robe, wearing a cross full of what appeared to be diamonds, walking slowly and completely engulfed in praises to God. As he drew near to Mother Erene, he explained that the Lord allowed her to see him in order to console her. Then suddenly she found herself standing in the very same place in her cell where she had been praying.

During this spiritual experience, the nun assigned to look after Mother Erene came to her cell at 10:00 am to administer her medication, but she was nowhere to be found. The nun searched everywhere for her but to no avail. So she decided to bring a chair and plop herself down in front of the door of Mother Erene's cell to see from where she would be coming. It was not until six hours later, at 4:00 pm, that the nun finally found Mother Erene in her cell again. "Where were you, Mother? I looked everywhere for you!" In her humility, Mother Erene was not at first forthcoming about her whereabouts. However, after much persistence, she finally divulged the experience to her pupil. Although she had been gone for at least six hours, Mother Erene told her, "I felt I was away for only 10 minutes."[28]

We see then the idea that time ceases to exist, but what will we do in Paradise? While it is regularly understood that in the heavenly abode people will be praising God, many today echo sentiments found among some early Fathers that people may also experience other sorts of spiritual advancement and growth in knowledge in the afterlife, as St. Irenaeus remarks: "[The righteous] ones receive the kingdom forever, and they make constant advancement in it."[29]

Bishop Youannis writes:

> I wish to add one more thing. When man was on earth, the created things gave him the desire and means to know God. Thus, St. Paul says, "For since the creation of the world His invisible attributes are clearly seen, being understood by the things that are made, even His eternal power and Godhead, so that they are without excuse" (Rom 1:20). We know God through the visible creation. In other words, we come to know God through what we see in creation. But the situation is reversed in heaven, for God will become the means by which we will know everything. It will be through Him that we know everything. He will be like a big telescope through which we can see, and in whom we can see all the minute details.[30]

Likewise, some early Christians believed that the righteous will increasingly ascertain knowledge about the universe as revealed by God. That is how Origen imagined it would be like in Paradise, where growing "by the grace of full knowledge, they may enjoy an unspeakable joy":

> I think it will be, so to speak, a classroom or school of souls, in which they are to be instructed regarding all the things that they had seen on earth. I think they will also receive some information respecting things that are to follow in the future. . . . When, then, the saints will have reached the

celestial abodes, . . . [God] will show to them, as to children, the causes of things and the power of His creation. He will explain why that star was placed in that particular quarter of the sky and why it was separated from another by so great an interval of space. . . . And, then, when they have finished all those matters that are connected with the stars and with the heavenly revolutions, they will come to those that are not seen and to those of whom we have only heard their names.[31]

As is evinced in several stories, another remarkable experience that appears will be granted is the ability to meet not just family and friends who pass on, but also famous saints and others who we yearn to meet face-to-face. St. Cyprian imagines the joy of this experience:

What will be the glory and how great the joy to be admitted to see God . . . [and] to greet Abraham, and Isaac, and Jacob, and all the patriarchs, and prophets, and apostles, and martyrs— to rejoice with the righteous and the friends of God in the kingdom of heaven, with the pleasure of immortality given to us.[32]

According to the following experiences by Mother Erene, it is suggested that there are other activities that the righteous will plausibly be exposed to: serving by praying for others, being aware of what is happening to those on earth, and maybe even covertly visiting places on earth that were never visited during life. Mother Erene relates this story:

Mother Martha passed away in 1982. One night I dreamt that she had come to me. So I asked her, "Are you here? I miss you very much."

And she said, "I have come to you because I felt that you wanted to see me."

I switched on the light and sat in my bed only to see her before me in my cell. She was dressed in white and looked so young, as if she were in her thirties. We both made the sign of the cross and spoke for two hours. I told her, "Tell me about heaven. How do you spend your time? I wanted to know details about heaven. You all say that you praise and pray. I want to know everything."

She said, "We spend all our time praising and singing hymns, and we pay visits to the saints. Sometimes we go to the Mother of God, another time to the martyr St. Demiana. And we also serve."

I asked her, "Do you serve in heaven? Is there service?"

She said, "Yes. For example, I have come to you now and I will sit with you and you will benefit from my visit. This is a form of service. And when you ask any martyr to pray for you, the martyr does so and says to God, 'So and so asked me to pray for him/her for that particular thing.' God will then tell him to go and do this and that. This is service...."

I asked her, "Mother Martha, do you feel for us? Do you know what is happening to us?"

She answered, "We know all news related to you, especially if someone is going to depart from the earth. They tell us in heaven so and so is coming, so we know ahead of time."

I said, "So you know everything?"

She said, "On earth as it is in heaven."[33]

On another occasion Mother Erene met with another departed nun, Mother Aziza:

> I saw myself walking in a desert and saw the door of an ancient monastery. I went in and found the door of a church that had ancient icons. The church reflected amazing and great spirituality. It was full of monks and there were three or four nuns; one of them was Mother Aziza. She looked much younger than her age when she passed away....
>
> [At the end of the Liturgy] I had Communion and was greatly consoled. Amazingly, there were foreign monks among those who were attending the Liturgy. It was God's gift that everyone heard the Liturgy in their own language. At the end, all the monks and nuns were gone, and Mother Aziza came towards me. I asked her, "Where is this place? Is it on earth or in heaven?"
>
> She said, "This is a monastery for monks; it is on earth, but not in Egypt. Some of these monks are still on earth, and some from heaven. All the nuns are from heaven and they all had great purity [when they were on earth]."
>
> I asked her, "Then what brought them from heaven to earth?"
>
> She replied, "When we depart to heaven, they take us to visit all places there. We visit the Mother of God and witness her glory. We also visit St. Demiana, and all our fathers and mothers, the martyrs, and the saints. I have just finished visiting all places in heaven. Afterwards, they show us every holy place that we have not seen on earth."
>
> I told her, "Now I can understand what the elderly nuns meant when they used to say, 'Whatever we miss seeing while

we are on earth, we will see when we are in heaven.'"³⁴

Traveling around Paradise

In so many afterlife stories, we find angels are usually present to guide us from one place to another within Paradise, and also that people may have a special designated place assigned to them. Are people free to move about in Paradise? Is the answer to that question dependent in part on how they lived their lives on earth?

We have already seen how an angel escorted Perpetua and Saturus in his heavenly vision. Rushdy, the man with the galabeya and takia, was escorted by an angel to visit saints as well as his parents. Likewise we find the nun who adored Mother Ilaria to have been continuously guided throughout Paradise, except when she was left alone with Mother Ilaria for a brief period. We also see Mother Erene was always accompanied by an angel in her brief sojourn in Paradise.

Bishop Makarious, who was just mentioned previously as having appeared to Mother Erene, appeared to one of his spiritual children who used to confess his sins to him.³⁵ This person was extremely sorrowful that his friend and father confessor, the bishop, had departed. Mother Erene tells us the story:

> One day an angel appeared and asked, "Why do you mourn for Abba Makarious? Come with me and I will show [you] the degree of glory that he possesses in Paradise. Do not mourn [for] him again." They went to Paradise, which is a beautiful place with pasture, light, joy, and wonderful peace. The friend of Abba Makarious found himself praising, and

he saw Abba Makarious from afar. He had heavenly attire and [was] holding a cross of precious stones. He told his friend about the glory he has and asked him not to weep again.

[Abba Makarious] asked him: "What do you think of the heavenly glory?"

His friend said that it is most excellent. . . . [He then] asked: "Is this your place?"

[Abba Makarious] told his friend that he is in the church of the firstborn and that he has the freedom to wander. [In the experience Mother Erene had where she saw Abba Makarious, she found him in a vast place full of green pasture. When she asked him about whether this was his place, he told her, "No, my place is more beautiful than this; this is only a vast place in which I walk, but my place is much more beautiful."][36]

The friend asked Abba Makarious: "Did I die?"

Abba Makarious replied: "You came with your flesh. I asked the Lord Jesus to show [you] my glory so that you will not cry again."

The friend asked: "Has the Paradise crosses from precious stones?"

Abba Makarious said: "No, the precious stones are symbols of virtues: simplicity, chastity, love, and humility."[37]

Notice the following: when the friend asked about whether the bishop had a particular designated place in heaven where he was required to abide, he responded by telling him he was given the "freedom to wander" about Paradise. One may inquire as to what the bishop meant by "the church of the firstborn," implying that it was that special designation that might have entitled him to the freedom of wandering about Paradise.

We hear mention of this phrase in St. Paul's Epistle to the Hebrews:

> But you have come to Mount Zion and to the city of the living God, the heavenly Jerusalem, to an innumerable company of angels, to the general assembly and church of the firstborn who are registered in heaven, to God the Judge of all, to the spirits of just men made perfect. (Heb 12:22–23)

Many understand this verse's mention of the "church of the firstborn" to refer to all of us Christians who walk in the manner Christ set out for us, but after reading the previous story, is there to be understood some distinction between the "church of the firstborn" and other designations in the passage above? Expounding upon these verses, Origen indicates his belief that there is a gradation of glory among people in Paradise, whereby the "church of the firstborn" is reserved for only the most holy:

> The apostle describes four orders of saints in heaven. He calls each of us to come to each of them. For not everyone comes to each of these places, but some come to "Mount Zion"; but those who are a little better than these come to the "city of the living God, the heavenly Jerusalem"; and those who are more eminent even than those come to the "multitude of praising angels"; and those who are beyond all those come to the "church of the firstborn ones, which is written in heaven."[38]

Still, others among the Church Fathers instead consider the term "firstborn" to refer to all Christians because Christ, being the

Son of the Father, is entitled to the Father's inheritance; and thus, in Christ, each of us can be counted as "an heir of God through Christ" (Gal 4:7) and members of the "church of the firstborn."[39]

What will your place in Paradise look like, and to what extent does the answer to that question depend on your actions on earth? The following chapter delves into those matters.

Varying Degrees of Reward and Glory

There is one glory of the sun, another glory of the moon, and another glory of the stars; for one star differs from another star in glory. So also is the resurrection of the dead. (1 Cor 15:41–42)

As Manifested in Our Outward Appearance

One extremely important feature the last few stories touched on is the fact that in the afterlife, God will "reward each according to his works" (Mt 16:27). It is in order to confer benefit on mankind, St. Irenaeus teaches, that God seeks our service, not because God *needs* our service: "God is in want of nothing," yet "for this reason does God demand service from men, in order that, since He is good and merciful, He may benefit those who continue in His service."[1]

> Service [rendered] to God does indeed profit God nothing, nor has God need of human obedience; but He grants to those who follow and serve Him life and incorruption and eternal

glory, bestowing benefit upon those who serve [Him] ... but does not receive any benefit from them.[2]

We often read in Scripture that we will receive glory and rewards commensurate with our actions performed during life on earth. Although much of what is written describes such rewards as belonging to what is to be given in heaven, after the judgment, the experiences you will read evince that in Paradise similar features of reward and glory are nonetheless manifest. However, as stated previously, keep in mind that what is received in Paradise is considered a pledge of what will be given to a fuller extent in heaven after the judgment: that is, as St. Augustine puts it, when people die now and go to Paradise, there "the good have joy; ... But when the resurrection takes place [on the day of judgment], the joy of the good will be fuller ... [because] all of them have still in the end to receive the fulfillment of the divine promises [in heaven]."[3]

Regarding these promises, Christ tells us of "treasure in heaven" (Lk 18:22) we should attempt to accumulate in order to be "rich toward God" (Lk 12:21), "for where your treasure is, there your heart will be also" (Mt 6:21). One way to amass treasure in heaven is to give up one's possessions and follow Christ, as He taught: "Sell whatever you have and give to the poor ... and ... take up the cross and follow Me" (Mk 10:21), to "provide for yourselves money bags which do not grow old, a treasure in the heavens that does not fail, where no thief approaches nor moth destroys" (Lk 12:33).

In other places in the Holy Bible we find Christ telling us about rewards we will receive corresponding to our righteous deeds, without explaining exactly what these rewards are: "Behold, I am coming quickly, and My reward is with Me, to give to every one according to his work" (Rev 22:12); "For the Son of Man will come in the glory of His Father with His angels, and then He will reward each according to his works" (Mt 16:27). If we endure persecution, Christ tells us to "rejoice and be exceedingly glad, for great is your reward in heaven" (Mt 5:12). If we pray, fast, or perform charitable deeds in secret, we will receive reward (Mt 6:4, 6, 16–18). Moreover, we are called to love all, even the most difficult of people to love, such as our enemies, because simply loving those who love us yields little to no reward in heaven: "For if you love those who love you, what reward have you?" (Mt 5:46). Hence, if you "love your enemies, do good, and lend, hoping for nothing in return . . . your reward will be great, and you will be sons of the Most High" (Lk 6:35).

Spreading Christ's message, the apostles also taught about how "each one will receive his own reward according to his own labor" (1 Cor 3:8). St. Paul told people to be careful so that "no one cheat you of your reward" (Col 2:18), because God "will render to each one according to his deeds," giving "glory, honor, and immortality" to those "who by patient continuance" remain committed to "doing good" (Rom 2:6–7). Likewise, St. John tells us all to remain steadfast in our path, taking heed that "we do not lose those things we worked for, but that we may receive a full reward" (2 Jn 1:8).

Elaborating further, the early Christians and Church Fathers expressed the notion of various degrees of reward in the afterlife. The ascetic Christian, Aphraates the Persian, taught the following (*c.* AD 300):

> [A person] who labored little shall receive his reward according to his remissness; and who ran well will be rewarded according to how he ran. . . . Know then, that even when the

sons of men shall enter into [eternal] life, still, reward shall exceed reward, and glory shall exceed glory, and recompense shall be greater than recompense.[4]

St. Jerome (*c.* AD 347–420) shared the same view, expressing how preposterous it would be if it were not the case:

> It is our task, according to our different virtues, to prepare for ourselves different rewards.... If we were all going to be equal in heaven it would be useless for us to humble ourselves here in order to have a greater place there.... Why should virgins persevere? Why should widows toil? Why should married women be continent? Let us all sin, and after we repent we shall be the same as the apostles are![5]

For this reason we find the early Christian bishop Papias (*c.* A.D. 70–163) (as quoted by Eusebius) indicating the following regarding the various abodes of the righteous in the afterlife: "As the presbyters say, . . . everywhere the Savior will be seen according to the worthiness of those who see Him," yet "there is a distinction between the habitation of those who produce a hundred-fold, and the habitation of those who produce sixty-fold, and the habitation of those who produce thirty-fold" (referring to the parable by Christ in Matthew 13:1–9).[6]

The following stories exemplify this notion with regard to those who choose the life of monasticism and asceticism, showing the reward some monastics receive in their outward adornment. Mother Erene tells us of a particular occasion when an angel took her to Paradise. She had been trying to understand what monastic discipline[7] she should set for her nuns in the convent. Then one day, she tells us:

> I saw right in front of me an angel who took me to Paradise. I knelt before the Lord of Glory; on His right was the ... Virgin. He said to the angel, "Take her to Abba Pachomius so that she will hear from him about the monastic discipline that I want her to follow." The angel took me with him down a long and brightly lit corridor where I saw a great throne decorated with crosses that shone like diamonds. Seated on it was a resplendent figure. He wore magnificent clothes adorned with golden crosses, and he held a cross in his hand. On both sides of the corridor I saw thousands of monks and nuns in white garments. The angel told me, "Go and greet Abba Pachomius. These are his children, those who took to the life of obedience to their father. They continuously come to him and sit with him."[8]

Mother Erene tells us also of a vision she saw of her aunt Mofida. This young woman desperately sought the monastic life, but her parents refused and forced her to get engaged. Before the wedding, as she cried before an image of St. Mary, she pleaded with her, saying, "O Mother of Light, they are going to make me marry and I want to be a nun."

St. Mary appeared as if she was coming out of the picture and told her, "Tell your mother, 'If you do not let me go to the convent, the Virgin will come and take me as a bride for the Lord of Glory, Jesus Christ.'"

Despite being told of this vision, her mother did not believe her, thinking she was lying simply to avoid marriage. Shortly before the wedding, while Mofida was baking cookies in preparation for it, she felt a severe headache and eventually fell down the stairs to her immediate death. Mother Erene, who was a young child at the time, wept bitterly over the loss of her beloved aunt.

> Then I saw a vision of many virgins who were all luminous and dressed in white garments. They had diamond crosses in their hands and crowns on their heads. Aunt Mofida was among them, so I felt so thrilled. She told me, "Is it right to cry for me in such a way? I am so happy in Paradise and I have a very beautiful place here. The most beautiful of all here is the Lord of Glory, Jesus Christ. He allowed you to see us to be consoled and happy, and to stop crying."
>
> I asked her, "Who are these girls?"
>
> She answered, "These are virgins who wanted to be nuns, but their wish did not come true. They lived in purity and struggled hard in the world; so God regarded them as if they had been actually consecrated nuns. We are going now to visit Demiana and the forty virgins to celebrate with them their feast."
>
> I told her, "I want to come with you."
>
> She said, "You have to ask your mother's permission first."
>
> I did, but my mother said, "No, do not go with them. We want you."
>
> I told my aunt, "My mother would not allow me."
>
> So she said, "You will become a nun and you will be the Mother Superior of a convent. You will have many daughters, and then you will come to us."[9]

Brightness of Our Appearance

There exists a notion that our bodies may emanate varying degrees of light to reflect our righteousness and deeds. This can be seen as being implied in the Bible where it speaks of heaven, which likewise it is plausible may be seen to some degree in Paradise. St. Paul teaches us about the differences between bodies of flesh and the "celestial bodies" we will have after we shed off our physical bodies (1 Cor 15:40). He speaks of how such celestial bodies may differ, likening it to a variation of brightness: "There is one glory of the sun, another glory of the moon, and another glory of the stars; for one star differs from another star in glory. So also is the resurrection of the dead" (1 Cor 15:41–42). This analogy echoes the prophet Daniel, who teaches us that "those who are wise shall shine like the brightness of the firmament, and those who turn many to righteousness like the stars forever and ever" (Dan 12:3). Tertullian associates such varied degrees of brightness with the variety of rewards merited: "How will there be many mansions in our Father's house if it is not according to a variety of deserts? How will one star differ from another star in glory, unless it is because of a disparity in their rays?"[10] Consider too the various stories passed down through the Church of saints who are seen exhibiting different degrees of radiance, often associated with their holiness in life (recall the previous mention of St. John the Short's departure, where he saw a host of radiant saints and angels, among whom was St. Anthony the Great, who exhibited a "magnificent light" which exceeded the others, being described as "shining like the sun.")[11]

St. Paul tells us also that we wait to receive a heavenly body like Christ's:

> For our citizenship is in heaven, from which we also eagerly wait for the Savior, the Lord Jesus Christ, who will transform our lowly body that it may be conformed to His glorious body, according to the working by which He is able even to subdue all things to Himself. (Phil 3:20–21)

"We shall all be changed," shedding off our "corruptible" and "mortal" bodies for a body of "incorruption" and "immortality" (1 Cor 15:51–53). "As was the man of dust, so also are those who are made of dust; and as is the heavenly Man, so also are those who are heavenly. And as we have borne the image of the man of dust, we shall also bear the image of the heavenly Man" (1 Cor 15:48–49). These heavenly bodies may be similar to those of angels, as Christ taught that "in the resurrection" people will be "like angels of God in heaven" (Mt 22:30).

Crowns

In the Orthodox Church, crowns are a familiar means to signify reward for our deeds on earth, as evinced in Scripture. Again, as similarly noted before, such crowns are often directly associated in Scripture with what will be awarded in heaven to the spiritually vigilant, yet there is ample evidence in Orthodox experiences of people in Paradise donning crowns upon their heads as well, which can be regarded as a solemn promise of the crowning to come.

In Revelation, God told us, "Behold, I am coming quickly! Hold fast what you have, that no one may take your crown" (Rev 3:11). God encouraged those who would suffer to the point of martyrdom for His name's sake, telling them that He is ready to reward them with a special crown:

Do not fear any of those things which you are about to suffer. Indeed, the devil is about to throw some of you into prison, that you may be tested, and you will have tribulation ten days. Be faithful until death, and I will give you the crown of life. (Rev 2:10)

St. Peter encouraged fellow bishops to serve as "examples to the flock, and when the Chief Shepherd appears you will receive the crown of glory that does not fade away" (1 Pet 5:3–4). St. James also tells us that those who endure temptation will likewise receive crowns: "Blessed is the man who endures temptation; for when he has been approved, he will receive the crown of life which the Lord has promised to those who love Him" (Jas 1:12). St. Paul echoes this notion, telling us to compete for the prize of eternal life, "to obtain . . . an imperishable crown" (1 Cor 9:25). Out of fear lest he neglect his own attempts at receiving such a crown, he tells us, "I discipline my body and bring it into subjection, lest, when I have preached to others, I myself should become disqualified" (1 Cor 9:27). Those who win the race—refraining from temptation and subduing the body's sinful desires throughout life until death—can say with St. Paul, "Finally, there is laid up for me the crown of righteousness, which the Lord, the righteous Judge, will give to me on that Day, and not to me only but also to all who have loved His appearing" (2 Tim 4:8).

Elaborating on this concept, St. John Chrysostom taught his congregation to accept suffering in order to gain crowns of glory in heaven:

> The present life is an arena: in the arena and in athletic contests the man who expects to be crowned cannot enjoy

relaxation. So if anyone wishes to win a crown, let him choose the hard and laborious life, in order that after he has striven a short time here he may enjoy lasting honor hereafter.[12]

He continues by teaching us,

If you see a righteous person suffering tribulation . . . do not lose heart: his misfortunes are preparing more brilliant crowns for him. . . . If it happens to the righteous, [it] makes their souls more splendid. A great benefit comes to each of them from tribulation, provided that they bear it with thanksgiving; for this is what is required.[13]

Crowns for Martyrdom

The association between crowns and reward for spiritual deeds is manifest through several stories of Christian martyrs recorded in early Christian texts. For example, the early Church historian and bishop Eusebius (c. AD 260–340) records for us the sudden conversion to Christianity of a soldier named Basilides due to an apparition of a Christian martyr (named Potamiaena) whom he had recently led to execution:

Basilides led her off to execution. But as the crowd tried to harass and insult her with obscenities, he pushed them back and drove them off, showing extreme pity and kindness to her. She accepted his sympathy and encouraged him, promising to ask her Lord for him after her departure and before long she would repay him for all he had done in her behalf. Having said this, she endured her end nobly when boiling tar was poured slowly, drop by drop, over various parts of her body from head to toe. Such was the contest won by this splendid girl.

Not long afterward, one of his fellow soldiers asked Basilides, for some reason, to take an oath, but he maintained that swearing was absolutely forbidden to him as a Christian, confessing it openly. At first they thought he was joking, but when he continued to affirm it, they brought him before the judge, who sent him to prison when he confirmed his beliefs. His brothers in God visited him and asked the reason for his sudden, incredible inclination, and he is reported to have said that three days after her martyrdom, Potamiaena appeared to him at night, wreathed his head with a crown, and said that she had prayed the Lord for him and obtained her request, and before long would take him to herself. At this the brethren conferred on him the seal of the Lord [in baptism], and the next day he gave a noble testimony for the Lord and was beheaded. They say that many others at Alexandria suddenly came to Christ at this time because Potamiaena appeared to them in dreams and invited them.[14]

One can turn to the Coptic Synaxarion for more. A cursory search through it expressly indicates that those who are killed in the name of Christ receive a special crown of martyrdom. Below are a few examples.

First we have the brief story of St. Marina of Antioch. When she was about to be beheaded, the executioner told her, "My lady Marina, I see the angel of the Lord and with him a crown of bright light."[15]

Also, St. Moses the Strong, after becoming a monk (and forgoing his previous life of sinfulness, including murders and robberies), went with some elders to visit St. Macarius the Great, who said to them, "I see among you one to whom belongs the crown of martyrdom," to which St. Moses replied, "Probably it is I, for it is written, 'all who take the sword will perish by the sword'" (Mt 26:52).[16] Sure enough, shortly after they returned to the monastery, some barbarians entered the monastery and killed St. Moses and seven others. One of the brethren was hiding out of fear, but then he saw an angel with a crown in his hand standing by and waiting for him. So he came out of his hiding place, showed himself to the barbarians, and was also martyred in order to receive the reward that awaited him.[17]

Another remarkable account in the Synaxarion is the martyrdom of the great saints Peter and Paul. After Emperor Nero had St. Peter killed by crucifying him with his head downwards (because, as is traditionally understood, St. Peter felt unworthy to be crucified in the same manner as Christ), the emperor seized St. Paul and ordered his head to be cut off. While St. Paul was passing along with the executioner towards the execution site, he asked a young woman (who was related to the emperor) for her veil to wrap his head with and cover it as he was being beheaded—a request with which she complied, weeping over his impending death. The executioner eventually cut off the saint's head and left it there with her veil still around it. The young woman saw the executioner on his way back to the emperor and asked him about St. Paul. He told her, "He is lying where I left him and his head is wrapped in your veil."

She told him, "You are lying, for he and Peter have just passed by me; they were arrayed in the apparel of kings, and had crowns decorated with jewels on their heads, and they gave me my veil, and here it is." It is recorded that this event caused both the young woman and the executioner to convert to Christianity.[18]

There is also an interesting story regarding forty individuals from a city named Sebastia.[19] When they confessed their faith to the governor in that region, he ordered that they be thrown into a nearby icy lake. Thirty-nine of them died as martyrs; however, one person, who could not withstand the cold, ran into a nearby bath house. The heat there melted the ice on his body, but he eventually died anyway and unfortunately lost his crown of martyrdom. One of the guards saw angels descending from heaven and in their hands crowns, which were placed over the heads of each of the thirty-nine martyrs. He noticed one crown remained in the hand of one of the angels, so the guard went down into the lake shouting, "I am Christian, I am Christian!" He eventually died and received that crown that was in the hand of the angel, being counted among the martyrs.

One day there was an attack on a monastery in Sheheet,[20] Egypt. One of the most respected monk elders there gave everyone the option to be killed by the Berbers or to hide. Including him, forty-nine monks living there were killed. As a layman was hiding, his son who was also hiding with him told his father, "I see spiritual beings putting crowns on the heads of the elders. I shall go to receive a crown like them." Both then came out of hiding and were killed, receiving crowns as well.[21]

Also, the great martyr St. Mina (also spelled Menas) was strengthened when one day he saw the heavens opened and martyrs with beautiful crowns. He heard a voice from heaven assuring him, "He who toils for the name of the Lord Christ shall receive these crowns."[22]

Crowns Signifying Virtues

St. Cyprian, the bishop of Carthage (d. AD 258), explains the notion of crowns signifying virtues:

> Let there be the divine reading in the hands, the Lord's thoughts in the mind; let constant prayer never cease at all; let saving labor persevere. Let us be occupied at all times in spiritual works, that as often as the enemy approaches, as often as he tries to come near, he may find our heart closed and armed against him. Actually, for the Christian there is not only one crown which is obtained in time of persecution. The time of peace, too, has its crowns, with which we are crowned as victors . . . after the adversary is laid low and overcome. To have conquered lust is the palm of continence [i.e., a reward for those who exercise sexual self-control]. To have struggled victoriously against anger and insult is the crown of patience. To spurn money is to triumph over avarice. To bear the adversities of the world by hope in the things to come is the praise of faith. . . . In this arena of the virtues we run daily, and to these palms and crowns of justice we attain without intermission [i.e., if we continually strive without a pause or a break].[23]

We have already read the story of the choir in Egypt that died. Recall that as Mother Erene watched in a vision the invisible aspects of their departure to Paradise, she saw the angels place a crown on each of their heads. They did not die as martyrs, yet received crowns.

A saint from Rome named Euphrasia (or Eupraxia), who was

related to the emperor Honorius, lived her life as a nun in extreme asceticism. One night the abbess of her convent saw in a vision multiple crowns which had been prepared, and she asked, "Who are these for?" She was told, "These crowns are for your daughter Euphrasia. She will be coming to us after a short while."[24]

There is a story arising out of the late third century about three saints: Abba Bidaba, bishop of Qift, Egypt, as well as two others, all of whom were martyred. As they awaited their turn to die for Christ's sake, Abba Bidaba could see other Christians being tortured, and he saw angels coming down from heaven. In their hands were crowns of life for the heads of those who were being martyred, and he saw them being raised to Paradise with great honor and glory. Later, just before his own martyrdom, Archangel Michael appeared to Abba Bidaba and said to him,

> "Hail to you, O honored one. Let your soul rejoice today, for God has accepted all your toil, asceticism, and struggle for the sake of the faith. You shall receive three crowns: the first, for your worship and asceticism since your young age; the second, for shepherding the flock on the straight path; and the third, for your martyrdom. You shall be crowned with these crowns, with glory and honor, to receive the heavenly glories."[25]

The following story about St. John the Short tells us about crowns for obedience. When he began his monastic life, his spiritual father Abba Pemwah decided to test him. They occupied the same abode together, but then one day Abba Pemwah expelled him saying, "I cannot live with you." In humility and obedience, St. John stayed outside by the entrance of the cell for seven days without grumbling. Each of those seven days, Abba Pemwah would exit and strike him firmly with a palm branch. St. John's response was simply to prostrate before him and say, "I have sinned." Finally, on the seventh day, as Abba Pemwah left his abode to go to church, he saw seven angels, each holding one crown, placing them on the head of Abba John.[26]

In modern times we find the story of a woman who dreamt consecutive recurring dreams of Bishop Makarious of Qena after his departure. It turns out that there was a monk, from a different city, who witnessed the same exact vision as well. In it, they found Bishop Makarious sitting on a great throne with a crown on his head, as if he were about to celebrate some festive liturgical occasion. So she asked him, "Are you going to pray the Divine Liturgy now?"

He answered, "Prayers here are continuous and without ceasing." He then went on to ask that a very important message be delivered: "Go to church, confess, and partake of the Communion all the time . . . so you can reach where I am, because those who confess and partake of the Eucharist have a great position with the saints in heaven."[27]

Among those saints we have Mother Erene. Shortly after her death it was reported by two children that they saw her receiving a crown on her head. Those children accompanied their mother to visit Mother Erene as she lay in an open coffin for people to view her one last time. When they came home, their father was very upset that two young children were taken to observe this. However, to his surprise, they told him that they saw Mother Erene appear as "a sleeping angel who was dressed in white. . . . Jesus was on one side and our Mother the Virgin was on the other. Both were placing a golden crown on [Mother Erene's] head."[28]

As Manifested in Ways Other than Our Outward Adornment

Aside from indications of reward demonstrated in our outward appearance, our glory in Paradise may be manifested by some other means outside of what we wear on our bodies, bear in our hands, or don on our heads.

Spiritual Cognizance of the Merits of Others

In heaven one may deduce that knowledge will be given to us whereby we may be spiritually cognizant of the merits of others without having lived with them or heard of them before. Maybe such cognizance could also be granted in Paradise. Hippolytus comments regarding the afterlife, that while the wicked are no longer "worthy of remembrance, . . . the righteous will remember . . . the righteous deeds by which they reached the heavenly kingdom."[29]

Bishop Youannis writes:

> There is no ignorance in heaven, [but] only perfect knowledge. We have been living in the body by faith in the world. Faith offers us knowledge, as in a mirror. . . . But in heaven, we shall live a life of visualization. We shall see everything face to face. As St. Paul says, "For we know in part and we prophesy in part. But when that which is perfect has come, then that which is in part will be done away. . . . For now we see in a mirror, dimly, but then face to face. Now I know in part, but then I shall know just as I also am known" (1 Cor 13:9–12).[30]

The Splendor of One's Designated Place

Recall the story about Mother Ilaria mentioned previously. As the nun who adored her was granted the opportunity to visit Mother Ilaria in Paradise, she asked her why the area she inhabited looked so drab. She explained that it was because she was a miser during life who did not allow others to borrow her possessions, and she did not adequately give to the needy. Later on, while the nun visiting Mother Ilaria gazed at Christ from a distance, an angel came back to her and told her that the Lord of glory commanded him to show her the places of the saints, her father, and her mother. What is astonishing is that, while both her parents had beautiful places in Paradise, her mother's dwelling in Paradise was more beautiful; she was told this was because her mother was more simple and pure.[31]

Another story that exhibits the two different places and degrees of glory a married couple may receive comes also from Mother Erene.[32] She explains that there lived a man she knew personally who was very humble and giving, and all of his good works would be done in a manner that would not be seen by anyone so that he would receive his reward from God rather than from men. He lived in one of the villages of Egypt, where he and his wife would visit widows and their children to help them with their material and spiritual needs as often as they had time. One day one of his relatives died, along with his wife, leaving behind a few children. This man and his wife took care of those children (who later went on to go live with their grandparents) as if they were their own.

Then one day, shortly before his death, the man saw a revelation that made him aware he was about to die and go to Paradise. Just before his death he visited his friends and relatives to bid them farewell. Whenever they would ask him why he was doing so, he would explain that he had seen a vision that informed him of his impending departure to Paradise. Shortly thereafter, he came home and simply collapsed and died. (Note that his wife had departed from this world some time before.) Mother Erene explains the rest of the story as she heard it from this man's son:

> One day, one of his children was praying [fervently] and asked, "Oh Lord, show me where he went. Is he with mom, or where is he?" (Because previously he saw a vision of where his mother was.) He spent the entire night praying. It came to his mind to pray the "Commemoration of Saints" from the Midnight Praises. So, for example, he would pray, "Oh my Lady the Virgin, pray for me that God forgives me my sins, and if it is Your will [O God] that I see Your servant [my father], then please show him to me." In the end, after finishing prayer [and asking each saint to pray for him], he saw the room suddenly filled with light, and then he saw his father.
>
> Immediately upon seeing him, his father told him [in a jovial tone], "Did you really have to ask all those saints to ask God that I come to you? So [because of that] He [i.e., Christ] told me, 'Go ahead and descend to him and see him.'"
>
> "How am I to know that you are actually my father?" Because the devil could have been hearing him during his prayers [and may have been tricking him].
>
> "How do you want to be assured that I am your father?"
>
> He replied, "Make the sign of the cross."
>
> His father signed the cross and then said, "You make the sign of the cross too," and he did so. "Convinced now?"
>
> [The son, in telling Mother Erene the story, says] I was

convinced because I felt peace.

[The father then proceeded to inquire of his son as for the reason he was so concerned for him.]

"I just wanted to ask you if you are in a good place," [his son told him].

[The father replied emphatically], "I am in such a good place, I could never have dreamed of it."

"What is the most useful thing to you [of the things you did while on earth?" asked his son].

He said, "Works of mercy."

"Well, are you with mom, or are you in one place and she in another?"

He said, "The truth is she is in a place that is more beautiful than mine, but we can see each other."

"But why? You were a very good person!"

He said, "She was more pure, simple, and penitent. I was different than her, but I am in a beautiful place and we see each other continually and we are both in the glory [of Paradise and] see our Lord Jesus Christ, to whom be the glory, forever. Amen."[33]

Christ Himself said that, "In My Father's house are many mansions; if it were not so, I would have told you. I go to prepare a place for you" (Jn 14:2). Clement of Alexandria expands on this notion: "There are various abodes, according to the worth of those who have believed."[34] Recall Nahed's account of her encounter with Christ, she attempted to describe the mansions she saw: they were "a marvel that words can never describe . . . like the castles we envision in our imagination. No, it was more marvelous than that. It was something that no imagination could grasp."

The Coptic Synaxarion also tells us of a few occasions when saints were granted the opportunity to see the mansions of Paradise. For example, St. Sergius of Atripe, who at the age of 20 desired to suffer and die as a martyr, was granted his wish when the governor commanded that he be tortured and cast into prison. There in prison, at night, he saw a vision "as if he was in heaven, and he saw the mansions of the saints," which gave him great comfort and encouragement to continue his strife; the Lord Christ healed him of his wounds (but he later died after being beheaded).[35]

Another example in the Synaxarion involves St. Eusebius, the son of Basilides (a minister in the Roman government).[36] He was exiled to Egypt, where the governor of the city called Qift tortured him severely and even dismembered him. The Lord, seeking to fortify his intent to strive for martyrdom, sent him an angel who healed his wounds and then allowed him to see "in a vision Paradise and the mansions of the saints, and the places that had been prepared for him, his father, and his brother."[37] This caused him to receive exceeding joy and motivation to continue.

Thrones

In the previously mentioned story of Habib Farag, the deacon who died young but lived a life full of spiritual riches while developing an extremely close relationship with the Mother of God, we learn that he saw in Paradise many thrones on which sat the saints, but one chair remained empty. He asked St. Mary, who brought him there, "Whose chair is this?" She told him, "Yours, if you follow the will of the Lord Jesus Christ."[38]

St. Maura (a third-century Christian martyr from the village of Perapa near Antinoe in Egypt) relates a similar experience she had while being crucified with her husband, St. Timothy:

> I . . . beheld a . . . man, very comely of appearance; his face shone like the sun. He took me by the hand, led me up to heaven and showed me a throne covered with white garments, and a crown, most beautiful in appearance. Amazed at such beauty, I asked the man that had led me up to heaven: "Whose is this, my Lord?"
>
> He told me: "This is the reward for your struggle. . . . But now return to your body. In the morning, at the sixth hour, the angels of God will come to take your soul up to heaven."[39]

Afterlife experiences provide support for this feature as being a part of Paradise, although it is spoken of in Scripture as being relegated to heaven. In the book of Revelation the Lord tells us, "To him who overcomes I will grant to sit with Me on My throne, as I also overcame and sat down with My Father on His throne" (Rev 3:21). This verse has usually been interpreted by the Church Fathers as being allegorical, expressing the notion that we shall have a share and participation in God's kingdom, reigning with Christ; as St. Paul said, "If we endure, we shall also reign with Him" (2 Tim 2:12).[40] However, there may be room for a more literal interpretation when one considers that Christ told His disciples that "in the regeneration [i.e., at the renewal of all things in heaven]" they will "sit on twelve thrones, judging the twelve tribes of Israel" (Mt 19:28), and in St. John's revelation we find the "twenty-four elders who sat before God on their thrones" (Rev 11:16).

Enduring Suffering and Tribulations

Mother Erene, as indicated previously, used to be extremely ill. Once she was asked why she did not pray for healing, while so many people were healed by the effectiveness of her prayers. She told the person that her physical maladies were something she sought and prayed for. It appears that a person can receive glory in heaven by enduring suffering on earth, even if that suffering seems to have nothing to do with Christ, such as sickness. Recall that, although St. Paul was afflicted with a "thorn in the flesh" (2 Cor 12:7), which is often understood to have been "physical infirmity" (Gal 4:13) that God allowed him to live with even though he asked three times for it to be taken away (2 Cor 12:8), yet he said, "most gladly I will rather boast in my infirmities, that the power of Christ may rest upon me" (2 Cor 12:9). When one denies one's flesh in this way, such a sacrifice is considered to align with what Christ taught about what was necessary to become His disciple: "Whoever desires to come after Me, let him deny himself, and take up his cross, and follow Me" (Mk 8:34).

Mother Erene, being aware of the great glory that martyrs receive, wanted to become a martyr herself. However, Abu Sefein appeared to her and told her,

> God has allowed you physical pains because this is a cross and you will gain glory for it. Bearing these pains with gratitude is considered martyrdom. Did you not always ask God to be a martyr for His sake? These pains are equal to martyrdom. I am praying for you and my God is with you.[41]

Another time, Abu Sefein appeared and also told her, "God will give you blessings and consolations. Patience and gratitude have a crown like that of the martyrs."[42] St. Mary herself visited her and addressed Mother Erene's prayer for martyrdom, telling her, "Indeed, whatever you put up with—be it pains, diseases, problems, anguish or stress—is martyrdom."[43] Even till her last breath, as she lay on her deathbed enduring excruciating pain, she kept repeating various prayers, including, "You know that the pains surpass my capacity. I am being martyred. Help me and support me."[44]

This notion of bloodless martyrdom, in the sense that a person receives glory akin to that of a martyr for Christ (without actually dying a martyr's death), is echoed in the sayings of the Church Fathers. St. Athanasius speaks of the monk St. Anthony the Great as having lived a life where he was "martyred daily."[45] St. John Chrysostom urged Christians:

> Mortify your body, and crucify it, and you will yourself receive the crown of martyrdom. For what in the other case the sword accomplishes [against one's will], then in this case, let a willing mind [accomplish the same].[46]

St. Augustine used to tell his congregation, "Let no one say 'I cannot be a martyr because there is now no persecution.'"[47]

In order to explain the notion of glory received from ailment, Mother Erene used to tell the following story:

> Sickness is a blessing. And a person who receives sickness with patience and gratitude, they will receive for it glory.... There was one person who was sick, and he was a very good man. He stayed stricken in sickness for four years, and then he went

to heaven. The Mother Superior who was [the head of the convent] before me, who was a saint and a blessing, used to love this person and pray for him a lot, and she would see Abu Sefein frequently.

So she told Abu Sefein, "Why, if this guy was so good and righteous, and we kept requesting your prayers, did you not come to do anything about it?"

Abu Sefein said, "Look, I will go get him for you and come back." So he went and brought him.

The man [came and] told the nun, "I wished that all my life I was like this, [bearing this sickness]. These four years that I was sick, you have no idea the extent of glory I received for it."[48]

For this reason, there are some who actually feel concerned when they experience periods of time in their lives that are devoid of tribulation or suffering, considering that God is somehow not "blessing" them with the opportunity to gain glory in heaven. They feel that if they lack hardship in their lives, it is as if God is absent, and maybe something is not quite right. They seek the chance to "endure hardship as a good soldier of Jesus Christ" (2 Tim 2:3), and to say with St. Paul, "I am filled with comfort. I am exceedingly joyful in all our tribulation" (2 Cor 7:4). That is why St. John Chrysostom tells us, "When you see a righteous person punished in this life, consider him fortunate."[49] Do not forget though to find comfort that "God is faithful, who will not allow you to be tempted beyond what you are able, but with the temptation will also make the way of escape, that you may be able to bear it" (1 Cor 10:13). Thus one can be consoled as St. Paul was: "For indeed . . . our bodies had no rest, but we were troubled on every side. Outside were conflicts, inside were fears. Nevertheless God, who comforts the downcast, comforted us" (2 Cor 7:5–6).

Although it may be difficult to accept the concept of finding fortune in suffering, after death we will know and even wish we could have endured more hardship because of the glory we would have received in Paradise. This was the case with St. Efymia (also spelled Euphemia), an early Christian martyr who endured much physical pain and suffering, yet, knowing what she came to find out about the glory in Paradise, would have endured more. See what the modern-day elder Paisios, from Mount Athos, heard her say when she appeared to him and told him about her life, as recounted by his disciple Father Maximos:

> [After the Holy Virgin St. Mary and St. John the evangelist appeared with Saint Efymia and then went away], Saint Efymia stayed behind to have a conversation with the elder [Paisios]. For eight continuous hours they discussed all sorts of issues, some related to her personal life and to theology. Old Paisios explained to me that listening to her describe her life was like watching a movie. Every episode of Saint Efymia's life paraded in front of his eyes in every minute detail. After he witnessed the torments she went through, the elder sighed and wondered how it was possible for a young woman to withstand so much suffering. Her response was: "Father, for the kingdom of heaven, that was nothing. Had I known at the time what awaited me in God I would have tolerated infinitely more."[50]

Understanding this, St. John Chrysostom encouraged people to give no thought to their present tribulations in light of the glory to come:

> Among the righteous those who suffer any misfortunes here will enjoy great honor hereafter.... If there are two righteous men, of whom one has endured greater tribulation, the other less, he who endures the greater tribulation is more fortunate, since "He will reward each one according to his works" [Mt 16:27].[51]
>
> [Therefore] when you see anyone cultivating virtue, but enduring a multitude of trials, call him lucky, envy him, because all his sins are being dissolved in this life, and a great reward for his endurance is being prepared in the next life.[52]

That is why St. John Chrysostom preached to his congregation that they should withstand all that befalls them: "if they stumble ... or fall ill with a chronic disease ... or any such ailment," they should not "blaspheme" their condition. "Give thanks instead of blasphemy, worship instead of despair. Confess to the Lord, cry out loudly in prayer, cry out loudly glorifying God."[53]

You may be wondering about the status or condition of one's spiritual form after death if one suffered much affliction or ailment in the physical body during life. As is readily understood, there is expected to be no sickness in heaven, as such maladies are related to the inherent limitations of the flesh and do not apply to one's spirit. One may interpret the prophet Isaiah to have prophesied about our abode in the hereafter, telling us that its "inhabitant will not say, 'I am sick'" (Is 33:24).[54] This aligns with what St. John tells us in the book of Revelation: "They shall neither hunger anymore nor thirst anymore; the sun shall not strike them, nor any heat" (Rev 7:16). Recall that Father Arseny, the Russian Orthodox priest whose story was mentioned earlier, was able to tell us about the relief he felt once his spirit left his old and sickness-ridden body. Both the Coptic as well as Eastern Orthodox Churches share a prayer that is substantially the same, which expresses belief that those who repose in Christ will find themselves in "a place of light, a place of green pasture, a place of repose, where all sickness, sorrow, and sighing have fled away."[55]

Moreover, observe the following account by Mother Erene about her beloved friend, the saintly blind monk Father Andrew of the St. Samuel Monastery in Egypt (1878–1988). She had a very special place in his heart, and he visited her convent often, which led her to say, "I should be visiting you. Still you are the one who always visits me." In response he promised her, "I will come to you even when I am carrying my own shroud." That is what happened on February 7, 1988.

> [Mother Erene] was praying in her cell when she saw Father Andrew standing before her and dressed in a white tunic. His eyes were open (though he was blind since the age of 4). And he told her, "As promised, I've come carrying my shroud to say goodbye. I am departing to heaven."
>
> So [Mother Erene] told him, "How come you would go and leave me? Take me with you."
>
> He told her, "No. Not now."
>
> Then she told him, "Your eyes are wide open Father?"
>
> He answered, "I am out of the body."
>
> She said, "Remember me before God Almighty."
>
> He replied, "I will. I will. I will."[56]

If Reward Is Based on Merits, Then What Happens with Infants and Where Do They Go after Death?

Scripture, the early Fathers, and the afterlife experiences shared thus far all agree that God in His justice and mercy compensates people for their choices made during life. What happens to infants though, who do not have the mental capacity to make such choices deserving of either blame or reward? Consider that the Bible likens the innocence of children in similar terms as when describing Adam and Eve before the fall who likewise did not understand the difference between right and wrong: "Your little ones and your children . . . have no knowledge of good and evil" (Deut 1:39). In the field of criminal law, it would be said that these children lack sufficient capacity to form any criminal intent, and as such they do not do anything knowingly or willfully to merit punishment. On the other hand, they likewise do not intentionally amass any virtues or choose to perform good deeds. So what happens to infants and young children if their life is cut short and they pass away?

While some may wish to shy away from this inquiry altogether, considering it be too speculative a venture to arrive at any comforting answer, this did not keep St. Gregory of Nyssa from expounding at length on this question as proposed to him:

> If the recompense of blessedness is assigned according to the principles of justice, in what class shall he be placed who has died in infancy without having laid in this life any foundation, good or bad, whereby any return according to his deserts may be given him?[57]

St. Gregory concludes that it makes just as little sense that a righteous follower of God perish as it would an infant who has done nothing:

> Having, then, all these considerations in our view, we hold that the soul of him who has reached every virtue in his course, and the soul of him whose portion of life has been simply nothing, are equally out of the reach of those sufferings which flow from wickedness. Nevertheless we do not conceive of the employment of their lives as on the same level at all.[58]

He also indicates that, in the sense of varying degrees of reward, people who have struggled to be righteous and increase in virtue will "proportionately" receive their due, but infants who have "never felt the taste of virtue" simply partake of the life beyond without obtaining the same extent and gradation of glory.[59]

St. Gregory then points out that the resurrection is not *only* for recompensing good and evil, but, as supported by the notion that infants are entitled to enjoy immortality and bliss, the resurrection primarily is "in its essence a heritage of humanity," and thus they are obtaining what is naturally theirs as God planned all along.[60] A few hundred years earlier we find the early Christian apologist Athenagoras expressing a nearly identical argument:

> If only a just judgment were the cause of the resurrection, it would of course follow that those who had done neither evil nor good—namely, very young children—would not rise again; but seeing that all are to rise again, those who have died in infancy as well as others, they too justify our

conclusion that the resurrection takes place not for the sake of the judgment as the primary reason, but in consequence of the purpose of God in forming men.[61]

There are a few stories that purport to provide some insight as to what may be the plight of children who die young. The first comes from a vision of a nun named Mother Safina who hailed from a very pious family (her aunt and sister were also nuns, the latter having been the head of the convent which she joined). She advanced in purity, simplicity, prayer, and much service. Once she even was taken by an angel on a chariot of light to visit holy sites where the Lord Jesus Christ lived and walked, as per her wish. It was clear that she knew of her death three days before it happened. At the young age of 29, on June 12, 1909, she passed away. After her departure, another nun, named Mother Mengeda, witnessed Mother Safina's place in heaven:

> An angel came to me and told me to come and see the soul of Mother Safina. He took me up to heaven and I found myself in a place filled with children who looked like angels. They were singing praises in great joy. Mother Safina was in the middle of these children. So I asked her, "What brought you here amid them?" And the angel replied, "Because she had the purity and simplicity of children; and this is the place of the pure hearted."[62]

Were these children just angels that happened to look like children, or vice versa? We can glean a plausible answer from a dream that Mother Erene had of Mother Martha, a nun who had passed away. She saw Mother Martha in her cell and exchanged in a lengthy dialogue. She tells us:

> While Mother Martha was talking with me, I saw an angel of light with a beautiful face approaching us. He was smiling, and he had the face and body of a child. He created an air of joy and was flapping his wings until he reached us. I said, "In the name of the Father, the Son, and the Holy Spirit. Mother Martha, this angel is coming to take you back."
>
> She said, "No, this is your brother George who passed away at the age of 2. All children in heaven take the shape of angels. Every family with a child that departed to heaven has an intercessor in heaven who intercedes for the whole family like an angel."
>
> I asked him, "How are you my love?" He was smiling but did not say a word. Then he flew away and Mother Martha stood up and went up high.[63]

The Hierarchy of Glory in Paradise (and Heaven)

Those who honor Me I will honor. (1 Sam 2:30)

We have seen that in Paradise, some people will be glorified more than others. The notion of rewarding people in proportion to their actions on earth, thereby creating varied hierarchies of glory, is implicit in several biblical passages. One such passage is the parable Christ told of some servants who were each given money by their master, and their reward corresponded to the return they made on their investment. The person who returned ten times the amount of money invested was given authority over ten cities; the person who returned five times the investment was given authority over five cities (Lk 19:12–27). Christ tells us clearly that some "shall be called least in the kingdom of heaven" and others "shall be called great in the kingdom of heaven," depending on the extent to which one fulfills His commandments (Mt 5:19).

St. John Chrysostom likewise tells us:

> Among all human beings that exist, some are sinners and the

rest are righteous. So attend also to the difference among the righteous. One person is righteous, but another is more righteous. One is sublime, but another is more so. Just as there are among the righteous, "There is one glory of the sun, another of the moon, and another glory of the stars" [1 Cor 15:41]. For one is greater in glory, but another is less.[1]

Of course, this does not mean that one who is exceedingly righteous is to be regarded as sinless. St. John Chrysostom warns against such an inference:

> Pay attention: if someone is righteous, even if he is ten thousand times righteous, and if he reaches the very height, so as to be freed from sin, he still cannot be clean of every spot; even if he is ten thousand times righteous, yet he is a human being. "For who will boast that he has a pure heart? Or who will say confidently that he is clean from sin?" [Prov 20:9]. . . .
>
> Even Paul the apostle, the chosen vessel, the temple of God, the mouth of Christ, the lyre of the Spirit, the teacher of the world, he who crossed land and sea, who drew out the thorns of sin, who sowed the seeds of piety, he who was richer than kings, mightier than the wealthy, stronger than a soldier, wiser than the philosophers, more eloquent than the orators, he who possessed nothing and yet had gained everything, . . . who put disease to flight by his garments, who won a victory on the sea, who was snatched up to the third heaven, who entered Paradise, who proclaimed Christ as God—he says, "I am not aware of anything against myself, but I am not thereby justified" [1 Cor 4:4]. He who has

gained so many and such great virtues still says, "It is the Lord who judges me" [1 Cor 4:4].[2]

Although variation in the glory people receive in the afterlife is inevitable, this does not mean that they will be jealous of one another out of a feeling of inferiority, or prideful because of their elevated status, as such sinful inclinations cease once they shed "the body of the sins of the flesh" (Col 2:11), "for he who has died has been freed from sin" (Rom 6:7). Isaac the Syrian tells us,

> He whose measure is less will not see the great measure of his neighbor's rank, . . . [whereby] this very thing should become for him a cause of sadness and mental anguish. Far be it that one should suppose such a thing to occur in that realm of delights! Each man inwardly takes delight in the gift and the lofty rank whereof he has been deemed worthy.[3]

Likewise Mother Erene once saw the recently deceased father of another nun, and upon showing her his place in Paradise he assured her: "Everyone is grateful and satisfied with the place he or she is in."[4] On another occasion Mother Erene was taken to Paradise and witnessed the following:

> [I] saw very big arches; in front of every one there was a very large hall that belonged to a monk or a nun, but they were all open [to] each other. At the end of every hall I saw our Lord Jesus Christ sitting on a throne. He is in very strong light and His beauty brings great joy. There were many monks and nuns. There was indescribable joy and peace in every

hall. There were some places that were very near to God, others were a bit further, and a third group was very far away. Everyone had a place depending on his or her struggle. But all places inspired joy and whoever entered them would feel peace, quietude, and assurance.[5]

We have already been introduced to the general gradation and hierarchy of the departed to a small degree in the story about the choir from Heliopolis. Notice the order of the procession to Paradise, which is unlikely to have been a mere coincidence. Rather, it appears to be a very telling indication about God's designation of the favor and preeminence of various people in heaven. St. Mary led the procession, followed by the angels, some saints, and then the choir.

This exemplifies something the Orthodox Church has exhibited in its prayer rites and traditions for centuries: there are different degrees of glory and reward in heaven and a general arrangement of rank and favor with God, commensurate with people's spiritual triumphs on earth. The general practice of the Church is to regard the saintly departed in a particular order (e.g., in hymns and icon placement), as a reflection of their labors of love for God. Of course, we do not know for certain exactly how God may arrange people and in what manner, but there seems to be sufficient support that some arrangement will occur.

Saint Mary and Her Remarkable Apparition in Egypt

One of the most popular contemporary books on the afterlife, *Heaven Is for Real*, written by a non-Orthodox (evangelical) Christian family about what they tout as being their son's afterlife

The Hierarchy of Glory in Paradise (and Heaven)

experience, admits in a small paragraph in the Epilogue that St. Mary was not only in Paradise, but was always seen standing right next to Christ! This is what it said:

> A lot of our Catholic friends have asked whether Colton saw Mary, the mother of Jesus. The answer to that is also yes. He saw Mary kneeling before the throne of God and at other times, standing beside Jesus. "She still loves him like a mom," Colton said.[6]

Some may question the legitimacy of the claim that St. Mary is entitled to preeminence above the saints and even the angels. However, this biblically founded truth is undeniable, as has already been exhibited in several experiences mentioned thus far.

Let us look at the life of the Muslim woman Nahed who, before her conversion to Christianity, doubted the favor attributed to St. Mary. However, a wonderful miracle changed all of that. Her Coptic friend Samiah was in her office once, and Nahed "noticed something glittering behind the cross she was wearing." Nahed recounts the story:

> I asked, "What is that?"
> "This is an icon of the Virgin Mary," she replied.
> I reflected on this matter, thinking out loud, "Were there photographers or painters at that time who portrayed her image for the record? How can they be sure about it? Oh, how gullible these Christians are! I could swear the picture is but the product of the imagination of some artist who painted it and promoted it as the portrait of the Virgin Mary. And as it

happened, all the Christians believed the artist."

I was hardly finished with my thoughts when the glitter disappeared and I saw a bright light in front of me. I sensed the aroma of burning incense as if it were a column of smoke. Through it I saw a beautiful lady, very fair in complexion with kind features standing in front of me, dressed in a heavenly garb, while her hands were stretched downwards towards me. She was looking at me. I could not help but murmur, "The Virgin Mary!" as if I were in a coma. I could not believe what I saw. But I had seen her and she immediately disappeared.

When I regained my composure, Samiah and I were in tears. I discovered that I was the gullible one and that she had the "Truth." Now, for the first time in my life I felt devastated. I felt as if I were nothing but straw bouncing around. "What should I do? O God help me!"[7]

The psalmist tells us that queens are the ones that stand next to kings: "At Your right hand stands the queen" (Ps 45:9). This verse is therefore regarded by Orthodox Christians as being associated with St. Mary. (For this reason you will find at the front of virtually all Orthodox churches an image of Christ in front of the sanctuary, and across the sanctuary on His right hand an icon of His mother, St. Mary.) Hence, she is not simply regarded as Mary, who merely happened to be the mother of a person named Jesus, who happened to also be God. Rather, she is revered for being the only woman preferred over all other women of all time to bear God incarnate in her womb. She was found worthy to carry God in her womb for nine months, and yet the fire of His divinity did not consume her. Therefore, she is often compared to the burning bush that Moses saw, which was "burning with fire, but . . . was not consumed" (Ex 3:2).[8]

Compare this with Isaiah the prophet, who merely saw a vision in which "a live coal" was "taken with the tongs from the altar" by a seraph, who caused the coal to touch the prophet's lips and said, "Behold, this has touched your lips; your iniquity is taken away" (Is 6:6–7). That little coal, which symbolizes Christ and the fire of His divinity,[9] was all he was allowed to bear on his lips alone.

Recall also how God spoke with Moses on Mount Sinai while it "was completely in smoke, because the Lord descended upon it in fire, and the whole mountain quaked greatly" (Ex 19:18); "all the people witnessed the thunderings, the lightning flashes . . . and the mountain smoking; and when the people saw it, they trembled and stood afar off" (Ex 20:18). God commanded that the people get nowhere near the mountain, telling Moses,

> You shall set bounds for the people all around, saying, "Take heed to yourselves that you do not go up to the mountain or touch its base. Whoever touches the mountain shall surely be put to death. Not a hand shall touch him, but he shall surely be stoned or shot with an arrow; whether man or beast, he shall not live." (Ex 19:12–13)

By contrast, the Mother of God actually carried the incarnate Son of God inside her womb.

St. Mary is the only person of whom the Scripture prophesies that "all generations will call [her] blessed" (Lk 1:48). We should join Elizabeth in her praise of St. Mary, "the mother of my Lord" (Lk 1:43), saying, "Blessed are you among women, and blessed is the fruit of your womb!" (Lk 1:42), and hearken to the herald angel of God, Gabriel, who greets her in the following manner:

"Rejoice, highly favored one, the Lord is with you; blessed are you among women" (Lk 1:28).

I would like to share a pertinent miracle that is very near and dear to us Egyptian Christians, which illustrates St. Mary's prominence and also provides a glimpse of her appearance after death.

The inception of this event is said to be in the 1920s when a man known as Khalil Ibrahim was planning to build a hotel in the spot where a church in the Cairo district of Zeitoun currently stands, and which is regarded as a site that is believed to have been visited by the holy family some 1900 years earlier.[10] St. Mary appeared to Khalil and told him to build a church in her name there, promising that a miracle would take place many years later at that site. That promise came to fruition on the night of Tuesday, April 2, 1968. A group of Muslim workmen across the street from the church spotted movement above the middle dome of the church. They noticed what they thought was a young girl about to commit suicide. In desperation one of the Muslim workmen exclaimed, "Lady, don't jump! Don't jump!" As a few individuals called the fire brigade and others went across the street to summon a Coptic priest for assistance, suddenly the lady rose to her feet and revealed herself in a luminous apparition dressed in shimmering robes of light. A Coptic woman at the scene recognized her and cried out, "Our Lady Mary!" From that moment onward there continued to be periodic apparitions, sometimes daily, the duration of which ranged from very short moments and at other times for as long as nine hours. News spread like wildfire across Egypt (and eventually reached many outside of Egypt), generating waves of intense excitement and attracting immense multitudes of Christians, Jews, Muslims, and others to Zeitoun to see the visions themselves. At times Christians from a variety of denominations were seen praying together with Muslims, all imploring St. Mary to pray on their behalf for various things.

My father was among those crowds. While he was about 13 years old, he would walk nearly five miles from the Cairo suburb of Ein Shams to Zeitoun at around 11:00 pm to meet up with thousands gathered to see St. Mary. He tells me of how he saw her himself on at least three occasions. He remembers how people would sing hymns in honor of St. Mary and then suddenly they would see her. She would appear wearing "a long white robe and veil of bluish-white light."[11] One eyewitness recounts how he vividly recalls seeing her wearing a crown above her head.[12] St. Mary was often seen bowing to a cross above the church, and frequently acknowledging the crowds of people by a gesture with her hand, a nod of her head, or sometimes holding out an olive branch to the multitude.

Accompanying visions of St. Mary there would also frequently appear luminous birds of some kind, emanating a bright white light, as if they were made of light; that too my father witnessed, describing them as doves of light whose wings would remain spread without flapping, and who would appear flying and then just vanish. People would occasionally see incense rising from around the dome of the church, often diffusing a pleasant aroma as well. Along with the visions, many individuals, Christian and non-Christians alike, were cured of their physical ailments.

The 116th archbishop of Alexandria, Pope Cyril VI, who sent a delegation to investigate the authenticity of this miracle, officially confirmed these apparitions as being true. Other Christian denominations issued their own statements endorsing the same. Additionally, many other eyewitnesses gave their own personal testaments to the reality of these apparitions, whose accounts were disseminated through a wide variety of media outlets.

Some of us believe without seeing, and Christ says they are "blessed . . . who have not seen and yet have believed" (Jn 20:29). But for those who need to see to believe, we have eyewitness accounts of the prominence of the saints and the eminence of St. Mary, which should minimize doubt about the manner in which God honors those who love Him. Christ told us that to honor the saints is to honor Him: "He who receives you receives Me" (Mt 10:40). Some would still prefer to reject the honor God chooses to give to His Mother and His saints. Christ was once challenged for seeming to be "unfair" in the way He thought to distribute His benevolence.[13] He responded firmly: "'Take what is yours and go your way. I wish to give to this last man the same as to you. Is it not lawful for me to do what I wish with my own things? Or is your eye evil because I am good?' So the last will be first, and the first last. For many are called, but few chosen" (Mt 20:14–16).

Paradise and the Garden of Eden

> You were in the Delight of the Paradise of God! [LXX]
> You have been in Eden—the Garden of God! [Hebrew]
> (Ezek 28:13)

Before proceeding with some remarkable stories in the next, concluding chapter, there is an inquiry worth first engaging in. All of the stories mentioned previously that describe Paradise as resembling some massive garden begs the question: is the Garden of Eden equivalent to the Paradise of Joy to which spirits depart? Otherwise, what is their connection, if any?

Many call the Garden of Eden "Paradise" and assume it correlates with the Paradise of Joy without realizing that this association does not come explicitly from many translations of the Bible in use today. For instance, if you search through the New King James Version of the Bible, the word "paradise" is nowhere to be found in the book of Genesis, or any other Old Testament book for that matter.

What then? Why have Christians since early Christendom

drawn a link between the two, understanding that the Paradise Adam and Eve were cast out of corresponds to the Paradise the spirits of the righteous are sent to, made accessible again by the blood of Christ? For two main reasons: first, according to the Greek version of the Old Testament available to and used by the apostles and first Christians, the term used in Genesis is "Paradise" of Eden; additionally, the contextual clues in the New Testament indicate an inseparable link between the two.

In Alexandria, Egypt, about two hundred years before Christ was born, it is said that seventy-two Jewish translators were enlisted to translate the first five books of the Old Testament into the commonly used language of the time: Greek. Further translation into Greek of the remainder of the Old Testament led to a compilation referred to as the Septuagint, from the Latin word *septuaginta*, meaning "seventy." (It is thus also referred to by the Roman numeral for 70, which is LXX.)

The LXX gives the translation "Paradise"[1] (Greek: παράδεισος—*paradeisos*) instead of "garden," and "delight" (or "joy") instead of "Eden." This can be seen, for example, in the following passages: in Genesis God planted a "Paradise eastward in Delight" (Gen 2:8), and then after Adam and Eve's transgression, God sent them "out of the Paradise of Delight" (Gen 3:23). The prophetic book of Isaiah indicates that God will transform the waste places and wilderness of Zion and make it like Eden, "like the Paradise of the Lord" (Is 51:3). Ezekiel also describes how the king of Tyre (considered to allegorically or metaphorically refer to Satan) had fallen from his former glory, speaking of him, saying, "you were in the Delight of the Paradise of God . . . from the day you were created" (Ezek 28:13; also see Ezek 31:8–9). The prophet Joel speaks of how the "day of the Lord is near" and how the land is like a "Paradise of

Delight" before God's people (Joel 2:1, 3).²

It is evident that the Septuagint was used by the New Testament writers, especially when one examines their quotations of Old Testament Scripture. The first Christians, also utilizing the Septuagint, easily associated Paradise in the afterlife with the Paradise that was in Eden. For example, St. Irenaeus writes about how God "made the heavens and the earth, and formed man, and placed him in Paradise," which is the same "Paradise" St. Paul refers to as "the third heaven" where he was taken up, in which God "made spiritual things . . . which it is not possible for a man to utter," (which view is also attested to by St. John Chrysostom).³ The bishop Methodius (d. *c.* AD 311) tells us, "The tree of life which Paradise once bore, the Church has now again produced for all."⁴

In a very clear testament to the beliefs of the early Christians, it is evident that St. Athanasius correlated the earthly Paradise from which humans were cast out with the heavenly Paradise to which they can now return:

> When on earth He [i.e., Christ] showed us light from out of darkness, salvation from error, life from the dead, an entrance to Paradise, from which Adam was cast out, and into which he again entered by means of the thief, as the Lord said, "This day shall you be with Me in Paradise" [Lk 23:43], into which Paul also once entered. [He showed us] also a way up to the heavens, whither the humanity of the Lord, in which He will judge the quick and the dead, entered as a precursor for us. . . .⁵

St. Gregory of Nyssa delivered a sermon in which he offered a concluding prayer to God about how He "recalled us" graciously to Paradise:

> You banished us from Paradise, and recalled us; You stripped us of the fig-tree leaves, and unseemly covering, and put upon us a costly garment; You opened the prison and released the condemned; You sprinkled us with clean water, and cleansed us from our filthiness. No longer shall Adam be confounded when called by You, nor hide himself, convicted by his conscience, cowering in the thicket of Paradise. Nor shall the flaming sword encircle Paradise around, and make the entrance inaccessible to those that draw near; but all is turned to joy for us that were the heirs of sin. Paradise, heaven itself may be trodden by man; and the creation, in the world and above the world, that once was at variance with itself, is knit together in friendship; and we men are made to join in the angels' song, offering the worship of their praise to God.[6]

St. Cyril of Jerusalem further elaborates on how, through the Church, a person can be restored to Paradise. In his instructions to individuals who were learning about the faith of the Church before being baptized, he explains that baptism is the gateway to re-enter Paradise, from which we were formerly cast out:

> When therefore you renounce Satan, utterly breaking... your covenant with him, that ancient league with hell, there is opened to you the Paradise of God, which He planted towards the east, when for his transgression our first father was banished.[7]

Then may the gate of Paradise be opened to every man and every woman among you. Then may you enjoy the Christ-bearing waters in their fragrance. Then may you receive the name of Christ, and the power of things divine. . . . Great is the baptism that lies before you: a ransom to captives; a remission of offenses; a death of sin; a new-birth of the soul; a garment of light; a holy indissoluble seal; a chariot to heaven; the delight of Paradise; a welcome into the kingdom; the gift of adoption!

I have long been wishing, O true-born and dearly beloved children of the Church ... [that] I might lead you by the hand into the brighter and more fragrant meadow of the Paradise before us; especially as you have been made fit to receive the more sacred mysteries [the body and blood of Christ] after having been found worthy of divine and life-giving baptism.[8]

The allegorical interpretation of the Fathers, associating an earthly Paradise with a heavenly one, should not be read so as to lead you to lose sight of the distinction between the two, as their writings evince. Nonetheless, having expounded upon the link between the Paradise of Eden and the Paradise of Joy, a few questions come to mind. Are the two identical, or are there two Paradises, one heavenly and one earthly? Upon death, do the righteous return to a physical Paradise with trees and rivers and such? Or was Paradise something that was on earth (in the form of the Garden of Eden) and then was taken from the earth and placed in an invisible realm, perhaps also being elevated in its glory and magnitude? Or, alternatively, was Paradise always in "heaven" and never actually on the physical earth as we know it?

The late Bishop Youannis delineates a few views on the matter:

One view says that Paradise [in the afterlife] is that . . . place which is mentioned in the book of Genesis where Adam and Eve were before being expelled as a result of their sin of disobedience. It was once a place on earth, but was then . . . lifted up to heaven—the one [referred to] . . . by Saint Paul as the third heaven. Another view . . . says that Paradise was in heaven and is still there. A third point of view says that Paradise was on earth, and is still on earth, but it is hidden from our eyes after it . . . adopted a special . . . spiritual existence that cannot be visible to, or even realized by, the physical eyes.[9]

In a very genuine admission of ambiguity and inconclusiveness, he continues:

We cannot say which of the three views is more convincing than the other. It is quite a mysterious matter to us, as long as the divine inspiration did not explain or reveal more. Saint Paul the Apostle said well and truthfully, "For now we see in a mirror, dimly, but then face to face. Now I know in part, but then I shall know just as I also am known" [1 Cor 13:12].[10]

Yet another view exists, which was presented to me by a prominent Orthodox scholar. Maybe there are two Paradises, with the one on earth made to resemble one that existed heavenly. This notion is founded on a similar argument that can be made regarding the earthly tabernacle and the ark of the covenant. In Revelation, St. John sees "The temple of God was opened in heaven, and the ark of His covenant was seen in His temple" (11:19). We also find

God telling Moses how to build a place of worship for God to include an ark, to be fashioned after what God was showing him (presumably from what was seen in heaven): "According to all that I show you, that is, the pattern of the tabernacle and the pattern of all its furnishings, just so you shall make it" (Ex 25:9). Later, the Epistle to the Hebrews ties all of this together, saying that priests of the Old Testament served "the copy and shadow of the heavenly things, as Moses was divinely instructed when he was about to make the tabernacle. For He said, 'See that you make all things according to the pattern shown you on the mountain'" (Heb 8:5).

Allow me to offer my own personal conjecture (which of course does not preclude you from having your own). Paradise used to be on earth, but then was taken away from earth and elevated to a spiritual realm after the fall of mankind. That same Paradise, albeit spiritual rather than physical, and transformed into a more glorious place, is now accessible to all who are righteous and participate in the redeeming mysteries necessary for salvation. Let me explain:

Since the book of Genesis delineated nearly the exact place on earth where the Garden of Eden—Paradise—existed, describing the great river that flowed out of Eden and split into four riverheads that reached into known earthly habitations (see Gen 2:10–14), I am convinced at its inception it was a real place on this planet, as is also expressed by many Church Fathers (e.g., Theophilus of Antioch remarks: "That Paradise is earth, and is planted on the earth, the Scripture states"; yet, in his view, "Paradise was made in respect of beauty intermediate between earth and heaven").[11] Having said that, let me remind you of the fact that earth is regarded to have been originally in a better state of existence than now. After the fall of man brought about by the sin of Adam and Eve, earth was demoted;[12] on the other hand it is my belief that the

Garden of Eden was likely taken away from the face of the earth and was promoted in stature, maybe because of its uniqueness in containing the tree of life. In Revelation, God says, "To him who overcomes I will give to eat from the tree of life, which is in the midst of the Paradise of God" (Rev 2:7). St. John sees a new city he called "New Jerusalem" (Rev 21:2), and "in the middle of its street, and on either side of the river, was the tree of life, which bore twelve fruits, each tree yielding its fruit every month" (Rev 22:2). Notice the unique feature shared by both of these places: the tree of life. Also, just like the Garden of Eden, the place known as "Paradise" in the New Testament seems to feature garden-like aspects, which is why a correlation is so easily made identifying the Garden of Eden with Paradise.

The earthly Paradise (the Garden of Eden) then, in my opinion, and the Paradise it was elevated to become in the afterlife, are one and the same, albeit distinguishable in glory. We know that Adam and Eve were banished from the Paradise of Eden and that no person who died from that point on was allowed to return there until Christ redeemed us by His life-giving sacrifice on the cross.[13] Now we know that through Christ, who reconciled mankind with the Father, the spirits of those who depart are allowed to enter into a place also called "Paradise" which gives the impression of being one massive garden, which contains the tree of life made accessible again. Whereas previously "the first man Adam became a living being" who eventually died and inhibited mankind's chance for an eternal, blissful life, now "the last Adam [i.e., Christ] became a life-giving spirit" so that all may live (1 Cor 15:45). Therefore, because of Christ's redeeming sufferings, He told the thief on the cross, as He can tell each of us, "Assuredly, I say to you, today you will be with Me in Paradise" (Lk 23:43).

I am not claiming to have the ultimate answer on this subject, but simply offer an attempt to make a rational guess about a mystery. Regardless, what I know for certain is that I hope you and I meet each other there one day.

Part Five

The Power to Direct Our Fate

Second Chance

> Be zealous for the fear of the Lord all the day; for surely there is a hereafter. (Prov 23:17–18)

> I have blotted out, like a thick cloud, your transgressions, and like a cloud, your sins. Return to Me, for I have redeemed you. (Is 44:22)

After death (but for a few exceptional cases, such as you have read and will read below) there is no second chance. This life is our only opportunity for repentance. Thus far we have been exposed to the journey of the afterlife—leaving the body, entering the Crossover Realm, and experiencing the tortures of Hades as well as the bliss of Paradise—so let us consider ourselves to have now revived and been allowed a second chance to live our lives without any regrets. Think about this: the last few seconds in which you have been reading these sentences is all the time a person in Hades wishes they could have back on this earth, to be given a second chance to offer a sincere and fervent repentance, to beg God to accept them in Paradise.

Let us listen, then, to the words of Abu Sefein, who tried to convince the sinning Christian husband (whose story was mentioned previously)[1] that it matters to live this one life you get the right way:

> Your deeds will not lead to your salvation. You have to think of your eternal life. Repent before the time comes when your sorrow will not make a difference. You have the opportunity now as long as you live. The door of mercy will be closed after you die. You do not know the hour of your death. The life of every person will end; the flesh will turn to dust, but the spirit is eternal and will go either to Paradise if the person [carried out] good works or to Hades and [suffer] torture that is unbearable.[2]

Let it not be true about us what Christ said, that we will not be persuaded even "if one goes to [us] from the dead" (Lk 16:30) and tells us about their afterlife experience, and warns us about paying attention to our conduct in this life, as several in this book have done.

One of the Christian monks of the Egyptian desert, Evagrius Ponticus (late fourth century), wrote about what we should keep in mind regarding the afterlife experience to motivate us to live a righteous life now:

> [Collect] your thoughts. Remember the day of your death. See then what the death of your body will be; let your spirit be heavy, take pains, condemn the vanity of the world, so as to be able to live always in the peace you have in view without weakening. Remember also what happens in hell and think about the state of the souls down there, their painful

silence, their most bitter groanings, their fear, their strife, their waiting. Think of their grief without end and the tears their souls shed eternally. But keep the day of resurrection and of presentation to God in remembrance also. Imagine the fearful and terrible judgment. Consider the fate kept for sinners: their shame before the face of God, and the angels and archangels, and all men; . . . [also] the punishments, the eternal fire, worms that rest not, the darkness, gnashing of teeth, fear and supplications. Consider also the good things in store for the righteous: confidence in the face of God the Father and His Son, the angels and archangels and all the people of the saints, the kingdom of heaven, and the gifts of that realm, joy and beatitude.

Keep in mind the remembrance of these two realities. Weep for the judgment of sinners, afflict yourself for fear lest you too feel these pains. But rejoice and be glad at the lot of the righteous. Strive to obtain those joys but be a stranger to those pains. . . . Be careful that the remembrance of those things never leaves you, so that, thanks to their remembrance, you may at least flee wrong and harmful thoughts.[3]

Therefore we are taught, "Whatever you do, remember that some day you must die. As long as you keep this in mind, you will never sin" (Sir 7:36).[4]

For many, the Orthodox Christian mindset of constantly remembering the imminence of death is quite off-putting. Yet, as Metropolitan Kallistos writes, this "was once normal also in Roman Catholic and Anglican spirituality, but . . . has now grown unfashionable in the West."[5] Instead of viewing this as a morbid sentiment, it should be seen as "an authentic expression of

Christian realism and hope":[6]

> As Christians we have every reason to oppose the death-denying culture around us. It can with justice be said that true humanism and an awareness of death are "dependent variables": only by confronting death, not by trying to ignore it, do we become genuinely human. Death should be a constant dimension and quality of our life, not just something that befalls us at the last moment. When death is deliberately kept out of sight, life becomes mean and mediocre. By trivializing death, we trivialize life as well. . . .
>
> [Remembering death in this way] is not negative but affirmative; it does not make our earthly existence drab and colorless, but has precisely the opposite effect. Because we keep death in mind . . . our daily words and actions acquire an eternal dimension that otherwise they would lack.[7]

The words of Isaac the Syrian present the typical Orthodox approach on this subject:

> When it is time for sleep and you approach your bed, say: "Bed, perhaps this night you will become my grave. I do not know. . . ."
>
> In your heart be always ready for your departure. If you are wise, you will expect it at every hour. Each day say to yourself: "Perhaps the messenger who comes to fetch me has already reached the door. What am I doing sitting here? I must depart forever. I cannot come back again."
>
> Go to sleep with these thoughts every night, and reflect

on them every day. And when the messenger arrives, go joyfully to meet him, saying: "Come in peace. I knew you would come, and I have not neglected anything that could help me on my journey."[8]

Such mindfulness of death helps ensure that the same level of necessary intensity and seriousness is present in all our daily encounters. This is needed because hardly anyone will die and then afterward be granted an opportunity to correct their ill-advised manner of life. Maybe that is because very few people, as Christ said, would be persuaded to change (cf. Lk 16:31). There are many who have been exposed to afterlife experiences (personally or otherwise) and seem to have lived their lives unaffected or, even worse, chosen a path that will likely lead to their eternal condemnation.

Fortunately, this was not the case with the man from Northumbria (mentioned in Chapter 5) who witnessed the torments of Hades and came back to life after being dead one whole night: "I have truly risen from the grasp of death, and I am allowed to live among men again. But henceforth I must not live as I used to, and must adopt a very different way of life."[9] He gave away all his possessions and retired to a monastery. Later he related that he had seen both Paradise and Hades,

> [but] this man of God would not discuss these and other things that he had seen with any apathetic or careless-living people, but only with those who were haunted by fear of punishment or gladdened by the hope of eternal joys, and were willing to take his words to heart and grow in holiness.[10]

Athanasius of the Kiev Caves (who lived during the twelfth century) was similarly shaken to repentance after dying and coming back to life two days later:

> [His fellow monks] were terrified seeing him come back to life; then they began to ask how he had come back to life, and what he had seen and heard while he had been apart from the body. To all questions he answered only with the words: "Save yourselves!" And when the brethren insistently asked him to tell them something profitable, he gave as his testament to them obedience and ceaseless repentance. Right after this Athanasius closed himself up in a cave, remained in it without leaving for twelve years, spending day and night in unceasing tears, eating a little bread and water every other day, and conversing with no one during all this time. When the hour of his death came, he repeated to the assembled brethren his instruction on obedience and repentance, and died with peace in the Lord.[11]

Moreover, we have an early Christian account from *The Paradise of the Fathers* of a woman who was exposed to the varied plights of her parents:

> A certain old man related the following story: There was a virgin who was far advanced in years. She had grown old in the fear of God. Having been asked by me to tell me the reason why she left the world, she began, with sighs, to speak to me as follows.
>
> She said, "Great and marvelous things have happened

to me. My father was a peasant man. He was modest in his disposition. He was a delicate man in health, and was always suffering from some kind of sickness. He lived entirely to himself, and never interfered in the affairs of other people. It was the greatest difficulty to induce him to see the people of his village. When he was in good health he devoted his attention unceasingly to the care of his estate, and occupied himself at all seasons with the cultivation of his fields. He finally was obliged to pass many long days of his life laid out on a bed of sickness. He was so quiet that those who were not acquainted with him would have thought that he was deaf.

"My mother was the opposite of my father in all her ways and manners. She used to do things which were beyond her capacity. She was very talkative. Her words to everyone were useless. She talked so much that everyone imagined that her body was composed wholly of tongues. Moreover, she had quarrels with her neighbors continually, and was always in a state of drunkenness. She drank shamelessly at all times with wanton folk. She managed the affairs of her house badly, in the manner of a harlot. . . . Though the house was well furnished with goods of every kind, it was with the greatest difficulty that people could find enough to supply our wants. She was very lax in the care for the things which my father required in his illness. She displayed the utmost attention in providing for her own body in a disgraceful manner. The people of the village at length fled before her shameless appearance. No illness ever came on her, and she had never been ill in the whole course of her life; from the day she was born, she was healthy in body until her death.

"When I, a wretched girl, lived for some time in

circumstances as these, it happened that, after struggling against a long illness, where my father was obliged to pass every day of his life in the infirmity of sickness, he departed from the world. At the very moment of his death, the weather changed. The rain poured down in torrents; lightnings and thunders were tearing through the air, disturbing it violently. It was impossible to tell whether it was day or night. My father, for this reason, lay dead on his bier for three days, as the weather did not permit us to bury him. Moreover, it made the people of the village shake their heads, and wondered, saying, 'Perhaps great wickednesses were committed by this man secretly, and he may have been found to be such an enemy of God that even the earth will not permit his burial.' But, in order that his body might not corrupt, even though the weather was gloomy and threatening, and the rain had not ceased, by some means or other, we carried him to the grave, and laid him there.

"My mother, as one who had found great relief, fulfilled unreproved her wanton lusts to the utmost. She straightaway turned my father's house into an abode of harlots. She lived there in such a state of luxury and lascivious pleasure that soon, of all the goods in it, only a mere remnant was left when I was very young. Then with difficulty death came to my mother. In my opinion, death was afraid to approach her, for great worms grew in her. With much trouble she was buried, the weather by its serenity and the sun by its splendor helping in the work.

"After the death of my mother, I was still a little girl. I left the world. During the period when I was a young woman the lusts of the body were stirred up within me, and goaded me severely. I used to rise up in the evening (or night) that I might lie down again and find a little relief from the disturbance of my mind. A struggle went on in my thoughts, for I wondered what manner of life I should choose for myself, how I should end the days of my life, and whether they would be passed in quietness and happiness, and fair chastity, as during my father's lifetime. Then my thoughts spoke to me thus, 'Behold, in this world your father did not enjoy any happiness whatsoever. He passed all his life in sickness and wretchedness. He departed from this world of trouble under the same circumstances. The earth, even, was unwilling to receive his body. What do men do to receive such a life as this? God, why did my father deserve such treatment? On the other hand, supposing I chose to lead a life like that of my mother, will that be any better to deliver my body over to fornication, and lasciviousness? What is the gratification of my lusts? For, behold, my mother left no kind of abominable wickedness she did not commit. She destroyed her whole life with her depravity. Yet she departed from this world having enjoyed health and prosperity every day of her life! What then? Is not it then right for me to live even as she lived? For it is better that I should believe with my own eyes, and that they should see for themselves the various endings of such matters. There is nothing better than to understand thoroughly what we see openly before our eyes.' I, the wretched girl, vainly imagined that such thoughts were the thoughts of truth. For this reason, I determined to prepare myself to live even as my mother lived.

"When the night had overtaken me, I slept thinking thoughts of this kind. During my sleep I dreamt; a certain man, of huge stature, stood up above me. His appearance was frightful, and his form trembled and terrified me. His face was hard. In a stern voice he asked me, saying, 'Tell me, what are these thoughts in your heart?' Because I was terrified by his appearance and form, I scarcely dared to look at him. In a voice sterner than before, he commanded me to reveal to him the things which I settled in my own mind to do.

"Being stupefied with fear, I forgot all my thoughts and I said to him, 'My lord, I do not know what you are saying.' Denying that I knew, he reminded me of everything which was in my mind, one after the other. Therefore, having rebuked myself, I turned, begged and entreated him that I might be held worthy of forgiveness. I related to him the reason for such thoughts.

"He straightaway said to me, 'I am about to show you both your father and your mother. You will see the different manner of life which they lead, the things each does, and you shall choose which life to lead.'

"He took me by my hands, drew me away, and carried me to an exceedingly great plain. There were many paradises,[12] and thick trees heavily laden with fruits. The appearance and beauty surpassed description. When I had entered into that plain, my father met me, embraced and kissed me. He conversed with me and called me 'my daughter.' While I was in his embrace, I besought him to remain with him. He said to me, 'At present it is impossible. If you desire to walk chastely in my footsteps you shall come here after no great time.'

"As I remained making my supplication to him, he who had brought me to this place took me. I was lifted up in his hands, and he said to me, 'Come and see your mother also in the fire which is blazing fiercely, so that you may know how to choose what is good, and what manner of life is useful and beneficial for you to incline to.' He showed me a fiery furnace which was burning fiercely. Every kind of cruel wrath surrounded the furnace. I heard the sound of weeping and gnashing of teeth coming from there. Having looked down into the furnace, I saw my mother sunk in fire up to her neck. She was weeping and gnashing her teeth. She was being consumed in the fire, and was being gnawed by a multitude of worms. When she saw me, she cried out with tears in a loud voice, saying, 'My daughter, woe is to me, O my daughter, for these things had happened to me because of my evil deeds. I ridiculed the things which were said to me concerning chastity and concerning the punishments declared to fall upon those who committed fornication and adultery. Behold, in return for my lascivious pleasure, I have to suffer torture because I did not think that vengeance was laid up [consequently]. Behold, in return for a little pleasure, the momentary gratification of my desire, is an everlasting punishment I have to endure. . . . Consider, moreover, that in return for the short-lived happiness I the wretched woman enjoyed, I have to pay a prolonged penalty. Because I despised God what evil wages I have to receive! All these things have overtaken me because I behaved rebelliously, but, behold, this is the time for helping me, O my daughter. Remember with what anxious care and attention your bringing up was carried out, the helpful things which I brought you, all the good things which I did for you. Have mercy upon the woman who burns in the fire. Have mercy upon the woman who is cast into tortures as these. Have pity upon me, O my daughter, stretch out your hand, and lift me up out of this place.' I excused myself from doing this on account of him that stood by my side. She wept and cried out to me, saying, 'O my daughter, help me. O my daughter, have pity upon me, and come to me. Do not neglect your mother who gnashes her teeth in pain. Do not treat her with indifference, for she suffers torment in Gehenna.'

"As, according to the human nature, I felt pain because of her tears and mournful voice, I began to cry out loudly, to sigh and moan bitterly. Then all those who were sleeping in our house awoke. When they had risen up, I told them the reason of the outcry and disturbance. I narrated to them everything which appeared to me. These are the things, by the rich mercy of God, [which led me to] choose to follow the life and works of my father. I was persuaded [thus] . . . and through divine providence I am confirmed in my belief that such punishments are laid up for those who desire to live an evil life."[13]

Let us return to the account of Mr. Uekskuell. When he was last mentioned, we were watching as he was being taken up towards a "kingdom, full of the power of light." He thought he would continue proceeding upwards and eventually enter into that kingdom of light, which one can deduce is Paradise. "But something different happened," he explains:

Majestically, without wrath, but authoritatively and firmly, the words resounded from above: "Not ready!" And after that thereafter an immediate stop came to our rapid flight upward—we quickly began to descend.

But before we left this realm, I was endowed with the capacity to learn of one of the most wonderful phenomena. Hardly had the said words resounded from above when everything in that world it seems, each particle of dust, each slightest atom, responded to these words with their accord, as though a multimillion echo repeated them in a tongue unable to be perceived by hearing, but perceived and understood by the heart and mind, expressing its unison with the decision so decreed. And in this unity of will there was such wonderful harmony, and in this harmony so much inexpressible, exalted happiness, before which all our earthly charms and raptures appeared like a gloomy day without sunlight. This multimillion echo resounded in the form of an inimitable musical chord, and one's whole soul extended out towards it, wholly responding to it in a state devoid of any cares and in an ardent transport of zeal to be at one with this omnipresent, most wonderful harmony.

I did not understand the real sense of the words that were directed to me; that is to say, I did not understand that I had to return to earth and again live just as previously. I thought that I was being carried to some other different parts, and a feeling of timid protest stirred within when before me, at first as hazily as in a morning mist, the outlines of a city were denoted before me, and following this, streets well known to me also became clearly visible. Here I saw the building of the hospital which was known to me. Exactly in the same manner as before, through the walls of the building and closed doors, I was carried into a room completely unknown to me. In this room there stood a row of tables which were coated with dark paint; and on one of them, covered over with something white, I saw myself lying, or more correctly, my dead, stiff body.

Not far from my table some gray-haired small old man in a brown jacket, moving a bent wax candle along the lines of large type, read the Psalter [i.e., the book of Psalms], and on the other side, on a black bench that stood against the wall, sat my sister who evidently had been notified of my death and already had arrived, and beside her, bent over and quietly saying something—her husband.

"Have you heard the decision of God?" leading me up to [the] table, my guardian angel, who hitherto had not spoken, addressed me. And after that pointing with his hand to my dead body, said: "Enter and prepare yourself."

And following this, both angels became invisible.[14]

How haunting are those words! This scene! For those who are wavering in their commitment to godliness, will this affect you and change your life as it did his? For after this, he left the world and became a monk; life on earth seemed so insignificant in comparison with the permanence of eternal life. And this man did not even see Paradise, but only its light!

St. Paul yearned for the afterlife, preferring it over this life: "We are confident, yes, well pleased rather to be absent from the body and to be present with the Lord" (2 Cor 5:8). See what Mr. Uekskuell goes on to say about his experience returning to his body and his feelings about returning to this vanishing world after the Lord pronounced he was "not ready" to enter Paradise:

> I recall with complete clarity how and what happened to me after these words.

At first I felt as though something pressed close about me; after this followed the sensation of unpleasant cold, and the return of this capacity (which was absent in me just before this) of feeling such things vividly brought back to life the conception of my previous life. A feeling of deep mourning came over me, as though I had lost something (I shall further note here, that this feeling has always remained with me after the above described occurrence).

The desire to return to my previous form of life, although up until now there was nothing especially sorrowful in it, did not once stir in me; in no way was I drawn to it; nothing in it attracted me.

Reader, have you ever had the occasion to see a photograph that had been lying for a considerable amount of time in a damp place? The image on it was preserved but faded from dampness, moldy, and in place of a definite beautiful image, one has a kind of continuous light-gray murkiness. In like manner life here has become faded for me, appearing like a kind of monotonous and watery picture, and appears so to my eyes even up to the present time.

How and why I suddenly felt this I do not know; but one thing is certain: it in no way had any attraction for me. The horror that I experienced earlier concerning my separation from the surrounding world, now, due to some reason, lost its strange significance for me. For example, I saw my sister and understood that I could not associate with her, but this in no way disturbed me. I was content with [just] seeing her. . . . Unlike previously, I even did not have the desire to somehow announce my presence.

And besides, this was not my main concern. The feeling

of being compressed from all sides caused me ever-increasing suffering. It seemed to me that I was being squeezed between pliers, and this sensation increased with time. On my part, I did not remain passive. Whether I did something, whether I struggled trying to free myself of it, or whether I made no exertion to free myself, to cope with and overcome it—I am not able to ascertain. I only remember that I felt a sensation of ever-increasing tightness about me, and, finally, I lost consciousness.

When I recovered consciousness, I . . . found myself lying on a bed in a hospital ward.[15]

We can read about the experience of returning to one's body in the story of the saintly Coptic bishop Abba Makarious, as told to us by Mother Erene:

One day, he had a heart attack. The people around him called the pope [of the Coptic Orthodox Church]. The pope told them to bring him to Cairo, Egypt. They told him that his health condition did not allow him to travel. He died at 1:00 am. . . . He felt pain at the time of the release of his spirit. His spirit saw the flesh of Makarious lying on the bed. The spirit takes the form of its flesh. He saw a procession of angels and many great saints: Abba Antonios [i.e., St. Anthony the Great], the three Abba Makarii [including St. Macarius the Great], Abba Pachomios, and Abba Shenouda [the Archimandrite].

St. Mary came to them halfway and told them to go back, [and so] they descended. The spirit of Bishop Makarious was again in front of his flesh, [awaiting to enter it]. [Then], the

Virgin stretched her hands and said, "My Great God, the Almighty, if [it is] Your will, let the spirit of Abba Makarious return to his flesh, because he asked me [that he does] not repose until he consecrates the church that he is building in my name." All . . . heard a strong sound saying, "Amen, so be it." The angels put the spirit of Abba Makarious back into his flesh, which was lying on the bed. He felt great pain again when his spirit entered his body.[16]

Mother Erene describes a similar "great pain" when she herself returned to life after dying in a hospital due to heart complications and organ failure. She was dead for almost an hour. Before she was revived, here is what she experienced:

> An angel came and flew with me to heaven. I entered with the angel into a place overflowing with joy. It was not simply that there was joy in that place. No. It was overflowing with joy, peace, and light . . . a beautiful white light. It is the light of our Lord Jesus Christ that fills Paradise. The place was very large. It was full of lovely flowers and green trees. It had rivers like crystal.
>
> I was transported with happiness. I waited for a little while; then I saw Abu Sefein. He escorted me with the angel and told me, "Come, kneel down before the mighty God." Then I saw the Lord of Glory on the throne. I made the sign of the cross, and knelt before Him three times. He in turn made the sign of the cross over me. Next to Him were our Lady the Virgin, the cherubim and the seraphim carrying the throne, and a multitude of angels kneeling before the throne. They sang, "Glory to God in the highest, peace on earth, and

good will towards men. Glory, greatness and power are Yours forever and ever. Amen."

They were repeating many hymns loudly and in a sweet voice. I cannot tell you how much joy I felt. Then the Lord looked at me with love, kindness and tenderness. He said, "Do not be upset that you are going back to earth." These were the first words He said to me.

I asked Him, "How is it Lord that I should leave You? How can I go back and leave You?"

The Lord of Glory pointed to the martyr Philopateer [Abu Sefein] and said, "Philopateer asked Me and I cannot turn him down. He has shed his blood for Me. Besides, the convent needs you and many souls glorify My name through you. You still have work to do." He mentioned certain matters.

While the Lord was talking with me, our Lady the Virgin was saying, "Amen, Amen, Amen," and the martyr Abu Sefein was kneeling down. Whenever he stood up, he would say, "I thank You my Lord Jesus Christ. I glorify You, I praise You, I honor You."

The Lord of Glory continued, "The nuns are at the church crying. They want you and I cannot stand their tears. The young nuns need you. You still have a mission with the people. You will go back for the glory of My name. In other words, your vocation is divided between the convent and the people."

I replied, "Lord let it be Your will."

Then the Lord of Glory told the martyr Abu Sefein, "Take her to visit her father and mother." All this happened while the angel was still with us. After the visit, the angel took me down to earth and my spirit re-entered my body. This was very difficult. Unexpectedly, my heart began beating once more, and suddenly the rest of my organs were also functioning.[17]

As our spirit still resides in our flesh, today is our second chance. St. John Chrysostom urges us to take advantage of our lives on earth for the sake of our eternal wellbeing, paying close attention to how we spend every moment of each day: "[Do not] neglect . . . the time of our earthly life which is given to us by God's kindness as the opportunity for our salvation."[18] Elsewhere he also reminds us:

> While we are here, we have good hopes; [however], when we depart to that place, we have no longer the option of repentance, nor of washing away our misdeeds. For this reason we must continually make ourselves ready for our departure from here. What if the Lord wishes to call us this evening? Or tomorrow? The future is unknown, to keep us always active in the struggle and prepared for that removal.[19]

St. Cyprian of Carthage echoes that sentiment when he writes:

> Here life is either lost or kept. Here, by the worship of God and by the fruit of faith, provision is made for eternal life. Let no one be kept back either by his sins or by his years from coming to obtain salvation. To him who still remains in this world there is no repentance that is too late.[20]

Therefore, "See then that you walk circumspectly, not as fools but as wise, redeeming the time, because the days are evil" (Eph 5:15–

16).

God gave us a conscience in order to judge ourselves before He judges us, as St. John Chrysostom teaches us:

> So in order not to be chastised hereafter, in order not to undergo punishment hereafter, let each of us enter into his own conscience, unfold the story of his life, examine all his transgressions accurately, condemn his soul which has committed such acts, correct his intentions, and afflict and straiten his thoughts. Let him seek a penalty for his sins by self-condemnation, by complete repentance, by tears, by confession, by fasting and almsgiving, by self-control and charity, so that in every way we may become able to put aside all our sins in this life and depart to the next life with full confidence.[21]

Allow me now to share with you the remarkable story of a young man—a baptized Coptic Christian—who decided to neglect his eternal wellbeing by delaying repentance.[22] That young man used to seek spiritual guidance from the monk Father Bishoy El-Antony in the 1980s, visiting him and confessing his sins. Because this individual is still alive at the time of writing this book, his identity is being kept confidential.

On one occasion he was visiting with Fr. Bishoy and relaying several deplorable sins that he was unwilling to actually give up, including adultery and other matters in which he severely displeased the Lord. Fr. Bishoy implored him to stop, explaining that true repentance requires a commitment to change one's life and that if he had decided to continue in this way, Fr. Bishoy could not keep hearing his insincere confessions. The young man responded with all sorts of excuses, telling Fr. Bishoy that he came from a rich family, he was an only son, good-looking and strong—"Why do you want me to repent now and stop sinning? I love sin and life is long—I can do whatever I want."

"Until when do you want to live that way?" asked Fr. Bishoy.

"I will repent before I die," he responded.

"When are you going to die?" Fr. Bishoy asked rhetorically.

The young man brazenly answered back, "I'll live to at least 60 for sure. When I turn 60 I will confess."

"You cannot guarantee that," Fr. Bishoy warned him. The young man remained unconvinced and was set on continuing to live his life just as he was. After about 20 years had passed without them speaking to each other, Fr. Bishoy noticed a number of voice messages that had been left for him by a man who was pleading to be contacted back. Eventually Fr. Bishoy returned the calls.

The man at first tried to remind him who he was. "Do you recall the guy who told you he would repent when he turned 60, before he died?" Fr. Bishoy immediately remembered because he was the only person who ever said such a thing to him. As it turned out, the person on the phone was the same young man, except at the time he was calling he was 42 years old. He had one bit of news of which he was desperate to inform Fr. Bishoy: "Father, I died."

The man elaborated as he erupted in tears, sobbing loudly as he explained what he had experienced, which now that you have read this book should sound quite familiar to you. He was at the hospital in order to have an operation on his appendix. He underwent anesthesia and then suddenly found himself standing next to his body, watching after the surgeons had finished the operation. He was bewildered as to how it could be that he was observing his own body while being present outside of it.

After realizing he was in his spirit, he unexpectedly found himself pulled away from this world with tremendous force and at an alarming rate. While words were inadequate in describing the experience, he likened the speed of his withdrawal from this world to a rocket. He was taken out of the earth into another realm: he saw himself taken out of the hospital room, then the hospital, then the city of Cairo, and eventually away from the entire earth. He felt that he was being squeezed out of a narrow tube. Suddenly, darkness surrounded him.

During this experience he observed his entire life, moment by moment; it was not just some faint recollection from memory, but it was there, laid out before him. While it would have taken forty-two years to go through his life on earth, in the realm he was in it felt like just an instant. He saw himself being held by his father and mother, going to school, arguing with his sister, visiting his priest, and visiting the monk—Fr. Bishoy El-Antony. As he saw the course of his life, he also saw himself sin, and each time he disobeyed God's commandment he noticed dark spots appearing on his spirit. His spirit looked as if it were transparent, and any sin would reveal a spot which blocked that transparency. As he watched his conduct in life, he realized that whenever he confessed any of his sins, those sins and their corresponding stains on his spirit would disappear. The things he never confessed remained. After the course of his life had ended, his spirit was left engulfed in stains. "After I left you," he told Fr. Bishoy, "the spots remained there and it covered me with darkness."

He felt such deep sorrow and remorse, crying while earnestly calling out to God and begging for mercy, yet no sound came out of him. Although he felt as though he were screaming from the depth of his soul, his voice was silenced by his new condition.

"I'm sorry, Lord. I thought You would give me another chance," he tried to express, but to no avail. He became aware that he was gravitating away from a light, and as that was happening he told Fr. Bishoy that evil and scary faces swarmed around him. Although the realm he was in was already dark, he found himself dropping down what seemed like a tunnel, going from darkness to even more darkness. No matter how dark, it kept getting darker. To illustrate his descent into the darkness, he told Fr. Bishoy, "Have you entered the pyramids from the top? I dropped level to level like I was entering the pyramids."

As he descended, he somehow felt as if others were falling with him, observing the wicked faces around him who appeared to be grabbing others like him to join in his descent, although he could not see those other spirits that were being brought down to their demise. As he suffered through this terrifying ordeal, he continued to yearn earnestly for a second chance and forgiveness. Then unexpectedly a voice resounded all around him. It was not just a voice that one hears in the ear, but with it was power and the sense that it encompassed everything around. That voice declared firmly, "I will give you another chance."

At this point in the story, I will share with you what a doctor in the hospital room observed, with whom Fr. Bishoy El-Antony spoke to get her perspective. She was the anesthesiologist and the only physician who at that point was still facing the man's body. The rest of the doctors were no longer paying attention to him because they were too busy blaming each other for the death of this patient after undergoing what should have been a successful, routine surgery. About six minutes had passed since he was declared dead, when suddenly the anesthesiologist saw the man's body begin to move, and then he sat up. The doctor began screaming because she was sure he was dead. As the man regained life and opened his eyes, he too let out a piercing scream as he begged over and over again for someone to turn on the lights. He felt so helpless in the darkness that enveloped him amidst the frightful evil spirits that when now his voice could be heard and he had some power over his surroundings, he sought to reverse the predicament immediately.

This entire ordeal and the memory of the darkness traumatized him so much that he had to undergo psychological treatment for two months after his surgery before being released, because he did not want to close his eyes. Eventually he recovered and has since completely changed his life around, forgoing his former life of sin so that he, along with his angelic wife and their two lovely children, may instead live in continual preparedness for the day of departure from this world.

Who of us can afford to delay our repentance? Who of us knows when the moment of death will come upon us? It is true that there are some who live such blessed lives that God reveals it to them. We already witnessed that in the life of Abba Makarious. There are even some exceptional cases where a person simply releases their spirit into the hands of their Creator when they are ready. That was the case with a monk known as Fr. Tadros El-Antony, a beloved and dear friend and fellow monk in the same monastery of Fr. Bishoy El-Antony. Fr. Tadros was an extremely simple and humble man. There was one thing he was always against: being taken to see a physician. Even when this man developed cancer in his stomach and the monks tried to persuade him to see a doctor, he refused, telling them that he accepted his illness and would only allow God to heal him if it was His will.

Eventually this monk became so ill that he fell into a coma. Fr. Bishoy El-Antony, who was in charge of the monastery at the time, placed Fr. Tadros in his car and began driving towards a hospital. During the drive, Fr. Tadros opened his eyes and asked, "Father, where are you going?"

Fr. Bishoy responded, "I am taking you to the hospital."

"No, no, take me back! I do not want to go to the hospital!" exclaimed Fr. Tadros.

But Fr. Bishoy kept on driving in hopes that he could convince him this was the appropriate course of action: "Father, you are very sick, and you need to go to the hospital. Please let me take you there and they will tell us what is going on with you."

"No," Fr. Tadros responded. "Please go back."

"Father, as you know, I am in charge now, and if something happens to you I will be very upset for the rest of my life. I will feel guilty as if I did not care enough about you."

"But Father, if you take me to the hospital, I too will feel upset for the rest of my life." Then Fr. Tadros proposed the following solution: "What if I die right now?"

"Father, do not say that! Death is not an option you can just choose, as if you are selecting it from a menu or something. No one just asks God to die and dies."

Fr. Tadros told him, "If I ask something from Christ, He will give it to me. Look Father, would you agree that I die? If I go to heaven then neither you nor I will be upset. We will both be happy that I departed to heaven."

Fr. Bishoy continued to refuse this whole idea, but then Fr. Tadros asked him, "Do you know any hymns about St. Mary?" Fr. Bishoy answered that he did, and then began to sing a hymn. He noticed that as he was singing, Fr. Tadros crossed his arms over his chest and at that moment died peacefully.[23]

Hardly any of us will be so blessed as to be able to choose the time and manner of our departure from this world. Instead, Christ laid out the path for us to depart and enter into His kingdom. He "has come in the flesh" (1 Jn 4:2) in order to give "us of His Spirit" (1 Jn 4:13). The divine Lord, in whom "dwells all the fullness of the Godhead bodily" (Col 2:9), became a partaker of human nature so that we in turn could be "partakers of the divine nature" (2 Pet 1:4). He took what was ours (our sin and the sentence of death) and gave us what is His (righteousness and eternal life). It is only through Christ cloaking us with His righteousness that we have "boldness and access with confidence through faith in Him" (Eph 3:12) "to enter the holy places [i.e., heaven] by the blood of Jesus" (Heb 10:19). Humanity was distanced from God when the first man and woman created by God—Adam and Eve—sinned, thereby causing all humans to suffer the same fate: no one would be allowed to live with God in heaven after death. After the Lord Jesus Christ sacrificed Himself on the cross to make atonement for the sins of humanity, He ascended into heaven so that He would "appear in the presence of God for us . . . to put away sin by the sacrifice of Himself" (Heb 9.24, 26). Having completed His mission to offer Himself on behalf of mankind to reconcile humanity with the divine, we are now given access to living after death, to receive "an inheritance incorruptible and undefiled and that does not fade away, reserved in heaven for you, who are kept by the power of God through faith for salvation ready to be revealed in the last time" (1 Pet 1:4). And all of this was afforded us not because we deserved it, but God graciously gave it to us: "God demonstrates His own love toward us, in that while we were still sinners, Christ died for us" (Rom 5:8).[24]

St. Athanasius the Great described the salvation accomplished by Christ in terms of having cleared the path for us so that after death we can pass through the throng of evil spirits and "the prince of the power of the air" (Eph 2:2), and enter the gates of Paradise which Christ opened for us:

> The enemy of our race, the devil, having fallen from heaven, wanders around these lower airs and, lording it here over the demons with him . . . [tries] to prevent [us] from rising upwards. . . . Yet Christ came that He might overthrow the devil, purify the air, and open up for us the way to heaven, as the Apostle said, "through the veil, that is, His flesh" (Heb 10:20). . . . By what other death would these things have happened except that which takes place in the air, I mean the cross? For only he that completes his life on the cross dies in the air. Therefore it was right that the Lord endured it. For being thus lifted up, He purified the air from the diabolical plots of all demons . . . and blazing the trail He made anew the way up to heaven, saying, "Lift up your gates, O princes of yours, and be raised up, everlasting gates" (Ps 24:7).[25] For it was not the Word Himself who needed the gates to be opened, since He is the Lord of all, nor was any made thing closed to its Maker; but we were those who needed it, who He Himself carried up through His own body. For as He offered death on behalf of all, so through it He opened up again the way to heaven.[26]

There are those of you reading this book who have been so blessed as to already know the truth, having been baptized in the true faith, receiving justification through Christ, and who have entered the "narrow" gate which, although it is "difficult," is nonetheless the "way which leads to life" (Mt 7:14). Scripture and the Fathers implore that we do not simply seek entrance into Paradise, but to pursue, more and more, a better extent of glory and reward to be given us when, by God's grace, we find ourselves there. This is what we can consider St. Paul to have alluded to when he wrote about Old Testament saints who sought "a better resurrection" (Heb 11:35). In that biblical passage you will find him mentioning people who were tortured for the sake of their adherence to the worship of the true God, who, although they could have accepted deliverance from their plight, sought instead to continue suffering "that they might obtain a better resurrection" (Heb 11:35). It is that kind of motivation that drives so many to pursue lives filled with self-imposed ascetic strife, such as those who choose the life of Christian monasticism, which St. Neilos the Ascetic comments on:

> What can be more stupid than to keep silent continually, live on vegetables, cover oneself with ragged garments of hair and spend one's days in a barrel, if one expects no recompense after death? If the rewards of virtue are restricted to this present life, then one is engaged in a contest where no prizes are ever offered, wrestling all one's life for no return but the toil and the sweat.[27]

Such a mindset, which is not satisfied with mere mediocrity in one's Christian path, is what St. Neilos' spiritual guide St. John Chrysostom means when he implores us to seek "a surplus of righteousness."[28] Are we seeking the minimum, just barely trying to get by? It is so interesting to reflect on how on earth people are constantly seeking a manner to be promoted in life (financially, work-wise, socially, etc.), but when it comes to heaven, people are comfortable with remaining last (just getting their foot in the door).

Therefore, as St. John Chrysostom tells us, let us keep our eyes fixed on heaven:

> Sweet is the present life and full of great pleasure—not for all, however, but only for those who feel an attachment for it. If a man has his eyes fixed on heaven and keeps looking at the beauties to be discovered there, he will quickly come to despise this life and will consider it of no account. Just as the beauty of an object is admired while none more beautiful is seen, but when a better appears, the former is despised. If then we would choose to look to that beauty, and observe the splendor of the kingdom there, we should soon free ourselves from our present chains; for a kind of chain it is, this sympathy with present things.
>
> Hear what Christ said to persuade us of this: "He who loves his life loses it; and he who hates his life in this world keeps it for eternal life. If anyone serves Me, let him follow Me; and where I am there also shall My servant be" [Jn 12:25–26]. The words seem like a riddle, yet they are not so, but are full of much wisdom. But how shall "he that loves his life, lose it"? When he carries out its improper desires, when he gratifies it where he should not. Therefore one exhorts us saying, "Do not walk in the desires of your soul" [Sir 18:30]. [Through this type of living] you will destroy your soul since it leads away from the path leading to virtue.
>
> On the contrary, "he who hates his life in this world will keep it for eternal life." But what does this mean, "he who hates his life?" He who does not yield to it when it commands

you to do what is evil. Yet He did not merely say, "He that does not yield to it," but "He who hates" it. For as we cannot endure even to hear the voice of those who we hate, nor to look upon them with pleasure, so we must forcefully turn away from the soul when it commands us to do things contrary to what is pleasing to God.[29]

In this way, we will have a more fulfilling life, as Christ promised us: "I have come that they may have life, and that they may have it more abundantly" (Jn 10:10).

Let us then seek a heavenly life here and now while we are still on earth, that we may "glorify God in [our] body and in [our] spirit, which are God's" (1 Cor 6:20). Although we reside on earth, "our citizenship is in heaven" (Phil 3:20). Therefore, we should live life as if we belong there, not here. Such a life is accessible now, as Christ tells each of us that "the kingdom of God is within you" (Lk 17:21). Elsewhere He says, "If anyone loves Me, he will keep My word; and My Father will love him, and We will come to him and make Our home with him" (Jn 14:23). Notice the previous verse and how it emphasizes that we should be motivated by "love" to seek God, arguably more so than the fear of punishment or the promise of rewards He is prepared to give us. The author of the influential text *The Way of a Pilgrim* elaborates on this point:

> Abstaining from sinful actions and fear of suffering are not sufficient for spiritual life; . . . only the guarding of the mind and purity of heart will free one's soul from sinful thoughts; . . . inner freedom can be attained only through interior prayer, . . . not through the fear of the sufferings of hell or even the desire for the bliss of heaven. The holy

Fathers consider even heroic deeds as the acts of a hireling. They claim that the fear of suffering is the way of a slave and that desire for a reward is the way of a hireling. But God wants us to come to Him on the path of a son; motivated by love and zeal for His glory, we should conduct ourselves with honor and enjoy His saving presence in our hearts and souls.[30]

Clement of Alexandria furthers this notion by indicating that rewards in the afterlife will be dependent in part on one's underlying motivation for why they performed any work for God:

> The same work, then, is different, depending on what prompted it. Was it because of fear, or was it accomplished because of love, faith, or knowledge? Rightly, therefore, their rewards are different.[31]

It behooves us then to look within ourselves and ponder: "If you cannot stand to live with God here on earth, how will you be able to live with Him in heaven?" That is the question His Holiness Pope Shenouda III posed in one of his sermons, and he explains why it is an important one to ask:

> If you cannot talk to the Lord for just half an hour a day here on earth, how will you be able to talk to Him when you go to eternity? Where will you go? If you had no relationship with the angels and the saints here on earth, how will you live with them when you meet them in heaven?
> If you love material possessions, crave the fulfillment of physical desires, and lust after worldly desires, what will

you do when you go to heaven and the material and physical desires are nonexistent? What will you say then? Will you apologize and say, "I am sorry. The heavens will not do for me. Send me back to earth!" That would be futile and useless, my beloved.

You should start establishing a relationship with eternity right away. You ought to familiarize yourself with the surroundings of eternity in this world. You should lead that spiritual life that you will eternally experience in the world to come. You should live with the Lord, His angels and His saints while you are here on earth for you will live with them there forever. What will that man who lives for the satisfaction of worldly desires do when the world and all its desires pass away [cf. 1 Jn 2:15–17]? What can he possibly do?

Form a relationship with the Lord because a relationship with Him starts here, but it will never end. Your relationship with the world will come to an end one day. It will end no matter how long you live. However, your relationship with the Lord, the angels, [and] the saints will not end. Neither will your relationship with righteousness, virtue and goodness. Never think that your life on this planet will last. Never! Life on earth will come to an end. Only the good and righteous deeds that were done in this life remain. God will scrutinize all your life and consider what goodness and love was manifested. These are the things that will last.[32]

To illustrate this point, the Coptic bishop Abba Bessada (of Akhmim, Egypt) tells a little story about three sisters.[33] Two of them were extremely religious, while one of them simply could not have cared less. The two girls tried repeatedly to persuade their sister to be more attentive to her spiritual life. One day, the sister who lacked spiritual fervor went to sleep and had a dream. She found herself in Paradise, where she saw a line of people passing in front of her as they were praising God. People in the line kept calling out to her, inviting her to join them in their procession and worship, yet she continually declined, expressing a lack of interest. Then, after the line ended, she saw the Lord Jesus Christ, who inquired as to why she was not willing to participate, inviting her again to join in worship. The girl made it clear that she had no interest in joining. Christ told her that in Paradise, this is what people do, and if she does not care for it, then there is no reason for her to be there. At this she woke up and told her other sisters about what she had seen. They rejoiced with the hope that this would finally change her. Unfortunately it did not, and a few days later she passed away.

Moreover we have the example given by the sixth-century archbishop of Rome, Gregory the Great, who tells in his *Dialogues* of a certain rich man who was a slave to numerous passions:

> A short time before he died, he saw hideous spirits standing before him, threatening fiercely to carry him to the depths of hell. . . . The entire family gathered round, weeping and lamenting. Though they could not actually see the evil spirits and their horrible attacks, they could tell from the sick man's own declarations, from the pallor on his face and from his trembling body, that the evil spirits were present. In mortal terror of these horrible images, he kept tossing from side to side on his bed. . . . And now, nearly worn out and despairing of any relief, he shouted, "Give me until morning! Hold off at least until morning!" With that his life was snatched away.[34]

Let us all consider the outcome of our conduct on earth and take advantage of our lives, "redeeming the time" while we have it (Col 4:5). I pray that both of us are ready for the afterlife and willing to respond to Christ's reminder, "Surely I am coming quickly," by proclaiming together: "Amen. Even so, come, Lord Jesus!" (Rev 22:20). Please pray for me, and for yourselves.

I conclude with the words of St. John Chrysostom in his sermon about Lazarus and the rich man (Lk 16:19–31):

> But lest we stretch out the sermon to a great length, it is enough to stop our teaching at this point, and to entreat your love not to pursue the wide gate or the easy road, nor always to seek comfort, but bearing in mind the end of each way, to flee the easy way, considering what befell this rich man, and to pursue the narrow gate and the way of tribulation, so that after tribulation here we may be able to reach the place of comfort. Flee, therefore, I beg of you, the spectacles of Satan and . . . harmful sights. . . . For the sake of those who have been enticed away and have walked towards the easy road I have been led to say these things, in order that they may learn to leave that road, and by traveling on the way of tribulation, I mean the way of virtue, that they may be counted worthy of the patriarch's bosom like Lazarus, and in order that all of us together, freed from the fire of hell, may enjoy those ineffable good things which eye has not seen nor ear heard.
>
> May we all attain to these, by the grace and love of our Lord Jesus Christ, with whom to the Father, together with the Holy Spirit, be glory, might, and honor, now and ever and unto ages of ages. Amen.[35]

Appendix A

The Life of Father Botros and His Afterlife Story

Before sharing with you the one story that changed the course of my life, it is first necessary to provide a preface. When I first used to share copies of my translation of Father Botros's afterlife experience with others, I would usually provide this caveat at the top of the page:

> NOTE: This document has not been officially approved by the church. What I know is that ... a friend of my family knew a monk who died and supposedly came back to life. He wrote down his experience from death to the next life. ... Whether this story is true, or whether it is fiction, the story is a compelling account of what it might be like after you die. It is a wonderful story. My mother translated this from a copy of the monk's handwritten account of his experiences after he died. It was in Arabic, and so she translated it and I typed it up and added a few verses here or there.

For nearly ten years I was reluctant to share this document as I did not know how to substantiate its authenticity and legitimacy. I will explain why now I am confident about its authenticity, but as for whether or not this is an actual afterlife experience or simply a meditative allegory, I will leave you to decide. For this, as with anything else, we are told to "test the spirits, whether they are of God" (1 Jn 4:1) and use spiritual discernment (cf. 1 Cor 2:10–16). The chapters of this book were meant to provide you an Orthodox Christian perspective so you may do just that.

As copies of this Egyptian monk's writing made its way to people's hands in Egypt and elsewhere, it was certainly met with polarizing reception. Some, among whom were several clergy members, adored and hailed it as a faultless vision, while others refused to read it simply due to its subject matter, or read it and questioned aspects of the experience. Still others, while understanding why certain aspects were deemed questionable, excused those aspects with some alternative explanation. Many, including some of Father Botros's fellow monks, concluded this must be allegorical, while others (including close friends and family) were convinced otherwise. For me it was touted as an actual account, and I believed it to be so, and it changed my life. As for what I think now, I will refrain from offering my point of view, beyond saying that this story changed my life and brought me back to God. I do not mean here to imply my mind has changed, or that it has not; I simply seek to refrain from influencing your view. Having read what has been provided to you in this book, you have been aided to decide for yourself what you prefer to believe. Nonetheless, with all of these varied views, you may ask then, why share this at all? Simply because, since my journey to explore the afterlife from an Orthodox Christian perspective began with reading this experience, I find it helpful to show you where my curiosity began, so that it may also help you understand where it led me. And also, whether you believe this to be a genuine experience or simply contemplative, it is a moving story.

Appendix A: Father Botros and His Afterlife Story

Allow me now to first introduce Father Botros to you.

The Life of Father Botros

The following biography of Father Botros, as well as his afterlife story, were published in a book, written in Arabic, titled *Biography of Love*.[1] It was written by an anonymous monk in January 2004.

Father Botros was born on December 9, 1950, in Cairo, Egypt. He was given the name Kamel Naguib El Masry at birth. His name was changed to Botros (the Arabic version of Peter) when he became a monk, in accordance with the Orthodox custom of treating monastic consecration as death to the world and a new life devoted entirely to God. This is conveyed in the Coptic Church by a striking ceremony in which the monk lies on the ground with a large curtain covering him as funeral prayers are recited. After his "death," he is given a new name to signify a new, heavenly life.

Kamel El Masry had two sisters, Magy and Samia (the latter of whom graciously gave me express permission to share her brother's story and afterlife experience). He grew up with two close friends in particular, who I had come to find out are closely tied to me. One, Magdy Abdelsayed, is the brother of a close family friend Rafik Abdelsayed, who gave my mother Father Botros's handwritten afterlife account. This Magdy is also the husband of Fr. Botros's sister Samia. The other friend is my aunt's husband, Atef Ghobrial. When I found out that Kamel, Magdy, and Atef were the best of friends, and even attended engineering school together at Ein Shams University in Cairo, I was elated and gained a newfound trust for Father Botros. (I even found a picture of Kamel and Atef while they were in engineering school, which, along with other images, can be found in Appendix B.)

Kamel was raised in a Christian home and taught to abide by the most fundamental of Christian precepts, such as obedience, respect for others, and providing for those in need. His father was much loved in the community, having been actively involved in various social activity clubs, as well as in several charitable organizations, with a particular focus on health care and caring for children.

Kamel and his father had a relationship akin to that of two good friends, although they were ages apart. His father would often entrust him with many important obligations; for example, at the age of 10, Kamel was sent to travel far from home by public transportation to take care of the needs of the family. Such moments in life taught him how to be responsible, and how to foster loving relationships.

Kamel was an intelligent and accomplished student. In Egypt, students who have completed general secondary school (as opposed to technical or vocational secondary school) take a national entrance exam for Egyptian public universities. The universities, and therefore careers, one is allowed to select from are directly related to one's score on this exam. Students with the highest scores are allowed to choose what is regarded (by most people) in Egypt as the best profession—medicine—or any other career they would like. What is commonly deemed as the second most reputable choice is engineering.

Kamel scored in the top percentages of the national entrance exam. Although most people in such a position would opt to pursue a medical degree, he was torn between medicine and engineering. Part of the reason for this was a promise that Kamel and one of his friends made with each other, that they would both go to medical school together. To help resolve the conflict, Kamel and his father

Appendix A: Father Botros and His Afterlife Story

decided to visit the saintly patriarch of Alexandria at that time, the miracle-working Pope Cyril VI.

As they approached to receive a blessing from His Holiness, Pope Cyril VI said to Kamel, "Welcome, engineer!" Kamel and his father were taken aback, as they had yet to mention their reason for meeting with His Holiness. Kamel's father informed him why they were there, and the pope kindly responded, "I have already greeted you, 'Engineer!' What else do you want? Now work hard so we can send you to work on our behalf." This last statement seemed to be a prophetic allusion to the fact that Kamel would later become a monk and work tirelessly for his Coptic Church and monastery, putting his engineering skills to good use.

So engineering it was. After graduating from Ein Shams University in 1973 at the top of his class, he worked as an associate professor at that same university. Students loved to attend his class, particularly because of his genuine approach to teaching. Commonly teachers and professors in Egypt earn very little, but help make up for that by providing private tutoring lessons for a sum of money. Kamel's students, however, were taught so well that they usually did not need extra tutoring; however, for those who nonetheless sought additional help, Kamel provided tutoring lessons free of charge, much to the chagrin of his peers. In spite of their insistence that he charge at least a nominal fee, he would tell them, "God is the one who gave me the knowledge in my mind, and He is capable also of taking it away. He did not give it to me so that I can make a profit out of it, but rather to convey it to others."

He used to spend much of his relatively high salary on serving the needy, to the extent that he would often run out of money and go to his mother to ask for more. Since in Egypt salaries are generally paid on the first of the month, his mother would often find him coming on the second or third day asking for money. Knowing that Kamel was not one to waste his money, she always complied with his requests without questioning him for even a moment, completely trusting his intentions.

His mother eventually learned the reason behind this after Kamel became a monk. One day a man came to his family's house and asked about an engineer he knew by the name of Kamel, not knowing he had already left and joined a monastery. The family discovered that this man was very sick and needed money to support himself and his family, which Kamel had provided; whenever Kamel's own resources were not enough, he turned to his mother. In that way, by keeping his good deeds secret, he chose the route of humility, following Christ's command, "When you do a charitable deed, do not let your left hand know what your right hand is doing, that your charitable deed may be in secret; and your Father who sees in secret will Himself reward you openly" (Mt 6:3–4).

Kamel was a very spiritual man, understanding the significance of one's spirit and the need to maintain an eternal perspective on life and death. One of his sisters recalls how he exhibited this on two occasions in particular: once while their father was ill, and another time just before their father died.

Kamel's sister used to sit by her father's sickbed; whenever he uttered anything, it was mostly incomprehensible due to the paralysis he suffered from a blood clot, followed by complications of a cerebral hemorrhage. Because of his condition, he was unable to lift himself up out of bed. When he wanted to go to the restroom, he would mumble to his daughter for Kamel or his wife to assist him, and she would go retrieve one of them. Once, as she waited outside the room after Kamel had entered, unexpectedly she overheard her father speak with a very clear, articulate voice, as if he was not sick at all, saying: "Kamel, I am going to Christ." Afterward he fell into a complete coma, and later passed away. It appears that God may have been responding to Kamel's constant supplication that He assures him about the eternal wellbeing of his father.

Kamel's sister also recalls the manner her brother handled the moments surrounding their father's death. In Egypt, usually death is accompanied with much visual spectacle with women wearing all black, wailing and groaning in obvious displays of anguish, sometimes slapping their faces with both hands simultaneously as everyone who gathers around to offer condolences watches and joins in empathy with those in grief. Christians, however, confident in "a living hope through the resurrection of Jesus Christ from the dead," and that we will receive "an inheritance incorruptible and undefiled and that does not fade away, reserved in heaven" for those "who are kept by the power of God through faith for salvation ready to be revealed in the last time" (1 Pet 1:3–5), should not engage in such spectacle but instead express the belief that death is merely a departure from this world to the next. Thus, while his father was on his deathbed, Kamel simply knelt down next to his bed and repeatedly prayed, "God, receive his soul in peace." Although tears welled up in Kamel's eyes, he never let a single tear fall to his cheek, in spite of the intense love and friendship they shared. When his father finally passed away, Kamel laid some flowers around him, placed a cross on his chest, and left the room, saying, "God's will was fulfilled." He refused to accept that anyone should cry or otherwise be too expressive in their sadness. He asked everyone who went in to see his father to simply pray and then exit peacefully.

Not too long after the death of his father, Kamel began to think about his own figurative death to this world and to contemplate a life of monasticism. He implored St. Macarius the Great to pray to God on his behalf for guidance in making his decision. During the summers, when his university job did not demand so much of his time, he visited the Monastery of St. Macarius frequently.

While there on one occasion during a liturgical service, feeling deeply conflicted about whether to become a monk or not, he yearned to hear God's voice giving him an answer. At this point a deacon came forward to read the psalm during the morning offering of incense: "Listen, O daughter, consider and incline your ear; forget your own people also, and your father's house; so the King will greatly desire your beauty; because He is your Lord, worship Him" (Ps 45:10–11). Immediately Kamel felt as if the voice of God was ringing in his heart, and when he tried to flee from this feeling, it would not leave him.

However, doubt just as suddenly flooded in, especially because this psalm is generally understood as being an invitation for all mankind. So he prayed that God would give him another sign, hoping to extinguish his renewed doubt. Then, in an extremely irregular turn of events, the deacon made some sort of mistake and was compelled to read the same psalm again. This finally caused Kamel to feel that a decision had been made, and so Pope Cyril VI's prophetic exhortation ("Now work hard so we can send you to work on our behalf") was about to come to fruition. Now Kamel could heartily join Jeremiah the prophet and say, "'The Lord is my portion,' says my soul, 'Therefore I hope in Him!'" (Lam 3:24).

Once he returned home, his first step towards his commitment to the life of monasticism was to write out his resignation from his teaching position at Ein Shams University. He kept the letter in his drawer for three months as he waited to determine the right time to leave the world and enter the monastery.

During the interim, the devil tried his best to keep him from becoming a monk. Satan's attempts took various forms and included an assortment of doubts. At times Kamel would feel tempted to stay in the world and enjoy making money and accumulating material possessions; other times he would recall that going to the monastery meant giving up the recognition he received for his scholastic achievements and intellectual prestige; he was under constant pressure to get married; and he still had a nagging concern for the welfare of his mother and two sisters, who would be left without a man in the house. (In Egypt, the cultural norm is for males to ensure that every female in their family is taken care of; thus, since his father died, he was the next male in charge, obligated in a cultural sense to ensure the three women left in his family would be provided for.)

What follows are a few of the hindrances that seemed to be traps set by the devil to undermine his resolve to enter the monastic life. For example, long before he decided on monasticism, Kamel and his friends had applied for the Canadian visa lottery program to eventually immigrate to Canada. At that time immigration to Canada was quite difficult. He finally received approval after he had decided to become a monk, and was encouraged by his family to take the opportunity. What might otherwise have been considered a blessing now was too coincidental not to be regarded as likely the work of the devil. However, this strengthened his resolve. Kamel thought to himself, if his family felt they could handle his absence while he would be away in Canada, then why would they not be able to also manage his absence if he left for the monastery?

Another temptation came by way of a lucrative opportunity

to make thousands of Egyptian pounds every month (when on average, in the early 1970s during which time this occurred, an Egyptian might make only about one to two thousand pounds in the entire year). His father's friend introduced him to the owner of a factory who wanted Kamel to build a large machine that would handle the production of different sorts of fabric. This machine was normally only found in very large companies, or the government, and was quite expensive. The owner, though, wanted Kamel to take a look at one of those large machines, and then to oversee the engineering and production of a similar, less expensive machine to be used locally. Kamel studied the matter, created a design for the machine, supervised its construction for about six months, and it was finally built and performed successfully, all for a fraction of the cost of buying it outright. Other companies who heard of Kamel's success sought a machine like this for themselves, and so the factory owner thought of venturing into the business of manufacturing and selling these machines. He planned on hiring Kamel's father's friend, and setting Kamel in the role of leading the entire effort. In spite of all of this financial opportunity, Kamel eventually apologized and told the factory owner that he could not go forward with the project, which was a response in line with the remarks of St. Paul to the Philippians regarding the insignificance of material possessions: "Yet indeed I also count all things loss for the excellence of the knowledge of Christ Jesus my Lord, for whom I have suffered the loss of all things, and count them as rubbish, that I may gain Christ" (Phil 3:8).

Another temptation was the subject of marriage, which suddenly became a matter of central importance in his household and a considerable preoccupation of his family. There was one girl in particular they thought would be a great match for Kamel. Her father was extremely wealthy. The girl and her family were usually out of the country; while she studied in London, her family lived elsewhere in Africa. They would come to Egypt maybe once every five to seven years, and when they visited they would usually stay at only the nicest hotels or resorts, where their friends would come to greet them.

Kamel was continually confronted with the idea of marrying this family's daughter, and just as often he refused. One day, as his family yet again tried to persuade him to consider this girl for marriage, he told them what he would require, "Let God send her this instant with her family to visit us. That is my final decision." Kamel's family, of course, thought this was an unfair ultimatum. Then, within moments of his exclamation, they heard a knock at the door. He answered the door and saw the girl and her mother standing there.

He stood there mute from his shock and dismay, and then he suddenly fled to his room, forgetting even to greet them. He remained there with his door closed, crying and praying to God to be saved from this situation. All the while his family was overjoyed, considering it a sign from God that he was meant to be married to the girl. Kamel's heart and mind struggled with what seemed to be the will of God having been revealed, but something deep within him remained resistant, not wanting to believe it or accept it.

He began to ruminate on these conflicting thoughts. Could it be that the devil somehow brought it into the mind of the mother from Africa and the girl from Europe to come to Egypt, while at the same moment causing his family to bring up the issue of him marrying this girl, and then causing him to say what he said? He just sat there pondering on all this, and eventually, after the girl and her mother left, he announced to his family that he had reached a final decision on the matter: he explained that he did not want to marry, and that this topic was no longer acceptable as a subject for discussion, argument, or any reasoning. From that moment, the family never brought it up again.

Later, when he eventually became a monk, the girl and her parents went to visit the monastery and congratulate him. The girl's father told Father Botros that he was always discontented with the notion of his little girl marrying someone he was not already familiar with, and so he felt safe giving his daughter away to him. However, he told Father Botros he was happier now that he had become a monk and prayed that God would bless him in his new life. About one month after this visit, the girl's father departed from this world.

After arranging all his affairs, Kamel finally submitted his resignation. On April 23, 1975, he left for St. Macarius's monastery. On his way there, as is not uncommon in Egypt, he saw several fatal car accidents, along with several gruesome scenes of accident victims lying dismembered on the ground. The sight of one dead man intensely impacted him, confirming his resolve to leave the world. Kamel thought to himself and offered a short prayer: "This person left the world, dying against his will, but I want to come to You and die by my own will."

While at the monastery as a brother (the title given to those who are awaiting approval to become monks), he was visited by his mother and youngest sister who were extremely upset by Kamel's sudden disappearance, as he never told them he was leaving. They implored his spiritual father to allow Kamel to stay with them for a while, at least until his sister's engagement. His spiritual father approached Kamel to inform him of what had transpired: "If it was for me, I would have taken you by your hands and feet and put you in a car to take you back home, but I do not want to pressure you. Your mom and sister talked to me and I am convinced that God accepted your sacrifice, but you need to go to them for the sake of love. If a family came to the monastery in need of someone to take care of them, do you not think we would send one of the monks to do so? Consider yourself a monk being sent to take care of the family because they do not have anyone."

In response, Kamel told him, "I know that monasticism is obedience; however, I ask that you please keep me from returning to the world, and I am confident that Jesus Christ will provide for their life's needs, and that He will not slumber nor sleep."[2] His spiritual father smiled and was convinced that he remains, but he asked that Kamel at least sit with his mother and attempt to comfort her. Kamel complied and spoke to her with words filled with grace, explaining that God Himself is more capable than any human to take care of her and the family. His mother eventually accepted the circumstances and departed peacefully from the monastery.

On August 25, 1975, on the day of the commemoration of St. Macarius the Great's departure to heaven, Kamel Naguib El Masry was finally admitted as a monk and given the name Botros El Macarii.[3]

As a monk, Father Botros was extremely pious and spiritual. He lived a life exhibiting an abundance of Christian virtues. Inside his cell, he slept on a hard, rough sleeping mat (made of plant leaves woven together and dried) rather than on a bed. He was known for his deep contemplations about God, which were published in the book written about him by the anonymous monk. One such contemplation was as follows:

I became estranged from my original country [heaven] and found myself here [in this world] as a stranger; I was estranged from this world and found myself in the monastery as a stranger; I was estranged from the monastery and found myself a stranger in my cell; then I was estranged from my cell and found myself peering into my heart, where I found You, O Christ, and the more time I spent there, the more I loved You.

Despite his intelligence and skillset, Father Botros spent 16 years in the monastery performing simple tasks serving other monks' immediate needs, with great humility. He served as their driver, taking them from location to location, refusing that anyone hire a driver. Over those long years he was assigned to buy things for the monastery, which he would unload without burdening other monks, expending much effort in hard labor. Father Botros worked diligently and patiently from early morning to late hours without grumbling or complaining. On various occasions Father Botros was also able to put his engineering skills to good use, as Pope Cyril VI prophesied about him, serving as the monastery's mechanic, repairing vehicles and various machines; for this reason his clothes were often stained with oil and gas.

Father Botros's errands for the monastery involved both domestic as well as international trips to retrieve things they needed. Once he was driving through Giza, Egypt, and a worker was walking across a busy street transporting pottery drinking vessels on a dolly. Father Botros noticed a wheel had broken off, and all of the pottery fell onto the street and shattered. The man stood there sobbing profusely because the items he was transporting did not belong to him; they were loaned to him by a factory owner to sell, and the man would receive a small profit for his efforts in return. In the middle of all this traffic, Father Botros reversed, exited his car, and came to the aid of the man by not only paying for all the pottery, but also giving him an equal sum of money to pay for another set of pottery. Father Botros then retrieved some tools from his vehicle and sat on the nearby curb to fix the wheel on the man's dolly as small crowds gathered around to watch. All the while the worker kept uttering phrases of tremendous gratitude.

On another occasion, his love was truly put to the test. As he was out driving on some errands for the monastery in the busy streets of Cairo, his car barely bumped a vehicle parked in front of a store. The owner stormed out of the store and became unreasonably irate, to the point of beating Father Botros with all his might, with both of his hands and remarkable violence, while cursing at him with the foulest language, until he became exhausted from exacting his excessive revenge upon the monk. This was being done as a crowd gathered to watch, and the entire time Father Botros remained quiet, without defending himself with one word, reminiscent of Christ: "As a sheep to the slaughter; and as a lamb before its shearer is silent, so He opened not His mouth" (Acts 8:32, quoting from Is 53:7).

Eventually, after the man had rested from his fury for a moment, Father Botros offered to fix his car right away and bear all costs. So the owner hopped into his car and drove with Father Botros to a body shop, and of course continued to complain and grumble the entire way there. When the owner of the body shop saw the insignificance of the damage to the car, he himself began to defend Father Botros, cursing the car owner and criticizing him for making so much fuss over such a minuscule collision.

Eventually the car owner returned to his senses and was

extremely embarrassed for what he had done, sincerely apologizing for his deplorable behavior. Father Botros responded in humility and told him, "Nothing happened, we are brothers." The monk kissed the man on the cheeks (as is the common manner of greeting in Egypt and elsewhere) and told him he would always be welcome in the monastery. From that day on, this man sent to the monastery all the electrical materials it needed, for free. In this way, Father Botros fulfilled the commandment of Christ: "But I tell you not to resist an evil person. But whoever slaps you on your right cheek, turn the other to him also" (Mt 5:39).

The devil never left Father Botros alone. Once, when he went to Spain, there was a prostitute that many youths were trying to beckon for their own interests. As he walked past, the woman tried speaking to Father Botros to get his attention. He did not speak Spanish, so he just kept on walking. Then one of the youths spoke to him in French, which he spoke fluently. He informed the monk that this woman was sexually attracted to him and sought his company. Immediately Father Botros marked himself with the sign of the cross and fled from there, reminiscent of Joseph who fled from Potiphar's wife: "'How then can I do this great wickedness, and sin against God?' . . . and so it was . . . he fled outside" (Gen 39:9, 13).

On another occasion the devil got involved in Father Botros's life, this time speaking in his presence by means of a demon-possessed girl. While he was at the monastery seeking a way to get to Cairo (because his car was not working at the time) to carry out some errands, there was a very devout family visiting that offered to give him a ride. On the way there he sat by the family's maid, a young girl, who suddenly exclaimed, "Get this monk away from me, get him away!" Father Botros asked the family the reason for her fear and screams, and they said that she was possessed by an evil spirit. Then the girl—or more accurately, the evil spirit possessing her—responded, "In his pocket there is a piece of wood that I am afraid of." When asked what she was referring to, Father Botros explained that he always carries a wooden cross with him everywhere he goes. Then the evil spirit spoke again: "I cannot stand the name you are always repeating, because it nearly burns me." The family understood that Father Botros and monks in general repeatedly recite the Jesus Prayer, and that the nature of God is a "consuming fire" (Heb 12:29) that the devils fear.

Eventually, after he had spent many years in spiritual strife against the wiles of the devil, Father Botros's life drew to a close. About six years before he died, the last monastery he visited outside of his own was the monastery of St. Anthony the Great, and then the monastery of St. Anthony's contemporary, St. Paul the First Hermit. It was as if he was paying his respects and saying goodbye to the founder of monasticism and his hermitic counterpart before he was to depart from this world.

Not too long before his own death, he was informed of his mother's passing. He initially refused to return to the city to console his sisters, recalling Christ's words when He said, "No one, having put his hand to the plow, and looking back, is fit for the kingdom of God" (Lk 9:62). However, his sisters kept their mother's body in the morgue two and a half days until he changed his mind and finally decided to join them.

This takes us now to the story of Father Botros's own death. When he felt like he was about to die and the sun of his life was setting, he began saying his goodbyes to his fellow monks with deep passion accompanied with intense tears, approaching each of the monks and prostrating himself before every one of them, as if he were about to leave for some distant place and never return. In reality, he would depart in three days: March 22, 1995.

On Sunday, March 19, 1995, he was in his cell. He remained there mostly immobilized because of a recent surgery on the bottom of his foot. A monk came by to visit him and see if he needed anything. On this day in particular Father Botros seemed happier than usual, singing hymns and songs about Paradise and about meeting Christ, to the point that when the monk tried to speak with him, Father Botros seemed to pay no heed to what he was saying. After a while the monk said he would be leaving. Then, just before he left, Father Botros brought himself to his feet with the help of his crutches, gave the monk an extremely affectionate hug accompanied with cheek kisses, and told him, "I am going to miss you very much."

The monk told him, "But I am right next to you, and if you ever need anything, just call for me and I will come to your aid right away." Father Botros then sat at his desk and began crying the deepest tears, so much that they were falling onto some paper on the desk in front of him. Although he did not say it, the visiting monk felt this was the last time he would greet Father Botros—that this was truly a farewell—but he tried to remove this thought from his mind.

On Monday, March 20, 1995, another monk came and sat with Father Botros, talking to him about Paradise and the glory of heaven. Father Botros told the monk that he was going to be leaving the world shortly, indicating his knowledge of his impending death.

On Tuesday, March 21, 1995, another monk that was very dear to Father Botros went to visit him. Again, as he had done previously, Father Botros greeted the monk with the most earnest affection and then told him, "I am going to miss you very much," accompanying his remarks with deep sobbing.

Another monk came by that same day and told him, "Try walking on your foot."

Father Botros responded ominously, "I will not walk after this day."

Later, after midnight Tuesday and into the early hours of Wednesday morning, a young boy, a carpenter's apprentice, saw a vision in which his boss made a large coffin to house a big-bodied monk who was placed into the coffin wearing white clothes. The monk's face was quite radiant with a heavenly light, and around his body was a white dove flapping its wings. When the young boy told his boss about this dream, he was rebuked and told to remain quiet. However, from that moment the boss began to worry about Father Botros, having previously heard that he was sick. He asked around about the monk's well-being, and everyone said he was fine. However, on the same day—Wednesday night—the vision came true. All of the previous three days had served as signs for Father Botros's impending departure.

In the afternoon of Wednesday, March 22, 1995, a few hours before Father Botros's departure, a blessed monk who was secluded in his cell during the Great Lent, heard a clear voice telling him three times: "Father Botros will depart today." He was very perplexed. Later he would come to find out that this was true.

Father Botros felt a severe pain in his chest accompanied by great shortness of breath. It appeared he was having a heart attack. Physicians used all their available resources to help him, but God's will prevailed over their skills. As he was dying (at around 7:00 pm), the last words he uttered were, "O Jesus, O Jesus, O Jesus."

When the other monks arrived, they found a brand new *tonya* (a white long-sleeved, floor-length tunic used during liturgical services, worn over the clothes to signify purity) that seemed tailored to fit his body perfectly. Until the time of writing the book published about his life (January 2004—nearly ten years after Father Botros's death), and as far as I am aware until now, they still have never found out how that *tonya* entered his cell.

They dressed him in the *tonya* they had found and moved his body to the church at 10:00 pm. They rang the church bells at that unusual time to gather the monks together, at which time everyone was informed of his departure. They prayed the Midnight Praises, then the funeral prayers, and then followed that late-night vigil with the Divine Liturgy, which ended at 4:30 Thursday morning.

A few interesting events came about after his departure. About a month later, on April 23, 1995, when the monks were chanting hymns in procession around the inside of the church, as is the rite of the Orthodox on the eve of the Feast of the Resurrection, a person who was well known and well loved by the monks (and highly trusted) said that he saw with his own eyes Father Botros wearing white clothes and holding a Bible in his hand, walking in front of the entire procession, singing along with them the well-known Orthodox hymn of the resurrection, "Christ is risen."

Also, on the anniversary of his departure, his sisters would usually go and visit the monastery. On one occasion his sister and the wife of one of his close friends saw the abbot, Father Matthew the Poor, and he told them to put the flowers they brought in front of the altar, and the picture they had of Father Botros over the place where the relics of St. John the Baptist's body are laid at the monastery.[4] During the entire liturgy, both of them saw a luminous vision of a *corban* (round loaf of bread offered for the Eucharist) appearing over his head in the picture which disappeared the moment the prayers concluded.

There is another interesting story in which a woman appears to have received the blessing of the prayers of the departed Father Botros. This woman used to serve his sisters around the house occasionally, and she was very fond of Father Botros, who used to help her family monetarily. She eventually needed to have surgery to remove her uterus, which was going to cost about 500 Egyptian pounds. After praying and asking the departed Father Botros to pray for her, she talked to his sister, who then spoke with many of the monk's friends to see if they could amass the money she needed. One friend actually provided the entire sum for the surgery straightaway.

The night before her surgery, she was praying and asking Father Botros for assistance when suddenly the room was filled with incense accompanied by a strong aroma. The same night, her daughter was also praying fervently and crying when, unexpectedly, she saw a vision of St. Mary, St. Bishoy, and also (as she described him) a very large monk. The girl prayed even more vehemently, asking St. Mary to cure her mother, and then our Lady, the Virgin, replied, "The three of us went to see her tonight, and we performed the surgery; there is nothing that will trouble her again. And the incense that your mother smelled tonight was a sign indicating this."

In the morning, the mother nonetheless went to have surgery done. Before surgery, the doctor performed an ultrasound and saw that her uterus lacked all indications of any tumor whatsoever. He described her uterus as looking as new as that of an 18-year-old girl, so there was nothing for him to perform surgery on. Upon hearing this wonderful news, she then asked the doctor to return the money she paid him, since there was no longer a need for surgery.

Surprisingly, he refused, although she urged him, informing him that this money had been given to her as alms. Nonetheless, he continued to stubbornly reject her request. Sadly, afterward, the doctor fell into a diabetic coma, was taken to intensive care, and a short time later died.

Father Botros's Afterlife Story

My entire life changed as this story was read to me and I typed the following translation:[5]

Someone was knocking on my door, so I answered. It was the angel of death who had come to claim my spirit, for my hour had come. I asked him[6] to wait a little bit so I could write these words. I requested to take a pen and some paper with me, so he permitted me, but on one condition: that I not write any secrets or words that are not lawful for a man to utter (2 Cor 12:4). So I thanked him because he accepted the intercession of the saints to give me this opportunity.

The truth is, the hour of death is terrifying, even though I have been waiting for it, watching and expecting it for a long time. But the feeling of dread is proportional to one's neglect in preparation for it. In other words, whoever puts it in front of his eyes (1 Cor 1:7) and prepares for it, striving every day, carrying his cross and continually mortifying[7] himself, the moment of departure becomes an occasion of great and boundless joy and happiness, as we have seen some saints whose faces are radiant or who are surrounded by angels as they behold the heavens opened, ready to receive them

(Acts 7:56).

As for those who neglect that moment, surprised by its arrival (Lk 17:20), [they are filled with a sense of] terrified dismay and horrified agitation. As for me, the joy of my imminent departure (2 Cor 5:2, 4) has been mixed with the dread of settling my account and repaying my debts [i.e., giving an account for what one has done with the life God entrusted them with][8] (Lk 19:15). The self, at that moment, fights between two overwhelming [and opposing] forces: [on the one hand] a great debt of sins, transgressions, and bad friends;[9] and [on the other hand] virtues, good deeds, and intercessions of saints and angels. The first drags you down into a deep pit by a rope of despair, while the second propels you up towards a better and more splendid life through the power of hope. These [two] forces continue to contend [with each other] until the situation is resolved, as I observed, which I am about to narrate.

I looked around me in my cell and out of my window and I could not find anything in the entire world that was worth taking along with me (Eccl 1:14; 2:11). And as I stared within the depth of my soul I could not find anything that could stand on its own feet: neither respect nor indignity, neither position nor stature, neither praise nor insults, neither money nor possessions (1 Pet 1:24). I was not allowed to take anything with me, whether beautiful or repulsive, except an old robe: its age was [exactly] my age.[10] No human eye can see it, but it is only seen in the spirit. It was [once] white but it became dirty, with many stains ranging from large to small. So I wore it to cover my nakedness and headed to the door in order to get out, thinking that was the way. And I am between the spirit and the body.

Then the angel of death stopped me and explained to me that the departure of the spirit is not through any earthly or material means, but rather it is a departure from a visible world to another that is invisible; from a limited world to another that is limitless; from narrowness to vastness. And then instantly I felt my spirit being squeezed as if trying to escape out of the infinitesimally narrow neck of a bottle into an unlimited expanse. And the spirit had departed to another world not bound by time and space, so that with one glance I saw the whole universe as a drop in the ocean of the Omnipotent or like a seed in the palm of the great Creator. The body remained lying on the ground in the dust from where it came (Gen 3:19). And I saw that at the same moment in which my spirit departed there was another spirit on its way, departing from somewhere else on that droplet that people call earth. This spirit was my companion in death,[11] whom I met at the ensuing moment of crossing over.

Curiosity prompted me to survey the faces, opinions, and feelings of my past acquaintances, friends and enemies, from relatives to close companions to my brethren in the Lord [i.e., fellow monks], regarding my departure.

I found the first [friend] sad and weeping, clearly evincing signs of spiritual shortsightedness. That poor one was groaning from the anguish of separation. So I smiled [at him] with compassion to reassure him, but he did not notice me. I had forgotten he could no longer see me. And I saw others gathered around him: some were weeping and sorrowful; some of them were simple at heart, truly empathizing with his pain, so that their words were like fresh dew on his grieving heart because they were being guided by the Holy Spirit to reach their proper place; and others were present [only] out of courtesy, but their hearts were far removed from participating in his grief so that their words returned back to them without benefit. That was the first group of people.

APPENDIX A: FATHER BOTROS AND HIS AFTERLIFE STORY

The second [person] was also crying, but the nature of his crying was different. He rushed to his cell. Around his head was a halo of bright light. I recognized he was enlightened [i.e., he came to the realization of his need to repent]. He was weeping and beating his chest while prostrating[12] before God. It appears what happened to me was compelling and moving him to ready himself through repentance.

A third [person] was in a state of extraordinary joy. He had always loved me and loved the brethren. He foresaw the advantages of eternal life, and was thus rejoicing with the heavens and [celebrating] with his beloved [friend] the end of his [earthly] struggle.

A fourth [person] was rejoicing, but his heart revealed depression and darkness because he thought of me as [being] a competitor for a position, and [hence he] was envious of God's graces [upon me].

The fifth and last one, afflicted with a bland spirit, was indifferent about what had happened, remaining content with [focusing on his own] concerns, responsibilities, and endless ambitions.

Here the angel of death stopped me saying to me that I had taken what no one else had [taken] and I had seen what had passed,[13] and that now I have to traverse the difficult crossing [over], and I have to pass through the most horrid experience for a human being to undergo.

I looked around me and beheld a group of devils standing, staring at me. They were hideous and were headed by a mighty devil whose heart was pierced by an arrow. His beard was [partially] plucked. He was standing there anxious and uneasy, awaiting the moment of crossing over and its outcome.

Opposite them I saw another group of luminous angels. They were very simple creatures, but fiery. They do not speak except through praises and hymns. Their voices were gentle, imparting peace to the heart. They were headed by an angel with whom I felt a strong bond. That group of angels outnumbered the group of the devils (2 Kg 6:16), and they were nearer to me. They were showing signs of assured, calm anticipation.

As for the group of devils, they were whispering to one another while pointing at the robe I was wearing. I looked closely at them and found they were carrying many different snares and traps. Some of their faces looked familiar to me, while others were companions along my [life's] path for [various] periods of time, [some] short and [some] long. Unfortunately, some of them left their mark on me so that I recognized them without a guide: that one was [a devil charged with tempting me to fall into the sin of] pride, that one lying, that one was theft, that one sexual immorality, and that one gossiping. So I recognized most of them.

I looked at what they were pointing at and found that each of the stains on my robe bore an image of one of them, without having realized it before; and I was overcome by fear. I drew closer to the head of the angels and asked him about the head of the devils. He explained to me that he had been trying to make me fall [into sin] with the help of the [other] devils and their snares. I sensed intense hatred on his [i.e., the head of the devils'] part; however, this was not a new feeling, but [rather] I instantly realized that it had been there since the day of my second birth ([since the time of the] rite of renouncing Satan during [the] baptism [ceremony, when during the mystery of baptism the priest has the candidate for baptism, or in the case of a child, the child's mother say, "I renounce you, Satan"]).

Then I asked the head of the angels about the arrow penetrating the [head] devil's heart and the reason why his beard was plucked; so he showed me a similar arrow, and I understood it was [as a result of] the monastic schema[14] ([from the] rite of ordaining [i.e., appointing][15] monks). Then I returned years back and saw him [i.e., the head-devil], the day I wore the schema, standing [there] grinding his teeth and plucking his beard, lamenting over what he had lost, intimidating and threatening. Truth is, I pitied him and wished he could repent, and sought an excuse for the intensity of his anger, considering it [due to] his evil outlook.

Then I returned again to the fearful situation [at hand], and I once more asked my guardian angel[16] regarding those devils whom I could not recognize. So my friend the angel explained to me that those were the ones whose voices I did not listen to and shut my ears based on the counsel of God's Holy Spirit and His angels, or I did listen to them and then offered sincere repentance so that their image and mention were erased off of my robe and from my memory by the grace of our Lord.

Then I looked at the angels, seeking peace during this dire situation, and I recognized in them love, meekness, simplicity, peace, and humility; and each of them carried [in one hand] a bouquet of various good deeds and virtues, which the Holy Spirit had been trying to entice me to acquire; and in the other hand [they were holding] a sharp sword (Eph 6:17), which has the authority to annihilate the armies of the devils and the angels of darkness and evil. As for that sword, it was every word that proceeds from the mouth of God [cf. Mt 4:4; Deut 8:3].

And I beheld the angel of death advancing, blowing a trumpet; then I saw in front of me towards the east a door leading to an area— if I may express it this way—that was very bright, beyond which

I could not see, but I felt a strong eagerness to enter it. Towards the west was another area that was [a] deep [pit], bottomless and extremely dark, inflicting terror in my heart. So I hastened to the eastern door yearning to enter it and escape, but as I approached it, there appeared two angels in soldier's attire preventing me from entering; and [they] pointed at the spots that stained my robe and said, "Those who practice such things will not inherit the kingdom of God" (Gal 5:21), and that I have a debt which I have not yet repaid,[17] so that the evil group [of demons] has the right [to take me] whereby I must go [with them] to the door in the west.[18] And indeed I began to feel a strong force pulling me towards the west. So I screamed in panic and asked the head of the angels for help. He explained that these stains [on my robe] are naturally attracted to the bottomless pit and that there is no way [for me] to erase them since the time of repentance had already passed.

To my surprise, I found that my companion, to whom the angel of death had also come, was undergoing the same ordeal. And although his robe had fewer stains in comparison to my robe, he was also being pulled towards the bottomless pit. So I screamed in my last moments [right] before my falling into the pit of darkness, "Where is the Christ of salvation!" And I was greatly remorseful for everything I had done, for staining my robe and the horrors that I had been dragged into [as a result]. There was no one who dared, not even from among the angels, to come to my rescue; and signs of victory loomed on the faces of the group of devils. As for my companion and I, we were weeping and wailing.

Then suddenly, when we were on the verge of [falling into] the bottomless pit, there appeared to us a great light, radiant and dazzling, and a person in a flame of fire, [so] glorious and beautiful in appearance, [and too] wonderful to describe, [that] I cannot express the immensity of His loveliness (2 Thess 1:7). He was surrounded by myriads of angels of a fiery nature, and saints; and I knew Him at once without being informed [of who He was]. So I fell on my face and prostrated before Him; then I lifted up my eyes towards Him, requesting His help yet without uttering a single word, for I knew Him, and knew His love without having seen Him [before] (1 Pet 1:8), and I experienced[19] Him plentifully and tried His help and His merciful hand. His image was in my heart. To my astonishment, I found that I resembled Him and bore His features, and I was in His image (Gal 6:17), with the exception of my stained robe. As for this image, I took it the day I was born of Him, and with regard to the stained robe, [I had acquired it] over [the course of] my life, the days I sinned with the hardness of my heart.

Oh, He is the most beautiful of all human beings! Yes, this is He who is the desire of my heart and all my hopes (Song 5:16). This is the moment that I have lived my [entire] life waiting for, but I was looking for it with eyes of hope. This is He in whom I believed and trusted. This is He who did not leave me for a [single] moment, so I handed over my entire life to Him. This is my beloved whom I have always called upon (Rev 22:20) and to whom I sang [praises]. This is He who is the hope of nations and the salvation of all peoples. I was confident in Him, and in His presence, and in His rescuing me because whoever believes on Him will not be put to shame (Rom 9:33; 10:11).

As soon as He extended His hand, wrapping [it] around me (Song 8:3), I saw in His palm the remnant of a deep wound—this is the fountain of salvation—and to my amazement, His wound was still bleeding. Then a drop from that wound fell—yes a drop of divine blood—and [just] a single drop was enough to erase all the filth of my sins (Eph 1:7) and the images of iniquity off my robe (1 Cor 15:52). And instantly the pit ceased attracting me towards impending doom. Thanks be to God who gives us victory though our Lord Jesus Christ (1 Cor 15:57).

Then suddenly a tremendous scream resounded and the head of the group of the devils fell down into the bottomless pit along with his entire group [of devils], bound in chains of deepest darkness, and they were cast into hell (2 Pet 2:4). For he [the head-devil] is darkness and is not drawn except to darkness and cannot remain as long as there is light (2 Cor 6:14).

And then I looked around me and found my companion in death with his robe still stained, and continuing to drift towards the pit; so I had pity on him, and I screamed at him, "This is Jesus!" But he did not understand what I meant. I was astounded that he was unable to recognize the source of salvation, nor believe in Him (Heb 3:19); this was because there was not in him the image of the Redeemer and [now, after death] he did not have time for believing in Him or getting to know Him. His saddened voice resonated as he plunged [down into the bottomless pit]; and I was saddened and wished if he had only known what I knew and believed in whom I believed he could have attained what I have obtained (Mk 16:16; Jn 8:24).

Then I looked at the robe I was wearing and it was not appropriate at all [for me to be wearing it] in the presence of God, so I was ashamed (1 Jn 2:28); but the Lord Jesus, my God and my beloved, knew all that I was thinking and quickly clothed me with a bright white robe (1 Cor 15:49; Phil 3:21; Col 3:10). As soon as I put it on, a few of the threads in its fabric began to shine.

Having worn the robe of His righteousness and His true holiness (Eph 4:24), with me still in His bosom, I saw what has been said about Him [which God has prepared for those who love Him], [things which] eye has not seen, nor ear heard, nor have entered into the heart of man (1 Cor 2:9 [also in Is 64:4]). Then the door in the east opened, and I heard the sounds of hymns of victory and salvation and the praises of angels and the voices of saints; I [also] smelled the aroma of pure prayers. And I wanted to write what I was seeing, but I found that human language would be unable to achieve this, and words fall short of expression.

Then I looked at the side of the Beloved and noticed His stab wound [where He had been pierced]; once I looked at it, a new life rushed through me and changed all of my senses, my mind, my perceptions, and it was revealed to me hidden mysteries about humankind and indescribable glories (2 Cor 3:18). Of the things revealed to me, I instantly learned the mystery behind why a few of the threads of the robe the Lord gave me were shining: some of the deeds I had done, guided by [God's] grace, despite their scarcity, matched [God's] divine nature (1 Jn 3:2) which I was clothed in with the robe of the righteousness of Christ, and which reflected the radiance and brightness of Christ upon it (2 Pet 1:4). Then I saw around me crowds of saints (Col 1:12; 1 Thess 3:13), and right away I knew them one by one, even though they [all] had one image and one form (Rom 8:29). And I also found that my image was the same as theirs (2 Cor 3:18), and that my form was the same [as well]. Each one of them was wearing a bright robe; [however], the intensity of glow [of their robes] varied from one to another (1 Cor 15:41).

And on the right hand of the Lord Christ (Ps 45:9) I saw a beautiful, gentle woman; her robe was exceedingly bright, as if woven with gold (Ps 45:13), because of the striking resemblance and harmony between her own life and the nature of God, until she rested and ceased dwelling [on earth]; so her robe was brighter than all other humans or even the angels. And I saw her, with motherly tenderness, sharing her robe without it being separated from her, clothing all those who ask for her [help] who had not yet finished their struggle; and thus their image would appear before God in the likeness of the Beloved's image, the image of the robe of the surpassing righteousness of Christ, [the] special [robe belonging] to the mother of the Son of God. In the same manner, all the saints and all those who had completed their struggles, in the midst of their incessant praise, were taking off their robes and putting it on all who requested [help], in [a display of] wondrous and loving fellowship. Whoever wears one of these robes is not overcome by any trap or snare of the evil one, but that does not prevent the repeated, envious attempts of Satan [to tempt them].

And then I saw a group of those who were perfected, distinguished by shining crowns on their heads. Among them I recognized the heroic Saint George, Saint Demiana, and many of whom I had never heard their stories on earth before, but [their deeds] were [nonetheless] written in the heavens. And I knew them as soon as I saw them, as if I had been [spending my entire life] living with them. From them exuded a wonderful and brilliant, ineffable aroma, which is the aroma of the blood they shed in the name of Christ; thus they attained the crown of martyrdom.

And I found another group—I would like to call them the Loving Group—and each one of them was holding a harp (Rev 5:8; 15:2) with which they praised, rejoicing for being in the everlasting presence of their beloved, sitting in His presence and also in Him! (Gal 2:20). And yet there was another group distinguished by the very luminous parts of their illuminated bodies: some had their abdomens brightened because of their asceticism; some had their heads illuminated because they had no place to rest them; some had their legs illuminated because they wandered, needing and distressed, in the wilderness [and] in the deserts while ministering and proclaiming the gospel of the kingdom [of heaven]; and others who were tortured and refused to accept release (Heb 11:35) were rewarded in place of their suffering with great glory and exceeding brightness so that the parts of their bodies that were cut off or tortured were illuminated.

As for me, one of the angels assigned to serve those who will inherit salvation (Heb 1:14) came to me and sat me down in the back of all the rows, because my robe was the least illuminated. But the truth is, I was [still] extremely joyful and content, because I did not consider myself worthy to be present in that place, or to participate with this heavenly chorus in their harmonious praise that is beyond description, or to see what I am seeing or live how I am living.

Then I became alert and I looked around me and I realized that I had not yet finished my struggle, and that I was still in the body; but my yearning and nostalgia for heaven was a fervent flame and I was filled with hope. I was determined to start washing my robe in the blood of the Lamb[20] to prepare myself for the day of meeting and because of my fear of the dreadful crossover.

I hope that the Lord has mercy on us and grants us salvation on the day of judgment. To Him is glory, praise, thanksgiving, and everlasting honor, forever. Amen.

Written by the departed monk Botros El Macarii[21] shortly before his departure.[22]

Appendix B

Photos & Images

A copy of the first page of Father Botros's experience as he wrote it by his own hand, in Arabic.[1]

Kamel (later known as Father Botros) with his sisters Magy and Samia in Egypt, 1959.²

Kamel with his final project for graduation from engineering school, 1973.³

APPENDIX B: PHOTOS & IMAGES

My uncle, Atef Ghobrial, with Kamel, his close friend, taken some time around the 1970s.[4]

Rafik Abdelsayed and his (now) wife Cindy visiting with Father Botros during their trip to Egypt together.[5]

Father Botros and his mother at the St. Macarius Monastery in 1987.[6]

Appendix B: Photos & Images

Father Botros (above).⁷ His final burial place (below).⁸

Photo taken by Wagih Rizk showing the apparition of St. Mary over the church named after her in Zeitoun, a district of Cairo, Egypt.⁹

Appendix B: Photos & Images

The late Mother Erene, Mother Superior of the convent of St. Philopateer Mercurius (Abu Sefein) in Old Cairo, Egypt.[10]

Icon of the early Christian martyr Philopateer Mercurius (also known as Abu Sefein).[11]

Appendix C

Glossary of Orthodox Christian People and Terminology Used in This Book

Abba. Also spelled and pronounced "Anba" among Arabic-speakers, this term today serves most commonly as a title of bishops in the churches of Egypt, Syria, and Ethiopia. It simply means "father." It is thought to derive originally from Aramaic. This word can also be used to designate certain elder monks, as it was most notably applied among third and fourth century monks of the Egyptian desert, particularly the oldest and most venerable.[1]

Abbot. Male head of a monastery, to whom all monks residing there owe unfailing obedience. It is derived from the word Abba, meaning father, and during the early periods of monasticism, where written rules were scarce or not in place, the abbot was very often a particularly charismatic character, inspiring other monks who gathered around him due to the prestige of his actions and holiness; later this role became more clearly defined and institutionalized.[2]

Abbess. Female nun who is the head of a convent, and is in all ways similar to an Abbot except that the Abbess is never a clergyperson. "Mother Superior" has the same meaning. For more, see "Abbot."

Abu Sefein. See "Philopateer Mercurius."

Agpeya. Derived from the Coptic word *tee-agp*, meaning "hour," this refers to the book promoted by the Coptic Church to be used as a guide for prayer by all people (whose Byzantine counterpart, to some degree, is the Horologian). It is arranged in canonical hours (which mark the divisions of the day in terms of periods of fixed prayer at regular intervals), with each hour with its own theme, and each containing mostly selections from the psalms, which are meant to be prayed. There are usually 12 psalms in each hour, the number of which can be traced back to a miracle involving Abba Pachomius of the Egyptian desert when an angel instructed him about the number of psalms to be prayed; another account involves an angel who appeared amid Egyptian monks gathered together in the early years of monasticism and chanted 12 psalms, then vanished, thus settling their dispute about the number of psalms to pray. For this reason the formula of 12 psalms has been given the name, "The Rule of the Angel."[3]

Anthony the Great (c. AD 251–356). This Egyptian Christian is regarded as the founder of monasticism (in the sense of living in the midst of the harsh deserts of Egypt rather than what other hermits were doing, living on the outskirts of cities). At age 20 he adopted an ascetic life, first in a village, then a tomb dug out of a mountainside near the Nile, then in an abandoned ruin in the middle of the desert. He lived a very devout and strictly ascetic manner of life, experienced countless encounters with the devil and evil spirits in a variety of ways, and was exposed to innumerable divine visions and revelations. After denying himself in order to be filled with Christ, he departed on a date he foreknew at the age of 105 years old. His biography was written by the famed St. Athanasius, the 20th archbishop of Alexandria.[4]

Apostle(s). This term, as used in this book, refers specifically to the twelve disciples and the seventy or so[5] others who lived during the time of Christ and were commissioned by God to establish and spread Christianity during its inception (Lk 10:1). This word is derived from the Classical Greek term ἀπόστολος (*apostolos*), meaning one who is sent forth or away, and usually is reserved to refer to those who Christ Himself chose; the Church usually attempts to use this term to distinguish those who are connected with the Church's origin and to a specific circle of witnesses of Christ (cf. 1 Cor. 15:1–11). In contrast, a disciple encompasses anyone who follows Christ and adheres to His teachings. Christ had many disciples, yet He chose some of them to be apostles, including His twelve (Lk 6:13). Apostolic Churches are those that are "built on the foundation of the apostles" whereby the "whole building" is a "dwelling place of God in the Spirit," Christ being the "chief cornerstone" (Eph 2:19–22).[6]

Athanasius the Apostolic, 20th pope of Alexandria (*c.* **AD 295/300–373).** Born in Egypt as a pagan, he eventually was taken under the care of the Coptic patriarch at the time and converted to Christianity. After the patriarch's death, St. Athanasius was chosen as his successor. He is most notable for opposing a heresy promulgated by an Alexandrian priest named Arius. Ensuring that the Church and its adherents for all time would not be shaken by this heresy, St. Athanasius firmly stood his ground and successfully promoted the correct belief about Christ's divinity and equality with the Father at the Council of Nicea. Because of his theological stance, he faced tremendous turbulence throughout his life, including at least four exiles. He was a contemporary of St. Anthony the Great, and many of his writings are still available today, including the *Life of St. Anthony* and also the fundamental Christian book titled *On the Incarnation* which in recent times has been widely proliferated with an introduction written by C. S. Lewis.[7]

Augustine of Hippo (*c*. AD 354–430). Aurelius Augustinus lived nearly all his life in Roman North Africa, serving as bishop of the seaport named Hippo (now Annaba in Algeria) for the last thirty-four years of his life. His writings which have survived to this day exceed in number that of any other surviving writings of any other early Church author and thus has not only influenced his contemporaries but also many others since his death. One of his most well-known and influential books is his autobiographical works that today have been compiled into a book titled *Confessions*, which tells us about his regret over his earlier sinful life and his movement towards Christianity, having been heavily influenced by St. Ambrose (bishop of Milan in the fourth century) and the prayers and support of his mother Monica.[8]

Basil the Great (*c*. AD 330–379). This is one of the most famous of all bishops in all of Christendom. St. Basil, who became the bishop of Caesarea in Cappadocia, along with his close friend Gregory Nazianzen, and his brother Gregory of Nyssa, are collectively known as the Cappadocian Fathers. He was very rich, but decided to be baptized and seek the teachings of various ascetic fathers, including monks in Egypt and Syria. Upon his return to Caesarea, he distributed his property among the poor and withdrew to a lonely district living like a monk in prayer, meditation, and study. In alignment with Pope Athanasius, he stood against Arianism. He left behind many invaluable writings.[9]

Bishop. Originally derived from the Greek word *episcopos*, which means "oversight," this refers to the highest clerical rank in the Church, being endowed with authority to expand the Church by ordaining others (as bishops, priests, and deacons) and to invoke the Holy Spirit to effectuate the mysteries of the Church. A bishop is considered legitimately authorized as such only if he can trace his ordination and authority to an apostle of Christ; this is termed Apostolic Succession.

Bishoy, "the perfect man" (fourth century). This fourth century Coptic saint lived as a monk in the Nitrian Desert. From a young age it was foretold that he would be particularly blessed. An angel appeared to his mother and chose who she considered to be her frailest son, assuring her, "This is whom the Lord has chosen." He lived a very ascetic life and a monastery in his name still exists in the place that an angel directed him to go live a solitary life. This saint is known to have seen the Lord Christ at least two times. On one occasion, he washed the feet of a passerby out of humility, whose appearance changed to reveal that He was in fact the Lord Christ. On another occasion, he carried a frail monk on his back who the rest of the monks ignored as they all rushed to see Christ who was to appear at a certain place and time. As he walked towards that place where Christ was to appear, the monk on St. Bishoy's back felt lighter and lighter until, when St. Bishoy finally arrived, all realized that this frail monk they ignored had actually been the Lord Christ in disguise.[10]

Bishoy El-Antony. After joining the St. Anthony monastery (in the eastern desert of Egypt) in 1978, this monk (who was eventually ordained as a priest as well) became heavily involved with assisting in the management and promulgation of Christian media production, including most recently the Christian Youth Channel (CYC). CYC produced a series titled "Stories" in which Fr. Bishoy relays remarkable experiences he personally witnessed that serve to invigorate and enliven the listener's walk with Christ. Having had the pleasure of meeting him recently, he graciously devoted time to let me interview him about afterlife experiences he was personally aware of, which he has allowed me to include in this book.

Calendar (Coptic). See "Coptic calendar."

Caught up. This term is derived from the biblical account in which St. Paul says "whether in the body . . . or out of the body," he was not exactly sure, but what he knew for certain was that he found himself "caught up to the third heaven . . . into Paradise" (2 Cor 12:2, 4). This phrase refers to those who experience a similar situation, which has not ceased to be a common occurrence for many saintly Christians, even to the present time, whereby someone finds themselves granted by God to experience heavenly or otherwise miraculous spiritual visions. It is sometimes referred to by the term "ecstasy" or simply "divine vision." St. Augustine refers to this state of ecstasy, which involves experiencing things that do not "derive from the senses of the body," describing a "peasant" he knew who experienced such an ecstatic vision.[11]

Chrismation. Also known by the term confirmation, this is one of the mysteries (or sacraments) of the Church, being one of the four regarded as required for salvation (along with baptism, repentance and confession, and the Eucharist), by which the Holy Spirit is invoked to enter into a person at some point after baptism, making that person a new creation (2 Cor 5:17) and a child of God (Gal 4), whereby they become a "temple of the Holy Spirit" (1 Cor 6:19). It is called chrismation, being derived from the Greek word *chrisma*, which means "anointing," because the newly baptized is anointed with holy oil—*myron* (a Greek word referring to fragrant oil)—to effectuate this mystery through the Holy Spirit. This was established in accompaniment or in lieu of the original manner by which the Holy Spirit used to be relayed to the newly baptized—the laying on of hands—at some point very early on in the history of Christianity.[12]

Church Father(s). While this term can be delineated in a number of ways, I use it in this book to refer to the early leaders of Christianity (clergymen, predominantly consisting of bishops, or in rare cases renown theologians) whose manner of life and teachings comport with apostolic tradition and who are trusted in expounding Christian teaching. Often the qualifications considered to merit this designation include: (1) brilliance of mind; (2) orthodoxy of doctrine; (3) holiness of life; and (4) belonging to the Church and not a schismatic.

Clement of Alexandria (*c.* AD 151–215). Regarded as a Church Father, he was a learned Christian teacher at Alexandria, Egypt, and was appointed as dean of the famed catechetical school there. Origen was one of his pupils.[13]

Clement of Rome (first century). Bishop of the church of Rome, he was likely a companion of both St. Peter and St. Paul, and is often associated with being the "Clement" who St. Paul mentions in his letter to the Philippians (4:3). In official lists of the bishops of Rome, he is regarded as the third successor to St. Peter, succeeding archbishops Linus and Anacletus. However, both Tertullian and Jerome regard him as St. Peter's immediate follower, consecrated by him.[14]

Commemoration of Saints. In the Coptic "Midnight Praise," which is a collection of hymns and praises that follow a certain order and rite, therein lies a prayer called the "Commemoration of Saints." It is sung in a particular tune and consists of requests that a commemorative list of saints, who are listed in a certain order, pray to God on our behalf that He forgives us our sins. The names of the saints would typically be incorporated in the hymn as follows: "Pray to the Lord on our behalf, [...], that He may forgive us our sins," with the name(s) of the saint(s) mentioned in place of the brackets. Another prayer by the same name can be found in the Divine Liturgy of the Coptic Church.

Constantine, emperor of Rome (c. AD 272–337). Prior to Emperor Constantine, many Roman citizens, and eventually several of the Roman emperors themselves, were ruthless in their discrimination and hatred of Christians, leading to the death of innumerable martyrs. Then, as is recorded by the historian Eusebius, and as was an established tradition during the emperor's lifetime, a miracle occurred that caused Emperor Constantine to look upon Christianity favorably (and, although hotly debated, it is deemed he "converted" to Christianity due to this event as well).

As he was marching at the head of his army from France to Italy, oppressed with anxiety due to a recent battle, he suddenly beheld a luminous cross in the air, accompanied with words inscribed on it that read, "By this overcome." Pondering on this event during the night, he asserted that the Lord Jesus Christ appeared to him in a vision and directed him to place the symbol of the cross on his military ensign. After overcoming in his military expeditions, he professed Christianity as the true faith and began to undo the wrongs of his predecessors, including issuing a decree allowing Christians to practice their faith. He and his mother Queen Helen utilized their power, wealth, and resources to advance Christianity and honor its treasures and saints. Constantine recognized the legal validity of Sunday as a day of rest, and took measures to address various schisms within the church, including the calling of the Council of Nicea to address one such schism that plagued the Church (that schism being Arianism).[15]

Coptic. In short, it means "Egyptian." It is the term used to denote the language of ancient Egypt, whose written script was changed from hieroglyphics and later replaced with an alphabet mostly borrowed from Greek; this word also refers to those Egyptians who are the truest descendants of the ancient Egyptians—the Coptic Christians.[16] The origin of the word "Coptic" can be traced in history to the Arabs who invaded Egypt; to distinguish themselves from the Egyptians, the Arabs referred to them in their Arabic language as "qibt," which came from the Greek word for Egyptian, Ai-gypt-os, whose etymology further leads you to the Egyptian word Ha-Ka-Ptah (meaning the house of Ptah, one of the earliest gods the Egyptians worshipped; this word referred to the country of Egypt).

Coptic calendar. Egyptians are proud to be among the earliest civilizations (and according to some, the first) to have measured time, dated the years and divided the years into months.[17] The Egyptians set 12 months of 30 days each, and a sixth one called the "small month" of five days (or six, if it is a leap year, which occurs every four years). The names of these months are derived from the names of various ancient Egyptian gods and festivals, often times also related to the usual climate or conditions that month is expected to bring. When Egyptians became Christian, they maintained use of this calendar, and so all of their Christian holidays and the commemoration of various Christian events were established according to it. The Coptic Church still adheres to this ancient calendar, which was re-dated to begin the year that the most infamous persecutor of Egyptian Christians—Emperor Diocletian—took the throne (AD 284 according to the Gregorian calendar). For this reason the Coptic calendar year is abbreviated A.M. (for Anno Martyrum or "Year of the Martyrs").[18]

Coptic Orthodox Christian. In short, this refers to a person who is baptized into the Egyptian Orthodox Church, which was established by St. Mark the evangelist and apostle in Alexandria in the first century.

Coptic New Year. See "Nayrouz."

Cyprian of Carthage (*c.* AD 200–258). He was the bishop of the church in Carthage, North Africa. As this time was one of severe persecution for Christians, he was eventually captured and died as a martyr at the hands of the Romans.[19]

Cyril VI, 116th pope of Alexandria (AD 1902–1971). Transliterated from Arabic and most commonly pronounced "Kyrillos," this is the 116th patriarch of Alexandria, with St. Mark the evangelist being regarded as the first. Born in 1902 in Gharbia, Egypt, he became a monk at the Baramous Monastery in 1931 and assumed the monastic name "Mina al-Mutawahhid al-Baramusi." He was eventually chosen to be the patriarch of the Coptic Church on April 19, 1959 and blessed us with his life until March 9, 1971 when he reposed in the Lord. This pope was renown for his close relationship with the great St. Mina (or Menas), and also for his divinely granted gift of performing countless numbers of miracles, which are published in a variety of books and well known to the Copts today and especially those who lived during his time. I was blessed to be related to a woman who was His Holiness's seamstress and had an extremely close relationship with him, and through whom His Holiness healed a family member of mine from the sudden onset of some curious illness.[20]

Deacon. The Church rank of deacon, ranking below a priest, has been around since the time of the apostles, being instituted by them (see Acts 6) and attested to elsewhere in the Bible (1 Tim 3:8–13; Phil 1:1). They differ from priests and bishops in that they are not able to invoke the Holy Spirit to effectuate any of the Church mysteries. The blessed Ignatius (who was a personal disciple of one or more of the apostles)[21] distinguishes between the three principal ranks (also known as Major Orders) of the Church—bishop, priest, and deacon—and states (*c.* AD 105), "apart from these there is no Church."[22] Chanters, readers, and subdeacons are below the rank of deacon. Note that, although in the Coptic Church the term "deacon" is confusingly applied to these minor orders, the true title of "deacon" is actually reserved for a very select few who can be regarded as similar to the rank given to the very first deacons in the book of Acts.[23]

Demiana and the forty virgins (early fourth century). St. Demiana is an Egyptian Christian from around the early fourth century who along with forty other virgins committed to living celibate lives in a makeshift convent built by her father, who was a governor in Egypt, which was part of the Roman Empire. After her father initially denied Emperor Diocletian's demand that he offer incense to his idols, he succumbed to the pressure and complied. His daughter Demiana sharply rebuked him and convinced him of his wrongdoing; afterward he returned to Emperor Diocletian and was beheaded. The emperor then turned his attention to St. Demiana, who was tortured severely as her forty virgin friends watched, and then, as none of them were persuaded to forsake Christ, all were beheaded and received the crown of martyrdom.[24]

Devil. This is the same entity depicted in the beginning of the Bible, in the book of Genesis, as a serpent who tricked the first woman and man into disobedience, as well as throughout the Bible as the enemy of God and all God's people, who at the end of time (according to the book of Revelation) will be cast into a "lake of fire" to suffer everlasting punishment. It is believed that he used to be an archangel who fell (along with some other fellow angels who followed his lead) from his position due to some prideful inclinations and some sort of struggle with God.[25]

Disciple. The Lord Jesus Christ personally selected twelve followers to be His disciples: Peter (also known as Simon), his brother Andrew, the brothers James and John (writer of the gospel ascribed to him), Philip, Bartholomew, Thomas, Matthew (writer of the gospel ascribed to him), another disciple named James (son of Alphaeus), Thaddaeus, another disciple named Simon (referred to as the Zealot or Cananite), and Judas Iscariot, who also betrayed Him but was later replaced by a disciple named Matthias to fill his office which had been vacated by his committing suicide (Mt 10:3; Mk 3:18; Lk 6:14; Acts 1:26). Aside from the Twelve, this term can also refer to any follower of Christ who adheres to His commandments (Lk 14:26).

Divine Liturgy. While the term "liturgy" can be understood according to its general meaning, which is understood from its Greek origin as referring to a public worship service, yet as Christianity developed, by the 4th century this term referred more specifically to the Eucharistic service (where Christians partake of the body and blood of Christ). Emphasis of this meaning is specifically expressed by adding the qualifying term "divine," whereby the Divine Liturgy particularly signifies the worship service focused on receiving the Eucharist.

Ecstasy. See "Caught up."

Eucharist. This word, derived from Greek and meaning "thanksgiving," refers to the body and blood of Christ, which people must partake of for salvation (cf. Jn 6).

Evening offering of incense. See "Offering of incense."

Father confessor (or Father of confession). In all Orthodox churches, this refers to the clergyman in whose presence a person confesses their sins to God. The frequency of required confession and the exact role the father confessor is expected to have in a Christian's life varies from parish to parish and from jurisdiction to jurisdiction. In the Coptic Church, members are encouraged and expected to develop a relationship with a clergyman who becomes their spiritual guide and to whom they confess their sins on a regular basis (the commonly understood recommendation is no less than once every 40 days). Like visiting a doctor to address our physical maladies, the father confessor acts as the physician of our spirits, providing us with a prognosis based on our current course of actions and also often providing a regiment we are asked to follow to help cure our spiritual vices and promote spiritual virtues.

Fasting. On certain pre-prescribed days in the year, Orthodox Christians fast by abstaining from food for a period of time, and then afterward breaking their fast but continuing to limit their food intake by quantity, quality, and also kind (e.g., no meat, dairy, or any other animal product or its derivatives may be consumed; different jurisdictions may vary in minor ways). Fasting has been a part of Christianity since its inception, as the Bible attests.

George, the Prince of Martyrs (d. AD 307). Historically it is problematic to derive what scholars would consider an accurate story of this saint's life, as there are several versions preserved in a variety of manuscripts. Here is an exemplary summary of his life: Born to Christian parents, he became distinguished among Emperor Diocletian's ranks, and then defied him when realizing the emperor was intent on persecuting Christians. After suffering several tortures, he was eventually beheaded, but not before (according to many sources) dying, coming back to life, and performing wondrous miracles. Many, including the emperor's wife, are said to have converted to Christianity and become martyrs as well because of St. George. After his martyrdom, his body was wrapped in expensive shrouds and taken to the city of Lydda, his home town (in present day Palestine), where a great church was said to have been built in his name by Emperor Constantine or at least during his reign; that church was later destroyed and the church that now stands in its stead is said to house his remains.[26]

Gregory the Wonder-worker (d. AD 270). While recent scholarship has cast some doubt as to an important source of the details of this saint's life story, what is related about him is as follows: Born to pagan parents, having learned the philosophy and wisdom of the world, he acquired knowledge about Christianity as a pupil of Origen. Being convinced of Christianity, he was baptized and eventually was chosen bishop (some sources say God's will for this to be so was made evident by an angel who appeared to him; Gregory of Nyssa is said to have written about St. Mary and St. John the evangelist appearing to him). He was widely known for performing wondrous miracles by the power of his prayers and favor with God.[27]

Habib Farag (1914–1941). This righteous person, who Bishop Youannis of Gharbia, Egypt called a "saint in St. Antony's Church in Shobra, Cairo," died at the very young age of 27 (the day of which he knew beforehand, as revealed in his personal diary). As a young man, he lived a life away from God. The servants of the St.

Antony Church (which was near his home) would continuously insist on his attending Bible study lessons. After refusing time and time again, he eventually succumbed to their insistence, laying out one condition: that he would attend only one lesson. If he enjoyed it, he would attend more, but if not, he did not want to see the faces of those servants again. The Bible study proved effective in moving his heart, by God's grace. Then, that same night, St. Mary appeared to him in a dream and showed him Hades, then Paradise. After coming to himself, he lived a life of chastity, constant prayer, and struggle to be granted entrance into eternal bliss.[28]

Hades. This is a place of torment where the spirits of those who have died and have been deemed unworthy to live in Paradise are sent to be reserved for judgment, awaiting God's judgment upon the world at which time He will set some aside to experience eternal bliss in heaven and the others to eternal punishment in hell.

Heaven. After we die, if we are counted worthy by God's grace, we will be allowed to wait in Paradise until Christ's Second Coming, after which time the righteous will be allowed to live eternally in heaven. Paradise and heaven refer to two different stages in eternal life, with the former being temporary and the latter continuing our blissful existence permanently where our full reward will be received. In this book, as much as possible, I have utilized the term heaven to signify the above-stated meaning. However, this term is often used indiscriminately as referring both to where the spirits of the deceased worthy of bliss abide just after death as well as their permanent home awaiting them after God's judgment of the world.

Hell. As distinguished from Hades, which is the temporary abode of sinners, hell is referred to in this book as the final, eternal condemnation and place of torment for the devil, evil spirits, and sinners, who will be sent there after Christ's Second Coming and judgment of all.

Hieromonk. A monk who is also a priest.

His Grace. Title of respect given to bishops, added as a prefix to their name.

Holy Synod. The ecclesiastical governing body of a church. Different Orthodox churches maintain their own local rules regarding membership. It is presided over by the head bishop over a particular ecclesiastical area. For example, in the Coptic Church, the Holy Synod is its highest authority rather than the pope of Alexandria. The pope, who presides over Holy Synod meetings as the first among equals, has the same voting power as the rest of the members, who consist of bishops from the Coptic Church.

Ignatius of Antioch (first century). This saintly bishop was a contemporary of the apostles. He was appointed to serve as the bishop of Antioch by one of the apostles, and he is believed to have been a friend of St. Polycarp and together with him also a disciple of St. John the evangelist, having travelled with St. John to various cities. His writings are valuable in that they are among the relatively few writings available from the first leaders of Christianity who took the helm of overseeing the Church immediately after the apostles. On his way to Rome, as a prisoner, he wrote several letters to various churches which provide much insight regarding the structure and beliefs of the churches in Asia Minor at the close of the apostolic age.[29]

Intercession. Orthodox Christians do not pray to saints. However, based on the premise that those in heaven are in a better condition than us, being continually in God's presence, and also because we consider ourselves to remain part of the one body of Christ, consisting of both the dead and the living, the striving and the victorious, we therefore have no problems speaking to those who are in Paradise and asking them to pray for us, just like we would ask someone on earth to do the same. Orthodox Christians have learned of the tried and true value of this throughout their experiences over the course of history, which has shed light on the undeniable efficacy of remaining in contact with those who are favored by God to implore Him on our behalf. As St. Jerome (*c.* AD 347–420) declares, "If the apostles and martyrs, while still in the body, can pray for others, at a time when they ought still to be anxious for themselves, how much more after their crowns, victories, and triumphs are won!"[30]

Irenaeus (*c.* AD 130–200). This bishop of the church at Lyons (in modern times located in France) was closely linked to the disciple of Christ, St. John the evangelist, having heard and learned from St. Polycarp, who was himself a disciple of St. John. He left us with several invaluable writings focused on combatting heresies prevalent at his time, which writings have also served as a wealth of insight into the mindset of an early Christian overseer and the Church.

John Chrysostom (*c.* AD 350–407). Known for his eloquence in preaching, St. John was given the Greek epithet *Chrysostomos* (Χρυσόστομος), meaning "golden mouth." St. John of the golden mouth was born at Antioch of Syria (a Christian community founded by St. Paul himself, visited by St. Peter, and led by St. Ignatius for a time) not long after Emperor Constantine established Christianity as the official religion of the Roman Empire. He was raised in a Christian home and was eventually baptized when he reached adulthood, after which he eventually undertook the ascetic life in the hills near Antioch where he spent roughly six years, four of which were under the guidance of an elderly Syrian monk, then two years isolated in a cave on his own. It is written about him that during his time as a monk a Syrian hermit had a vision in which he observed the apostles Peter and John approaching St. John Chrysostom and handing him a Bible while being told, "Do not be afraid, whosoever you shall bind shall be bound, and whosoever you loose shall be loosed" (cf. Mt 18:18). This vision confirmed the blessedness of this great saint. He was eventually ordained a reader, deacon, priest, and finally was appointed to serve as archbishop of Constantinople from AD 398 until his death on September 14, 407. He spent the latter part of his life preaching to the masses, and was evidently greatly loved by them (although he suffered strife, including forced exile, as a result of his unwavering steadfastness in preaching the truth to everyone, even if they were among the higher echelons of society). His sermons were very popular (usually very practical) and his congregation often interrupted him with applause. He is beloved by all apostolic churches as one of the greatest Christian teachers of all time.[31]

Kallistos Ware, metropolitan. Formerly known as Timothy Ware, this Eastern Orthodox bishop is one of the best-known contemporary Eastern Orthodox theologians. After leaving the Anglican faith and embracing Orthodoxy in his early 20s, he was ordained a deacon, ordained to the priesthood in 1966, tonsured as a monk, and given the new name "Kallistos." He was later consecrated as bishop, and then elevated to metropolitan. He served as the Spalding Lecturer in Eastern Orthodox Studies at Oxford University for 35 years until his retirement in 2005. He has authored several books, including the extremely popular title, *The Orthodox Church*.[32]

Kyrillos VI. See "Cyril VI."

Layman. This refers to any person who has not been ordained by a canonical bishop to some rank in the Church, or otherwise appointed to a special life of consecration or service; generally, anyone who is not a deacon, priest, or bishop (or a monk, nun, or some consecrated servant).

Liturgy of the Eucharist. See "Divine Liturgy."

Macarius the Great (d. AD 392). A contemporary of St. Anthony the Great, this Egyptian Christian who was forced into marriage was given the opportunity by God to live a life of celibacy as a monk (his wife having died before consummating the marriage), which eventually led him to the Nitrian desert of Egypt by the guidance of a cherub who appeared to him and said, "God has given this desert to you and your sons for an inheritance." There he became the spiritual father of many monks, as was divinely revealed to be God's will.[33]

Makarious, bishop of Qena (AD 1923–91). He was a Coptic Christian, born September 10, 1923. At age 27 he was consecrated as a monk at the Baramous Monastery, then later ordained as a priest. He served as a personal secretary to His Holiness Pope Cyril VI, who eventually ordained him as the bishop of Qena, Dishana, Nakada, Kous, Qift, and the Red Sea (all in Egypt). It is said that he would visit 50 to 100 homes of his congregation a day. He is renown among Copts as being the bishop who was granted his wish: to die during the Divine Liturgy. On February 3, 1991, after 26 years of strenuous service for the Lord, he died as he was holding the body of the Lord in his hand (after it had already been sanctified by the Holy Spirit). As he fell backwards to the floor in front of the altar, the body of Christ also began to fall with him; then suddenly and miraculously, by divine power and without the assistance of any human effort, the blessed *corban* was raised back to the altar and was kept from falling to the ground. While His Grace normally forbade the videotaping of any Divine Liturgy he prayed in, that was the one time he allowed it, and the video depicting this miraculous event is readily available (including on popular internet video sites). It is said that the money raised from selling the videotapes of this event helped complete the church he was praying in, which was still under construction.[34]

Mary, the Mother of God. St. Mary is revered by Orthodox Christians for being the only person in all the world of all time to be deemed worthy of bearing God within her womb, from whom He took flesh and was incarnate. Her favor with God was expressed clearly in the Bible when the angel said to her, "Rejoice, highly favored one, the Lord is with you; blessed are you among women!" (Lk 1:28). Our reverence of her is fulfillment of prophesy in Scripture, as she said, "Henceforth all generations will call me blessed" (Lk 1:48). To do otherwise would be to deny Scripture and obstruct God's wishes. The early Church gave her the title "Mother of God" (Theotokos, as transliterated from Greek), since she did not simply bear the human aspect of Christ in her womb, but the fullness of His humanity and divinity dwelt in her.

Midnight Praises. Also known by its Arabic name pronounced "*Tasbeha*" (which simply means praises), this is a collection of hymns, doxologies, prayers, and other manners of worship and praise that the Coptic Church abides by. It is considered to be a preparatory part of the Divine Liturgy, and is therefore supposed to take place prior to it. In most Coptic churches today, the Midnight Praises occur after Saturday night's evening offering of incense and Agpeya prayers, and then after going home to rest for the night, the congregation returns on Sunday for the Divine Liturgy. In monasteries and convents (and as was the norm long ago among the Copts), monks and nuns pray the Midnight Praises daily before the Divine Liturgy in a continuous night-long vigil that is completed by partaking of the Eucharist at the end of the entire service early in the morning.

Mina the Wonder-worker (also known as Menas; *c*. AD 285–309). His barren mother Euphemia wept before the icon of our Lady St. Mary imploring to be granted a child when she suddenly heard a voice emitting from the icon saying, "Amen." Her prayer was granted and Mina was born in the city of Nakiyos in Egypt, whose name was derived from the voice his mother heard. His parents died while he was still young. He joined the Roman empire, taking his father's place. When the infamous Emperor Diocletian issued orders that all were to worship pagan idols, St. Mina left his position and focused on the true worship of God in the desert. He saw a vision compelling him to receive the heavenly crown of the martyrs. He returned to the city and remained steadfast as he suffered through torture until he was finally beheaded. After paying a large sum, his sister recovered his body, which relics the Coptic Church still retains. Many miracles occurred after his death and still occur today due to the prayers of this saint. Pope Cyril VI, whose close relationship with this saint was well-known, built an elaborate monastery in his name in Egypt.[35]

Monastery of St. Macarius. Known in Arabic as *Dair Abu Maqar*, this is the southernmost monastery in the Nitrian Desert. After the death of his disciples Maximus and Domitius, St. Macarius the Great was led by an angel to a certain rock, and there he built a church. Eventually, as the cells of different monks began to spread around the church, this became the foundation of the present-day monastery.[36]

Mother Erene (1936–2006). She was the Mother Superior of the St. Philopateer Mercurius (Abu Sefein) Convent in Old Cairo, Egypt from October 15, 1962 until her departure on October 31, 2006. In recent times she is best known as someone who had many close friends in Paradise, many of whom appeared to her quite frequently, including the Lord Jesus Christ first and foremost, as well as the blessed Virgin Mary, and the beloved patron saint of the convent, Abu Sefein himself, and so many others (e.g., St.

Anthony the Great). Many books about this jewel from heaven have been published by the nuns she left behind, attesting to Mother Erene's life which was full of spirituality, miracles, and wonder. As a young child, her family was commonly exposed to divine revelations and apparitions, including the appearance of St. Mary who on one occasion foretold that Mother Erene was to become a nun. As Abbess, the convent flourished. In her last days she gave us the privilege to hear of many various wondrous events and miraculous incidents, that God may be glorified through His saints, by allowing the narration of such events and incidents to be recorded in writing, audio, and video (many of which are in my personal possession and serve as the source for many stories in this book). Mother Erene had always wished to receive the blessing of martyrdom, but she was assured by St. Mary and Abu Sefein that accepting and enduring suffering in this world, including the pain of illness, has a reward in the afterlife akin to that of a martyr. Thus, Mother Erene is known to have lived a life riddled with ailments throughout her body, including suffering from cancer. Regardless of the tremendous suffering that she endured, she continued to praise and glorify God, as this was what she asked for. Though deprived, according to her own desire, of healing for her own conditions, God granted healing through her prayers to many others, usually effectuated through the intercessions and prayers of the saints, particularly Abu Sefein. In her last moments dying while experiencing severe pain, she asked God to accept her suffering as martyrdom until finally she departed to Paradise on October 31, 2006.[37]

Mystery. In the Church there are mysteries, or "sacraments," in which the Holy Spirit mysteriously bestows some benefit upon the believer through some visible means. For example, in the mystery of chrismation, the holy chrism by which a person is anointed serves as the visible accompaniment of the mysterious indwelling of the Holy Spirit in the believer accomplished by this mystery. Four mysteries are regarded as fundamentally necessary for the purpose of obtaining eternal salvation, according to the teachings of Christ and as understood by the Church: baptism, chrismation, repentance and confession, and the partaking of the Eucharist. Other mysteries include marriage, unction of the sick, and priesthood. Many regard the limitation of the mysteries to just seven as being inconsistent with Orthodox beliefs. At minimum, the seven mentioned are recognized and practiced by Orthodox Christians.

Nayrouz. According to the Coptic calendar, the Coptic New Year falls on the corresponding Gregorian calendar date of September 11th (or September 12th if the previous Coptic year was a leap year). The name is not considered to derive from the Coptic language, but rather a Persian word, *nowruz*, which means "new day."[38]

Offering of incense. In the Coptic Church, as well as to some degree other Orthodox churches, there are two services that focus on the use of a censer to spread the smoke of incense around the church along with prayers. The services are supposed to be held the evening before every Divine Liturgy as well as during the morning before the Divine Liturgy proper. This practice of offering incense as a part of worship dates back to the very first place of worship of the true God and the very first priests (Ex 30:7–10). God taught that such offerings of incense are supposed to continue "throughout . . . generations" (Ex 30:10), and not just among the Israelites, but that it would be offered by Christians through the Church to God in all places: "My name shall be great among the Gentiles; in every place incense shall be offered to My name" (Mal 1:11). Burning incense is not only to be practiced on earth, but continues to be a feature in heaven as the book of Revelation tells us (Rev 5 and 8). Incense signifies our prayers rising before God as a "sweet-smelling aroma" (Eph 5:2; Phil 4:18). As incense can be found in heaven, so too there is a sense of an otherworldly, heavenly atmosphere as the sight and smell of incense pervades the inside of the church.

Origen (c. AD 185–254). Born in Egypt, he was brought up in a Christian home and studied the Bible and other Christian texts thoroughly while retaining a very inquisitive mind. He was a student at the famed Catechetical School of Alexandria, and then later appointed its dean. Although the most eminent of saints and even to the present time all apostolic churches agree that he was one of the greatest teachers of Christianity, due to some controversies that occurred during his life (whose verity is difficult to ascertain), he is not regarded as a saint and Church Father, so as not to give the impression of approval for any of the controversies that may have actually been true. Regardless, he is deserving of the utmost esteem. It is also interesting to note that many famous Church Fathers were his pupils, including St. Gregory the Wonder-worker and Pope Dionysius of Alexandria.[39]

Pachomius (c. AD 292–348). During the formative years of monasticism many monks lived solitary lives as hermits or adopted a variant of hermitic life by gathering monks within the vicinity of each other (usually under the guidance of some spiritual father, such as St. Anthony the Great or St. Macarius the Great), yet ensuring they spent the overwhelming majority of their time separately in private contemplation and prayers. Abba Pachomius, who was born a pagan but converted to Christianity after personally experiencing sublime and unanticipated kindness from the Copts in Egypt, became a monk and is regarded as the founder of the cenobitic lifestyle and communal, monastic life (*koinonia*), which he implemented after personal contemplation about the life of hermits (and reportedly culminated in the apparition of an angel delineating its rules).[40]

Paradise. In this book, this term is, as much as possible, used to refer to the temporary abode of spirits after death where the righteous will await Christ's Second Coming while experiencing bliss, joy, and peace. This term is distinguished from the word "heaven," or "kingdom of heaven," which is the eternal dwelling place where people will live after Christ returns and renders His final judgment.

Patriarch. See "Pope."

Paul, the First Hermit (d. *c.* AD 341). While St. Anthony is known as the Father of Monasticism, he is not known as the first hermit. That honor goes to St. Paul of Thebes. Just as St. Athanasius wrote *The Life of St. Anthony*, St. Jerome (a great Christian writer and Bible translator) wrote about St. Anthony's contemporary in a work titled, *Life of Saint Paul, the First Hermit*. Born in Egypt, he forsook his inheritance after his father died, having been affected by the sight of a funeral procession, which caused him to ponder about the transience of life and vanity of material possessions. Eventually he was led by an angel to the wilderness and lived there for seventy years without seeing a single human being, all the while living in extreme asceticism (being fed half a loaf of bread which was brought to him by a raven, and being clothed in a palm-fiber tunic). St. Anthony eventually learned of him, visited him, and came to him after he died, observing two lions as they miraculously were sent to dig his grave. After his death, St. Paul appeared to St. Athanasius asking him not to attempt to locate his relics. Instead, the palm-fiber tunic that St. Paul was wearing, which was retrieved by St. Anthony, was given to Pope Athanasius who used to wear it three times a year during the Divine Liturgy, to heighten people's awareness of the holiness of the tunic's owner. On one occasion, the tunic was placed over a dead man who rose up alive instantly.[41]

Philopateer Mercurius (also known as Abu Sefein; *c.* AD 224–250). This saint was a member of the Roman army and was promoted to the rank of general after fighting valiantly and succeeding in a battle against some barbarians, with the help of a sword provided by an angel who appeared to him in the midst of the engagement. Bearing two swords (his own and the one provided by the angel) is the reason he is affectionately referred to in Arabic as "Abu Sefein," (which means bearer of the two swords). The Roman emperor, Decius, rewarded his valiant triumph by promoting him to the rank of general and placing him in charge of the army. After being reminded by an angel to remember the true crown of victory that awaits us in God's heavenly kingdom, this saint defied the emperor in front of several dignitaries by proclaiming his Christian faith. After refusing the emperor's attempts to persuade him to present offerings to the pagan god Artemis, the emperor ordered that he be tortured. When finally he grew weary of the saint's resilience and miraculous recovery from his wounds, he sent him to Cappadocia to be beheaded. Shortly before his death the Lord Christ appeared to him for encouragement. It is recorded that at the time of his death, in AD 250, his body became white like snow and emitted a sweet smell of myrrh and incense, which caused many to believe in Christ. Many miracles have occurred since his death until the present time. One of the most notable miracles that took place explains why in his icon he is depicted as killing an emperor, while in the background a bishop with his staff can be seen witnessing it. It is recorded that St. Basil the Great saw in a dream the heavens open and Christ seated on His throne saying, "Mercurius, go and kill the emperor Julian, who is against the Christians." (This emperor wanted to return the empire from promoting Christianity [due to Emperor Constantine] back to its pagan roots, and thus he is called "Julian the Apostate.") After the Lord's remarks, St. Basil saw Abu Sefein standing before God's throne, disappear, and then re-appear and tell him, "The emperor Julian has been fatally wounded and has died, as You commanded, Lord."[42]

Polycarp (c. AD 69–155). St. Polycarp was the bishop of Smyrna, regarded as being "the angel of the church in Smyrna" to whom Christ addressed His remarks in St. John's Revelation (2:8). His close relationship with St. John, the disciple of Jesus, was attested to by Tertullian,[43] indicating that the church of Smyrna maintained records as of the time of his writing (around the end of the second century) crediting St. John with placing St. Polycarp in Smyrna to serve as its bishop. The Roman historian and bishop, Eusebius, notable for his writings about the history of the early Church, writes about the close relationship between St. Irenaeus and St. Polycarp. There he tells us that St. Irenaeus personally attested to this relationship and how he faithfully transmitted the doctrines of the apostles which he heard from St. Polycarp, who, according to St. Irenaeus, related all things in harmony with the Scriptures.

Pope (or patriarch). While many associate the term "pope" with the Roman Catholic Church, it is a historical fact that this term originally was the honorific title of solely the archbishop of Alexandria. The Roman archbishop of the Catholic Church began to be designated with this term as early as the fourth century and its origin has since become a matter of antiquity and lost in the consciousness of most people today. The word "pope" comes from the Greek word *papas* (whose Coptic counterpart is *papa*), which literally means "father." All clergy are considered to be spiritual fathers, but the head of all clergy, the pope, is the father among fathers, and is therefore also called the "patriarch," which is the title given to Orthodox archbishops of a particular jurisdiction. It is worthy to note that, unlike the pope of the Catholic Church, the patriarchs of the Orthodox Church are not regarded as infallible in any way.[44] (For more information regarding a particular pope mentioned in this book, look in this appendix for their first name: e.g., Cyril VI.)

Psalmody. This refers to the book used in the Coptic Church in the service (usually called "Midnight Praises") that precedes the Divine Liturgy, consisting of hymns and praises that are sung according to a certain order and certain rituals. The most ancient manuscript of the Psalmody in existence is among the collection at the monastery of the Archangel Michael in Hamuli (in Al Fayoum), Upper Egypt, and is dated *c.* AD 892. See also "Midnight Praises."[45]

Salvation. When we die, our spirits will have to go somewhere. Christians believe that before Christ came to earth, as a result of the first man and woman's sin, all humanity was condemned, whereby their spirits would not be allowed to exist in God's heavenly abode but rather be cast into Hades. Moreover, humans lost their formerly pure nature and sin became rampant. Christ came to earth and reconciled humanity with God again, so that those who abide by Christ's teachings would, upon death, be allowed to live in Paradise and eventually heaven with Him. Hence, Christ saved us from our former lowly state and from eternal damnation, allowing us to renew our image and also gain the salvation of our souls, as children of God and heirs to the kingdom of heaven.

Saint(s) (abbreviated "St."). Originally, Scriptural use of the term "saint" (Greek: ἅγιος—*agios* or some variant derivative thereof, meaning "holy," "set apart," "sacred") referred to all faithful believers (cf. Rom 12:13; 15:25; 1 Cor 14:33; 2 Cor 1:1; 8:4; 9:1, 12; Philem 1:7; Heb 3:1; Jude 1:3). Nowadays the Orthodox Church (and some other denominations, notably the Catholic Church) assigns the term to certain people who are regarded as worthy to be imitated and revered due to the extent and manner of their devotion to God. Scripture commands us to "imitate those who through faith and patience inherit the promises" (Heb 6:12). Just like we give people on earth titles as a prefix to their name to indicate their status, much more deservedly are those who have accomplished true success by remaining "steadfast to the end" (Heb 3:14) to be called holy (which is the meaning of the word "saint") and who are worthy of such a designation. Moreover, to call someone holy is a means of recognition that they fulfilled God's commandment for all of us to be holy: "As He who called you is holy, you also be holy in all your conduct, because it is written, 'Be holy, for I am holy'" (1 Pet 1:15–16). God has always shown varying degrees of favor with different people based on their virtues and conduct, as is clear throughout the Bible and also as has been evident since the inception of Christianity as seen in the way that Christians have continuously venerated saints and reaped the benefit of their prayers. Thus, it is fitting to honor the holiest of Christians with the title "saint," as a mark of distinction in accordance with a life, devoted to Christ, that went beyond the norm.

Sacrament. See "Mystery."

Satan. See "Devil."

Shenouda III, 117th pope of Alexandria (AD 1923–2012). This blessed successor of St. Mark the evangelist (the founder of the Church of Alexandria) was chosen and consecrated as the 117th pope and patriarch of Alexandria on November 14, 1971. Born August 3, 1923 and given the name Nazir (or Nazer) Gayed, he was raised by his brother Raphael after his mother died shortly after his birth, followed by the death of his father a few years later. In July of 1954, Nazir entered the Monastery of the Syrians (a Coptic monastery in Egypt known in Arabic as *Dair al-Surian*), being given the name Antonious (after they appointed him for the life of monasticism). He lived his monastic life as a hermit. Eventually, after being ordained pope, he experienced a number of tribulations due to the environment of religious and political persecution that existed at the time in Egypt, suffering numerous house arrests and exiles. His Holiness is known for his poetry and theological prowess, having begun his adult life as a teacher and then devoting his evenings at the theological seminary in Egypt. Pope Shenouda III retained his scholarly interests and wrote many books and delivered innumerable sermons (including those he gave on a weekly basis at the Cathedral in Cairo, Egypt). No words can describe the love and affection that the members of the Coptic Church have for their beloved spiritual father, His Holiness Pope Shenouda. That love was evident when millions of mourning Copts poured out onto the streets of Egypt to say farewell to His Holiness who departed to Paradise on March 17, 2012, visiting his body which remained on the throne of the Coptic Cathedral in Cairo, Egypt for three days after his death for people to view one final time (as is the traditional practice of the Coptic Church) before he was buried at the Monastery of St. Bishoy in the Nitrian Desert of Egypt.[46]

Shenouda the Archimandrite (*c.* AD 347–431). This Egyptian saint was the head of a large group of monasteries (which is why he is called "the Archimandrite"). He was born in the city of Shenalolet in the district of Akhmim, in Egypt. Growing up he showed an interest in fasting and asceticism, and so his maternal uncle, a monk named Abba Bigoul (also spelled Bigal, Bgoul, or Pgol), helped initiate him into monasticism. After St. Bigoul's death in AD 385, St. Shenouda took his place and became the abbot of the monastery. St. Shenouda maintained the Pachomian rules that were set in place by St. Bigoul, adding to it also a pledge the monk had to sign before joining the monastery. That monastery flourished during St. Shenouda's time, with about 2,200 monks being associated with it, and today it is known as "The White Monastery," near Suhag, Egypt. It is regarded that another monastery (known today as "The Red Monastery") was also associated with this saint. St. Shenouda attended the Ecumenical Council at Ephesus in AD 431 and joined Pope Cyril the Great (the 24th patriarch of Alexandria) in admonishing Nestorius (the patriarch of Constantinople). The writings of St. Shenouda are of great importance.[47]

Synaxarion. Notable events in Christian history, as well as many other remarkable stories of Orthodox Christian saints, are collected in the Coptic Synaxarion (from the Greek word Συναξάριον, whose base meaning is "to bring together"). These stories are arranged over a calendar year, so that each day a different set of saints and events are remembered, usually corresponding to the exact day that the saint departed or the event occurred. Unlike other Christian churches that arrange their Synaxarion and celebration of religious events according to the Gregorian calendar, the Coptic Church still uses an ancient Egyptian calendar (see "Coptic calendar").

Tertullian (*c.* AD 160–230). Little is known about the life of this prolific Latin Christian writer except what St. Jerome tells us, which includes that he "was a native of the province of Africa and city of Carthage, the son of a proconsular centurion: he was a man of a sharp and vehement temper, . . . and wrote numerous works." He even went on to say that St. Cyprian of Carthage "never passed a day without reading some portion of Tertullian's works." He was a convert from heathenism and once despised the Gospel. As a heathen, he enjoyed watching the savage sports of the gladiators and fell into the grossest of sins. Some sources, including St. Jerome, say he was ordained a priest. Due to an indication of some leanings (*c.* AD 201) toward a movement known as Montanism, Tertullian is therefore not regarded as a saint or Church Father, out of an abundance of caution so as not to give the impression that all of his beliefs can generally be held in high regard without any additional scrutiny. Nonetheless, it is important to note that his Montanist influences became more evident during his later years, so that his earlier writings are less tainted by that movement. His works are still extremely valuable in understanding much of the mindset of the Christians that lived at that time.[48]

Youannis, bishop of Tanta and its vicinity (d. AD 1987). While living a life of monasticism at the Monastery of the Syrians in Egypt (*Dair al-Surian*), Bishop Youannis was ordained on December 12, 1971 to serve as bishop over Gharbia, Egypt, and its suburbs (also known as Tanta and its vicinity), which was the first ordination of a bishop by Pope Shenouda III in his first year of enthronement. His Grace Bishop Youannis (whose name is pronounced according to the Coptic spelling of "John"), served as a personal secretary of the blessed Pope Cyril VI, and was tasked with teaching about Church history and rituals, among other subjects, in the theological seminary in Cairo (*El Eclerekia*). He was a prolific writer; one of his most notable books was about the Church during the era of the apostles, and another titled *Heaven* was translated into the English language in 2007. Bishop Youannis established a theological seminary in Tanta, Egypt. He departed this life on November 4, 1987.[49]

Youssef, Metropolitan of the Coptic Diocese of the Southern United States. Listening to the call of the Lord Jesus Christ, His Eminence Metropolitan Youssef entered the monastic life in 1986 at the Monastery of the Syrians (*Dair al-Surian*). He was ordained into the priesthood in 1988. Then in 1989, he came to the United States under the auspices of His Holiness Pope Shenouda III, the 117th pope of the Holy See of St. Mark. He was appointed resident priest to serve the Coptic congregation of St. Mary's Church in Dallas/Fort Worth, Texas. After being ordained as a general bishop in 1992, he was appointed as the first bishop to oversee the newly established Coptic Orthodox Diocese of the Southern United States of America the following year and was officially enthroned to serve in that capacity in 1995. In 2022 His Eminence was elevated to the rank of metropolitan by His Holiness Pope Tawadros II. He is greatly beloved by his congregation and has gained a reputation for his wisdom, insight, and spiritual prowess. The innumerable fruits of his tremendous efforts in his diocese and elsewhere are a testimony to his fervent love for Christ and His Church.[50]

Notes

PREFACE

1. St. John Chrysostom clearly understands this experience as being that of St. Paul and believed that the "Paradise" he was caught up into was the same place that Christ mentioned to the thief as being the place where he would go with Christ after death. John Chrysostom *Homily on 2 Corinthians* 26.1–2. In *Nicene and Post-Nicene Fathers: First Series* 12, Philip Schaff, ed. (1886–1889; repr. New York, NY: Cosimo, Inc., 2007), 398–399 (henceforth cited as NPNF[1]).
2. In order, you may find references for all of these events as follows: 1 Kg 17:17–22; 2 Kg 4:32–35; 13:20–21; Lk 7:11–15; 8:41–55; Jn 11:1–44; Acts 9:36–41; 20:9–10.
3. *Against Heresies* 2.31.2. In *The Ante-Nicene Fathers* 1, Alexander Roberts and James Donaldson, eds. (Buffalo, NY: The Christian Literature Company, 1885), 407 (henceforth cited as ANF).

CHAPTER 1. UNDERSTANDING THE MYSTERIES HEREIN

1. Gregory of Nyssa *On Infants' Early Deaths*. In *Nicene and Post-Nicene Fathers: Second Series* 5, Philip Schaff, ed. (1886–1889; repr. New York, NY: Cosimo, Inc., 2007), 374–375 (henceforth cited as NPNF[2]).

CHAPTER 2. DEATH

1. Obviously, in this definition of death, the presumed belief is that mankind is constituted of both a physical body and a spirit. St. Irenaeus demonstrated this generally accepted principle when he wrote: "Man is a mixed organization of soul and flesh, who was formed after the likeness of God, and molded by His hands, that is, by the Son and Holy Spirit, to whom also

He said, 'Let Us make man' [Gen 1:26]." *Against Heresies* 4.Preface.4 (ANF 1:463). The physical body was given when God "formed man out of the dust of the ground" (Gen 2:7). The spirit is that invisible part of humanity that stays with the body during life and upon death is released, leaving the physical body to return to dust ("For out of it you were taken; for dust you are, and to dust you shall return."—Gen 3:19; "Then the dust will return to the earth as it was and the spirit will return to God who gave it."—Eccl 12:7); it is that aspect of one's self that remains alive, experiencing life after the death of one's body. The spirit was distinctly given to humans only (and not to animals or any other living thing), as we are the only ones that received the "breath [i.e., spirit] of life" from God when we were created: "The Lord God . . . breathed into his nostrils the breath of life; and man became a living being" (Gen 2:7). It is immortal and has no necessary connection with the body and consequently is unaffected by the death of the body. It is this which distinguishes man from brute creation, allying him with higher intelligences such as those around the throne of God.

2. Athenagoras *The Resurrection of the Dead* 16 (ANF 2:158).

3. Ibid., 20 (ANF 2:160).

4. Ibid., 16 (ANF 2:156).

5. Ambrose *On Belief in the Resurrection* 73 (NPNF[2] 10:185).

6. Augustine *On the Soul and Its Origin* 2.8 (NPNF[1] 5:334).

7. Greek: Ἅιδης—transliterated "hades"; Coptic: ⲁⲙⲉⲛⲧ—transliterated "amenti."

8. There is often much confusion as to what is meant exactly by a "new heaven" and "new earth." The book of Revelation is not the only place where we find mention of this notion. The early Fathers often quote Isaiah where God tells him: "Behold, I create new heavens and a new earth" (Is 65:17). Elsewhere, in the New Testament, as St. Irenaeus points out (Irenaeus *Against Heresies* 5.35.2 [ANF 1:565–566]) we find Christ mentioning that "heaven and earth shall pass away" (Mt 24:35) and St. Paul indicating that "the form of this world is passing away" (1 Cor 7:31). Understandably, there is much ambiguity as to what this means exactly. The early Christians varied in their understanding of what this all means as well. For example, Origen and Methodius regarded it not as a complete destruction of heaven and earth but more so a change to something better (cf. Origen *De Principiis* [*On First Principles*] 1.6.4 [ANF 4:262]; Methodius *Discourse on the Resurrection* 1.8 ANF 6:366). Others exhibited difficulty in coming to their own understanding (cf. Augustine *The City of God* 20.16 [NPNF[1] 2:435–436]). Today, some consider references to a "new heaven"

and "new earth" as more allegorical than literal, while others read it more literally as meaning that heaven and earth as we know it will cease to exist and will be entirely replaced with something new. It may be best to simply conclude, as Origen did: "How things will be, however, is known with certainty to God alone, and to those who are His friends through Christ and the Holy Spirit" (Origen *De Principiis* [*On First Principles*] 1.6.4 [ANF 4:262]).

9. Note that this word, translated "hell" in some versions of the Bible, is derived from the Greek word *tartarosas* [ταρταρώσας—translated in English as Tartarus], which literally refers to simply a place of punishment reserved for demons; in Greek mythology, this word referred to a place of punishment under the earth. For an extensive treatment of this term and how to understand it in the Orthodox concept of the afterlife, please refer to Chapter 4.

10. Homily of Abba John Chrysostom, Liturgy of the Waters, Covenant Thursday. (2016). In CopticReader for Apple iOS (Version 2.54.1) [Mobile application software]. (Retrieved June 6, 2016).

11. David Bercot, *Dictionary of Early Christian Beliefs* (Peabody, MA: Hendrickson Publishers, Inc., 2010), 192 (henceforth cited as Bercot, *DECB*) (quoting Irenaeus *Against Heresies* 2.34.1 [ANF 1:411]).

12. Ibid., 196 (quoting Cyprian of Carthage *The Epistles of Cyprian* 51.20 [ANF 5:332]).

13. Ibid., 245 (quoting Tertullian *The Soul's Testimony* 4 [ANF 3:177]).

14. For more explanation, see the entry for "caught up" in Appendix C.

15. St. John Chrysostom clearly understands this experience as being that of St. Paul and believed that the "Paradise" he was caught up into was the same place that Christ mentioned to the thief as being the place where he would go with Christ after death. John Chrysostom *Homily on 2 Corinthians* 26.1–2 (NPNF[1] 12:398–399).

16. *Against Heresies* 2.30.7 (ANF 1:405).

17. Fr. Seraphim Rose, *The Soul After Death* (Platina, CA: St. Herman of Alaska Brotherhood, 2009), 9.

18. Mr. K. Uekskuell's account can be found in *Orthodox Life* 26.4 (July–August 1976): 1–36. Typos and punctuation have been edited.

19. Born with the name Sabry Younan Abd El Malek in El Maragha, Sohag, Egypt, he was ordained a priest on July 18, 1976 and given the name Father Makary. As of the time of this publication, he continues to serve in the St. Mark Church in Azbakia, Cairo, Egypt. He has become famous in recent

times, especially with the advent of Coptic and other Arabic Christian television channels, for purportedly healing the sick and casting out demons from Christians and Muslims alike, who flock to the church or are brought by their families for help. These displays of healing are played out on television and internet sites for people to watch in a very dramatic and to some degree frightening fashion. He is also very well known for the fervent manner in which he leads his congregation in prayers and spiritual songs.

20. Bercot, *DECB*, 192 (quoting Irenaeus *Against Heresies* 2.34.1 [ANF 1:411]).

21. Alexander servant of God, *Father Arseny, 1893–1973: Priest, Prisoner, Spiritual Father* (Crestwood, NY: St. Vladimir's Seminary Press, 1998), 43–46.

22. Augustine, *City of God*, Marcus Dods, trans. (New York, NY: Modern Library, 1950), 781.

23. Bercot, *DECB*, 192 (quoting Irenaeus *Against Heresies* 2.34.1 [ANF 1:411]).

24. "The Meeting Between Mother Irini and the Families of the Choir in 1999 AD," *Abba Antony Magazine*, 16.12 (December 2006): 9. Used with the much-appreciated permission of Fr. Anastasi St. Antony.

25. The convent of the great martyr St. Philopater Mercurius, *Tamav Erene: A Monastic Life Kindled with Love at the Feet of Christ—Book 3* (Old Cairo, Egypt: The Convent of the Great Martyr St. Philopater Mercurius "Abi Seifein" for nuns, 2010), 78–79. Used with permission, thanks to His Eminence Metropolitan Youssef.

26. The convent of the great martyr St. Philopater Mercurius, *Tamav Erene and Glorious Horizons in Monastic Life, Part II* (Old Cairo, Egypt: The Convent of the Great Martyr St. Philopater Mercurius "Abi Seifein" for nuns, 2009), 52. Used with permission, thanks to His Eminence Metropolitan Youssef.

27. Fr. Seraphim Rose, *The Soul After Death* (Platina, CA: St. Herman of Alaska Brotherhood, 2009), 178–179 (quoting First Conference, ch. 14, in *Works of St. John Cassian the Roman*, Bishop Peter, trans., Moscow, 1892, 178–179).

CHAPTER 3. CROSSING OVER

1. Kyriacos C. Markides, *The Mountain of Silence* (New York, NY: Doubleday, 2001), 110.

2. Bercot, *DECB*, 17 (quoting *Shepherd of Hermas* 2.6.2 [ANF 2:24]).

3. Ambrose *Concerning Widows* 9.52 (NPNF[2] 10:400).

4. Bercot, *DECB*, 17 (quoting Origen *De Principiis* [*On First Principles*] 2.10.7 [ANF 4:296]).
5. Gregory of Nyssa *The Life of Moses* 2. In William A. Jurgens, *The Faith of the Early Fathers* 2 (Collegeville, MN: The Liturgical Press, 1979), 45.
6. Coptic Orthodox Church of Saint Mark, *The Holy Pascha According to the Rites of the Coptic Orthodox Church* (Jersey City, NJ: Coptic Orthodox Church of Saint Mark, 2008), 57–58.
7. The convent of the great martyr St. Philopater Mercurius, *Tamav Erene: The Jewel of Heaven and the Beacon of Monasticism* (Old Cairo, Egypt: The Convent of the Great Martyr St. Philopater Mercurius Abi Seifein, 2007), 79–80. Used with permission, thanks to His Eminence Metropolitan Youssef.
8. *Pope Kyrollos the Sixth—A Melody from Heaven* (Scarborough, Ontario: Mina Printing, 2001), 16.
9. Fr. Markos Hanna, *The Coptic Offices for the Coptic Orthodox Church, Part IV: Funeral Services* (Los Angeles, CA: St. Mark Coptic Orthodox Church, 1995), 33.
10. Ibid., 52.
11. Synaxarion is the more appropriate manner to align with the way this word is spelled in Greek (Συναξάριον). The spelling derived from Latin is Synaxarium. For the main text in this book, the former manner of spelling is used.
12. Entry for the 26th day of the Coptic month of Hatour (also spelled Hathor). In *Coptic Synaxarium* 1 (Chicago, IL: St. George Coptic Orthodox Church, 1987), 112; henceforth cited as *Coptic Synaxarium* (future references will include the Coptic day and month in parenthesis, and a volume number preceding the page; for example—*Coptic Synaxarium* (26th of Hatour), 1:112.
13. Ibid., (2nd of Misra), 4:459. Also see *Sayings of the Desert Fathers: The Alphabetical Collection*, Benidicta Ward, trans. (Trappist, Kentucky: Cistercian Publications, 2006), 93–94.
14. Ward, ibid., 94.
15. *Coptic Synaxarium* (22nd of Tubah), 2:195. "Place of rest" was substituted for "perpetual rest" in accordance with René Basset's *Le Synaxaire Arabe Jacobite* in *Patrologia Orientalis* 11 (Paris, France: Paris Firmin-Didot, 1915), 666.
16. Ibid., (20th of Babah), 1:59.
17. Bishop Ignatius Brianchaninov, *Collected Works* 3, Tuzov, ed. (St. Petersburg,

Russia: [publisher unknown] 1883), 107–108. Taken from Fr. Seraphim Rose, *The Soul After Death* (Platina, CA: St. Herman of Alaska Brotherhood, 2009), 168.

18. *On Wealth and Poverty*, Catharine Roth, trans. (Crestwood, NY: St. Vladimir's Seminary Press, 1999), 44.

CHAPTER 4. THE TERRIFYING ORDEAL

1. We know from Scripture that the devil can change his form, even to appear as an angel of light (2 Cor 11:14). Likewise, St. Athanasius, who wrote extensively about the devil in his *Life of Antony*, explains: "Again they are treacherous, and are ready to change themselves into all forms and assume all appearances." Athanasius *Life of Antony* 25 (NPNF² 4:203).

2. Fr. Markos Hanna, *The Coptic Offices for the Coptic Orthodox Church, Part IV: Funeral Services* (Los Angeles, CA: St. Mark Coptic Orthodox Church, 1995), 52.

3. Canticle 6. In Fr. Seraphim Rose, *The Soul After Death* (Platina, CA: St. Herman of Alaska Brotherhood, 2009), 186.

4. Ibid.

5. St. Cyprian of Carthage: "The devil bore impatiently the fact that man was made in the image of God; and that is why he was the first to perish and the first to bring others to perdition. Adam, contrary to the heavenly command, was impatient in regard to the deadly food, and fell into death; nor did he preserve, under the guardianship of patience, the grace received from God." Cyprian of Carthage *The Advantage of Patience* 19. In William A. Jurgens, *The Faith of the Early Fathers* 1 (Collegeville, MN: The Liturgical Press, 1978), 225. St. Augustine of Hippo: "Some say the devil fell from his place on high because he was envious of man, who was made in the image of God. Certainly, however, envy does not precede pride, but follows it; for envy is not the cause of one's being proud, but pride is the cause of one's being envious." Augustine *On the Literal Interpretation of Genesis* 11.14.18. In William A. Jurgens, *The Faith of the Early Fathers* 3 (Collegeville, MN: The Liturgical Press, 1979), 87.

6. The archangel who now has charge over the angels is regarded to be Archangel Michael, who will fight against the former archangel Satan and his fallen angels: "And war broke in heaven: Michael and his angels fought with the dragon; and the dragon and his angels fought" (Rev 12:7). Satan

(considered to be the shortened or alternate version of the word Sataniel, meaning enemy of God) is understood by some to have been a rank of the cherubim: "It seems that Satan, called Sataniel, was an archangel, one of the cherubim. The rank of cherubim, as we pray in the Divine Liturgy, was a high position of the angels whose service was to the throne of God." H.G. Bishop Youannis, *Heaven: An Orthodox Christian Perspective* (Los Angeles, CA: Saint Paul Brotherhood, 2007); compare Ezek 28:14.

7. In the Septuagint one may also find this term used in Job 40:20 and 41:32 (or 41:24, depending on the numbering scheme).

8. Oskar Seyffert, *A Dictionary of Classical Antiquities: Mythology, Religion, Literature and Art* (London, ENG: Swan Sonnenschein and Co.; New York, NY: Macmillan and Co., 1895), 612–613.

9. Ibid., 264, 266.

10. This belief is founded on several Scriptural passages as well as writings of early Christians. For example, Hippolytus of Rome writes: "Whomsoever, therefore, Satan bound in chains, these did the Lord on His coming loose from the bonds of death, having bound our strong adversary and delivered humanity." *Fragments from Commentaries* 2.18 (ANF 5:181). St. Athanasius writes, "And he was bound by the Lord as a sparrow, that we should mock him. And with him are placed the demons his fellows, like serpents and scorpions to be trodden underfoot by us Christians." Athanasius *Life of Antony* 24 (NPNF² 4:203). Cf. Athanasius *On the Incarnation* 25.5 (NPNF² 4:50—"The Lord came to cast down the devil" by means of "the cross"). See also Heb 2:14; Col 2:15; Rev 20:3; Jn 12:31, 32; 1 Jn 3:8; Mt 12:28, 29.

11. Jerome *Letters* 23 (NPNF² 6:41).

12. Bercot, *DECB*, 246 (quoting Hippolytus of Rome *The Refutation of All Heresies* 30 [ANF 5:153]).

13. Bercot, *DECB*, 594 (quoting Origen *De Principiis* [*On First Principles*] 1.5.5 [ANF 4:259]).

14. Ibid. Note that the word "Satan" is derived from the Hebrew word for "apostate." Jeffrey Burton Russell, *Satan: The Early Christian Tradition* (New York, NY: Cornell University Press, 1981), 66.

15. Cyprian of Carthage *Treatise X: On Jealousy and Envy* 4 (ANF 5:492).

16. Bercot, *DECB*, 243 (quoting Irenaeus *Against Heresies* 3.23.3 [ANF 1:456]). Yet, while Irenaeus says the *original intent* of God was to prepare eternal fire for Satan and those angels who would follow him, he still regards the purpose for God's preparation of eternal fire to have included the punishment of sinners: "That eternal fire is prepared for sinners, both the

Lord has plainly declared, and the rest of the Scriptures demonstrate. And that God foreknew this would happen, the Scriptures do in like manner demonstrate, since He prepared eternal fire from the beginning for those who were [afterwards] to transgress [His commandments]." *Against Heresies* 2.28.7 (ANF 1:401).

17. Gregory of Nyssa *On the Baptism of Christ* (NPNF[2] 5:524).
18. Some regard this Hermas to be the one mentioned in the Bible (Rom 6:14), while others consider him to be an early Christian who wrote what has been titled "Shepherd of Hermas" some time in the first or second century.
19. *Shepherd of Hermas* 2.6.2 (ANF 2:24).
20. Ibid.
21. Justin Martyr *Dialogue with Trypho* 105 (ANF 1:252).
22. *On Wealth and Poverty*, Catharine Roth, trans. (Crestwood, NY: St. Vladimir's Seminary Press, 1999), 44.
23. Athanasius, *St. Athanasius: The Life of St. Antony*, Walter Burghardt and Robert Meyer, trans. (New York, NY: The Newman Press, 1950), 74–75. (Note that the name Antony was substituted with Anthony.)
24. Ibid., 75–76.
25. *Coptic Synaxarium* (27th of Baramhat), 3:277–280.
26. St. Adamnan, *Life of St. Columba,* Wentworth Huyshe, trans. (London, ENG: George Routledge & Sons, Ltd., 1939), 207.
27. *Lives of Saints* (April 5), Demetrius of Rostov ed. (Moscow, Russia: Synodal Printshop, 1902). In Fr. Seraphim Rose, *The Soul After Death* (Platina, CA: St. Herman of Alaska Brotherhood, 2009), 134.
28. *The Letters of Saint Boniface,* Ephraim Emerton, trans. (New York, NY: Farrar, Strauss and Giroux, 1973), 25–27.
29. *Ladder of Divine Ascent*, Archimandrite Lazarus Moore, trans. (Willits, CA: Eastern Orthodox Books, 1977), 120–121.
30. *Sayings of the Desert Fathers: The Alphabetical Collection*, Benedicta Ward, trans. (Trappist, KY: Cistercian Publications, 2006), 104.
31. Archimandrite Tikhon, *Everyday Saints and Other Stories* (Moscow, Russia: Pokrov Publications, 2012), 271–272.
32. Justin Martyr *First Apology* 12 (ANF 1:166).
33. Transcribed from *The Oprah Winfrey Show* which headlined a story titled "The woman without a face" (originally aired May 25, 2006).

34. Bercot, *DECB*, 195–196 (quoting Hippolytus of Rome *Against Plato, on the Cause of the Universe* 1 [ANF 5:222]).
35. *On Wealth and Poverty*, Catharine Roth, trans. (Crestwood, NY: St. Vladimir's Seminary Press, 1999), 43–44.
36. Fr. Seraphim Rose, *The Soul After Death* (Platina, CA: St. Herman of Alaska Brotherhood, 2009), 73.
37. Basil the Great, *Exegetic Homilies*, Agnes Clare Way, trans. (Washington, DC: CUA Press, 1963), 167–168.
38. *Sayings of the Desert Fathers: The Alphabetical Collection*, Benedicta Ward, trans. (Trappist, KY: Cistercian Publications, 2006), 81–82.

CHAPTER 5. HADES

1. Bercot, *DECB*, 196 (quoting Hippolytus of Rome *Against Plato, on the Cause of the Universe* 2 [ANF 5:222]).
2. *Coptic Synaxarium* (14th of Bashans), 3:345.
3. Justin Martyr *First Apology* 20 (ANF 1:170).
4. Ibid., 242.
5. Ignatius of Antioch *Letter to the Ephesians* 16.1. In William A. Jurgens, *The Faith of the Early Fathers* 1 (Collegeville, MN: The Liturgical Press, 1979), 18.
6. Justin Martyr *First Apology* 12.21, 52. Ibid., 51.
7. Irenaeus *Against Heresies* 1.10.1. Ibid., 84.
8. Cyprian of Carthage *Treatises of Cyprian* 5.24 (ANF 5.464).
9. Basil the Great *Rules Briefly Treated* 267. In William A. Jurgens, *The Faith of the Early Fathers* 2 (Collegeville, MN: The Liturgical Press, 1979), 26.
10. Irenaeus *Against Heresies* 4.39.4 (ANF 1:523).
11. Bercot, *DECB*, 249 (quoting Cyprian of Carthage *The Epistles of Cyprian* 55.10 [ANF 5.350]).
12. John Chrysostom *Homilies on First Corinthians* 9.1–2 (NPNF[1] 12:49).
13. *On Wealth and Poverty*, Catharine Roth, trans. (Crestwood, NY: St. Vladimir's Seminary Press, 1999), 87–88.
14. Ibid., 88.

15. Ibid., 95–96.

16. Bercot, *DECB*, 243 (quoting Theophilus of Antioch *Letter to Autolycus* 14 [ANF 2:93]).

17. Archbishop Hilarion Alfeyev, *The Spiritual World of Isaac the Syrian* (Collegeville, MN: Cistercian Publications, 2009). Also see *The Ascetical Homilies of St. Isaac the Syrian*, Dana Miller, trans. (Boston, MA: Holy Transfiguration Monastery, 1984), 56–57.

18. Bercot, *DECB*, 196 (quoting Victorinus of Syria *Commentary on the Apocalypse* 6.9 [ANF 7:351]).

19. *On Wealth and Poverty*, Catharine Roth, trans. (Crestwood, NY: St. Vladimir's Seminary Press, 1999), 45.

20. Cyprian of Carthage *To Demetrian* 24–25. In William A. Jurgens, *The Faith of the Early Fathers* 1 (Collegeville, MN: The Liturgical Press, 1979), 223.

21. Basil the Great *Oration on the Wealthy* 7.8. In William A. Jurgens, *The Faith of the Early Fathers* 2 (Collegeville, MN: The Liturgical Press, 1979), 23.

22. Gregory Nazianzen *Oration on the Destruction of the Crops by Hail after a Prolonged Drought and a Deadly Cattle Plague* 16.7. Ibid., 28.

23. Cyril of Jerusalem *Catechetical Lectures* 23. *Mystagogic* 5.9–10. In William A. Jurgens, *The Faith of the Early Fathers* 1 (Collegeville, MN: The Liturgical Press, 1979), 363.

24. Epiphanius Salamis *Against All Heresies* 75.8. In William A. Jurgens, *The Faith of the Early Fathers* 2 (Collegeville, MN: The Liturgical Press, 1979), 76.

25. H.H. Pope Shenouda III, *Many Years with the People's Questions, Part IV* (El Kawmia, Cairo, Egypt: Dar El Tebaa, 1993), 32–35. Pope Shenouda also indicates that the Church does not pray for those who died as a result of committing certain sins, such as suicide.

26. Fr. Seraphim Rose, *The Soul After Death* (Platina, CA: St. Herman of Alaska Brotherhood, 2009), 200.

27. *Sayings of the Desert Fathers: The Alphabetical Collection*, Benedicta Ward, trans. (London, ENG: A.R. Mowbray & Co., 1975), 115–116. Note that some academic sources challenge the historicity and veracity of this account.

28. *On Wealth and Poverty*, Catharine Roth, trans. (Crestwood, NY: St. Vladimir's Seminary Press, 1999), 14. Catherine references an article by Metropolitan Kallistos Ware, where he points out that many Orthodox Christians hold on to the hope that release from Hades may be possible;

nonetheless, implicit in his article is his belief that the majority Orthodox view is that praying for the departed is "not for the actual release of the dead from hell, but only for a diminution of their suffering," as he indicates is made clear in the Eastern Orthodox "Vespers of Kneeling prayer" on the evening of the Sunday of Pentecost. "'One Body in Christ': Death and the Communion of Saints," *Sobornost/ECR* 3.2 (1981): 190.

29. This comment was derived from a conversation I had with Abba Youssef as we read through this book together.

30. Epiphanius of Salamis *Against All Heresies* 75.8. In William A. Jurgens, *The Faith of the Early Fathers* 2 (Collegeville, MN: The Liturgical Press, 1979), 76. In this excerpt, Bishop Epiphanius indicates that one aim of prayers commemorating saints is to distinguish between the high regard deservedly given to the righteous and the exalted reverence due only to God: "We make commemoration of the just and of sinners: of sinners, begging God's mercy for them; of the just and the fathers and patriarchs and prophets and apostles and evangelists and martyrs and confessors, and of bishops and solitaries, and of the whole list of them, so that we may set the Lord Jesus Christ apart from the ranks of men because of the honor due Him, and give reverence to Him, while keeping in mind that the Lord is not to be equated with any man, even if that man live in a justice that is boundless and limitless."

31. The convent of the great martyr St. Philopater Mercurius, *Tamav Erene: A Monastic Life Kindled with Love at the Feet of Christ—Book 3* (Old Cairo, Egypt: The Convent of the Great Martyr St. Philopater Mercurius "Abi Seifein" for nuns, 2010), 54.

32. "'One Body in Christ': Death and the Communion of Saints," *Sobornost/ECR* 3.2 (1981): 189.

33. Ibid., 190.

34. John Chrysostom *Homilies on Romans* 31.3–4 (NPNF[1] 11:551).

35. In all of the verses in this paragraph, "hell" has been translated Hades, in accordance with the Septuagint.

36. Everyone who died prior to Jesus Christ's loving and redemptive act on the cross was not allowed to enter into heaven, including some of the most favored of God, such as Abraham, Moses, and King David, because "death reigned" (Rom 5:12) over all mankind after the fall of man caused by the sin of Adam, precipitated by the persuasion of Eve. The punishment for this sin was set out in no uncertain terms to Adam and Eve: "Of the tree of the knowledge of good and evil you shall not eat, for in the day that you eat of it you shall surely die" (Gen 2:17). The term "surely" exemplifies the

notion that the death spoken of here meant more than just physical death, but also no access to eternal life in heaven and a condemnation upon all humanity to live eternally away from God after death in Hades, a point with which the earliest Christians are in agreement, as illustrated by the remarks of Pope Alexander of Alexandria, Egypt (c. AD 324): "When man afterwards had inclined to death, because of the fall, it was necessary that man's form be recreated anew to salvation by the same Maker. For the form [i.e., the body] lay rotting in the ground. However, that inspiration [i.e., the spirit] that had been as the breath of life—it was detained separately from the body in a dark place that is called Hades. So there was a separation of the soul [i.e., spirit] from the body . . . banished to Hades while the body was returned back to dust." *Epistles on the Arian Heresy* 3.3 (ANF 6:300). The Coptic Church also reflects these beliefs during worship services in a variety of places, such as the Ninth Hour Exposition of Great Friday: "Rejoice Today, all you righteous, prophets, and patriarchs! The first man. . . . God is the Word, in its perfection, and went to Hades by the soul which He took from Adam's nature and made it one with Himself. He lifted with Him the souls that were in captivity according to His great mercy." See also H.H. Pope Shenouda III, *Many Years with the People's Questions*, Part *II* (El Kawmia, Cairo, Egypt: Dar El Tebaa, 1993), 155–56; Eusebius of Caesarea *Proof of the Gospel* 4.12; Basil the Great *Psalms* 49.14; Clement of Alexandria *Stromata* 6.6; Hilary of Poitiers *On the Trinity* 10.34, *On the Councils* 85, *On Psalm 53* 14; Cyril of Jerusalem *Catechetical Lectures* 4.11, 14.18–19.

37. Bercot, *DECB*, 192 (quoting Irenaeus *Against Heresies* 5.31.2 [ANF 1:560]).

38. Bishop Alexander Mileant, *Life After Death* (pamphlet, Los Angeles, CA: Holy Protection Russian Orthodox Church, 1999).

39. H.G. Bishop Youannis, *Heaven: An Orthodox Christian Perspective* (Los Angeles, CA: Saint Paul Brotherhood, 2007).

40. Maurice Rawlings, *Beyond Death's Door* (Nashville, TN: Thomas Nelson, Inc., 1978), 24–25.

41. Ibid., 65.

42. Ibid., 63–64.

43. Ibid., 103–110.

44. Gregory the Great *Dialogues* 4.37. In *The Fathers of the Church: A New Translation* 39, Odo John Zimmerman, trans. (Washington, DC: CUA Press, 2000), 237.

45. Ibid.

46. John Chrysostom *Homily 53 on St. Matthew* (NPNF[1] 10:331–332).

47. H.G. Bishop Youannis, *Heaven: An Orthodox Christian Perspective* (Los Angeles, CA: Saint Paul Brotherhood, 2007). (Note that the name Antony was substituted with Anthony.)

48. Pope Kyrollos VI Sons, *St. Mary's Modern Miracles* (Maryut, Egypt: St. Mena Monastery, 2003), 9–10.

49. See Appendix C for an explanation.

50. Translated and transcribed from an audio recording in my possession of Mother Erene giving a talk to a Coptic congregation in Boston, Massachusetts about various miracles. Exact date of recording unknown.

51. Fr. Seraphim Rose, *The Soul After Death* (Platina, CA: St. Herman of Alaska Brotherhood, 2009), 147–148.

52. Archbishop Hilarion Alfeyev, *The Spiritual World of Isaac the Syrian* (Collegeville, MN: Cistercian Publications, 2009). Also see *The Ascetical Homilies of St. Isaac the Syrian*, Dana Miller, trans. (Boston, MA: Holy Transfiguration Monastery, 1984), 141.

53. Hippolytus of Rome *Against Plato, on the Cause of the Universe* 1, 3 (ANF 5:222–223).

54. Bercot, *DECB*, 246 (quoting Origen *De Principiis* [*On First Principles*] 2.10.4 [ANF 4:294]).

55. Note: in the preceding two verses, "hell" has been translated Hades, in accordance with the Septuagint.

56. Basil the Great *Rules Briefly Treated* 267. In William A. Jurgens, *The Faith of the Early Fathers* 2 (Collegeville, MN: The Liturgical Press, 1979), 25.

57. Archbishop Hilarion Alfeyev, *The Spiritual World of Isaac the Syrian* (Collegeville, MN: Cistercian Publications, 2009). Also see *The Ascetical Homilies of St. Isaac the Syrian*, Dana Miller, trans. (Boston, MA: Holy Transfiguration Monastery, 1984), 56.

58. Bercot, *DECB*, 196 (quoting Origen *De Principiis* [*On First Principles*] 1.6.2 [ANF 4:261]).

59. *On Wealth and Poverty*, Catharine Roth, trans. (Crestwood, NY: St. Vladimir's Seminary Press, 1999), 87.

60. Aphraates the Persian *Treatises* 22.22. In William A. Jurgens, *The Faith of the Early Fathers* 1 (Collegeville, MN: The Liturgical Press, 1979), 305.

61. *Sayings of the Desert Fathers: The Alphabetical Collection*, Benedicta Ward, trans. (London, ENG: A.R. Mowbray & Co., 1975), 115–116.

62. Bercot, *DECB*, 242 (quoting *Shepherd of Hermas* 3.9.18 [ANF 2:50]).
63. Alexander of Alexandria *Epistles on the Arian Heresy* 3.3 (ANF 6:300).
64. Bercot, *DECB*, 243 (quoting Irenaeus *Against Heresies* 4.39.4 [ANF 1:523]).
65. *Coptic Synaxarium* (11th of Baramhat), 3:254.
66. Justin Martyr *Dialogue with Trypho* 130 (ANF 1:264–265).
67. Fr. Markos Hanna, *The Coptic Offices for the Coptic Orthodox Church, Part IV: Funeral Services* (Los Angeles, CA: St. Mark Coptic Orthodox Church, 1995), 52.
68. Claimed (albeit disputed): Karl Baedeker, *Palestine and Syria, Handbook for Travelers* (London, ENG: Dulau and Co., 1876), 228; Sylvanus Cobb, *The New Testament of Our Lord and Savior Jesus Christ with Explanatory Notes and Practical Observations* (Boston, MA: [self-published by Cobb] 1864), 116.
69. Fr. Seraphim Rose, *The Soul After Death* (Platina, CA: St. Herman of Alaska Brotherhood, 2009), 146–147.
70. Bishop Alexander Mileant, *Life After Death* (pamphlet, Los Angeles, CA: Holy Protection Russian Orthodox Church, 1999). According to this source, this excerpt was originally taken from a publication titled *Eternal Mysteries from Beyond the Grave* by the St. Panteleimon Monastery on Mount Athos.

CHAPTER 6. PARADISE

1. St. John Chrysostom clearly understands this experience as being that of St. Paul and believed that the "Paradise" he was caught up into was the same place that Christ mentioned to the thief as being the place where he would go with Christ after death. John Chrysostom *Homily on 2 Corinthians* 26.1–2 (NPNF[1] 12:398–399).
2. Abba Youssef indicates that while this verse is traditionally regarded by the Coptic Church as being associated with Paradise, it is possible it actually refers to the glory prepared for us in heaven, which follows Paradise. Certainly the previous reference where St. Paul speaks about being caught up to Paradise and the inexpressible words he heard there relate to Paradise specifically.
3. Clement of Rome *The First Epistle of Clement to the Corinthians* 35 (ANF 1:14).
4. H.G. Bishop Youannis, *Heaven: An Orthodox Christian Perspective* (Los

Angeles, CA: Saint Paul Brotherhood, 2007).

5. Ibid.

6. Ibid.

7. The Coptic corpus includes twenty letters which in Arabic are attributed to St. Anthony the Great, evident from the notes in the Arabic manuscripts, as well as from a reference by the late medieval Coptic encyclopedist Abu-l-Barakat Ibn Kabar to a Coptic version of twenty letters by St. Anthony still extant in his lifetime. One of these additional letters is found in a quotation in the writings of St. Shenouda the Archimandrite. According to Greek and Syriac sources, however, only seven letters are attributed to St. Anthony the Great, but the others to Ammonas, his disciple. A Coptic version of all seven letters is attested by Jerome, who writes about seven letters translated from Coptic into Greek. Samuel Rubenson, *The Letters of St. Antony: Monasticism and the Making of a Saint* (London, ENG: A&C Black, 1995), 16.

8. According to this source, authorship is attributed to Anthony the Great, from his *Thirteenth Letter*, The convent of the great martyr St. Philopater Mercurius, *Tamav Erene and Glorious Horizons in Monastic Life, Part II* (Old Cairo, Egypt: The Convent of the Great Martyr St. Philopater Mercurius "Abi Seifein" for nuns, 2009), 61.

9. His Holiness Pope Shenouda III expresses how, when the Lord responded "in Paradise," He was correcting the theological error of the thief to his right who asked to be in His "kingdom," delineating a difference between Paradise and the kingdom of heaven, the former being the temporary abode of the righteous, and the latter serving as their eternal abode after the day of judgment. H.H. Pope Shenouda III, *The Seven Words of Our Lord on the Cross* (El Kawmia, Cairo: Dar El Tebaa, 1991), 32–33. Also note, although Holy Scripture does not provide the name of this thief, Holy Tradition identifies him as Demas (or Dismas). It is not mentioned in Holy Scripture which literal side, Christ's right or left, he was crucified, but Holy Tradition refers to him as the thief on the right, likely because of the symbolic meaning of "the right" being power, righteousness, strength, all which is pertinent to him in his confession of Christ.

10. H.G. Bishop Youannis, *Heaven: An Orthodox Christian Perspective* (Los Angeles, CA: Saint Paul Brotherhood, 2007).

11. H.H. Pope Shenouda III, *Many Years with the People's Questions, Part I* (El Kawmia, Cairo: Dar El Tebaa, 1993), 78–79.

12. Augustine *Tractates on the Gospel According to St. John* 49.10 (NPNF[1] 7:273–274).

13. Gregory of Nyssa *On the Baptism of Christ* (NPNF² 5:522–523).
14. This interpretation was derived from an exposition read as a part of the Coptic Pascha prayer rite, during the first hour of the eve of Wednesday.
15. Tertullian *On the Resurrection of the Flesh* 27 (NPNF² 3:565).
16. Ambrose *Concerning Repentance* 1.7 (NPNF² 10:334).
17. Cyril of Jerusalem *Procatechesis (Prologue to the Catechetical Lectures)* 4 (NPNF² 7:2).
18. John Chrysostom *Homily LXIX on the Gospel of St. Matthew* (NPNF¹ 10:423).
19. John Chrysostom *Homily on Eutropius, and the Vanity of Riches* 2.14 (NPNF¹ 9:262).
20. Ibid.
21. Augustine *Sermon XL about Matthew* 22.4–6 (NPNF¹ 6:393–394).
22. *Ancient Christian Texts: Greek Commentaries on Revelation (Oecumenius and Andrew of Caesarea)*, William C. Weinrich, trans., Thomas C. Oden, ed. (Downers Grove, IL: IVP Academic, 2011), 128.
23. This was translated and adapted from a video recording in my possession of an interview of Layla, conducted by the Coptic television station known as CTV, which aired on or around April 1, 2012.
24. Micaiah the prophet had a similar vision of God in heaven, surrounded by such angels and a multitude more: "I saw the Lord sitting on His throne, and all the host of heaven standing on His right hand and His left" (2 Chr 18:18).
25. Bercot, *DECB*, 195 (quoting Hippolytus of Rome *Against Plato, on the Cause of the Universe* 1 [ANF 5:221]).
26. *The Passion of The Holy Martyrs Perpetua and Felicitas* (ANF 3:703).
27. "The Meeting Between Mother Irini and the Families of the Choir in 1999 AD," *Abba Antony Magazine*, 16.12 (December 2006): 9. (Text slightly edited to improve readability.)
28. "The Man with Galibiya and Takia," *Abba Antony Magazine* 16.12 (December 2006): 9. (Text slightly edited to improve readability.)
29. Ibid.
30. Fr. Markos Hanna, *The Coptic Offices for the Coptic Orthodox Church, Part IV: Funeral Services* (Los Angeles, CA: St. Mark Coptic Orthodox Church, 1995), 33.
31. Ibid., 83.

32. This theme, that our actions should comport with our calling to be children of light, may be found in several verses, including the following: "Therefore take heed that the light which is in you is not darkness. If then your whole body is full of light, having no part dark, the whole body will be full of light, as when the bright shining of a lamp gives you light" (Lk 11:35–36). "The darkness is passing away, and the true light is already shining. He who says he is in the light, and hates his brother, is in darkness until now" (1 Jn 2:8–9). "Walk while you have the light, lest darkness overtake you; he who walks in darkness does not know where he is going. While you have the light, believe in the light, that you may become sons of light" (Jn 12:35–36).

33. Bercot, *DECB*, 195 (quoting Hippolytus of Rome *Against Plato, on the Cause of the Universe* 1 [ANF 5:221–222]).

34. Fr. Markos Hanna, *The Coptic Offices for the Coptic Orthodox Church, Part IV: Funeral Services* (Los Angeles, CA: St. Mark Coptic Orthodox Church, 1995), 83.

35. Ibid., 199.

36. The convent of the great martyr St. Philopater Mercurius, *Tamav Erene: The Jewel of Heaven and the Beacon of Monasticism* (Old Cairo, Egypt: The Convent of the Great Martyr St. Philopater Mercurius Abi Seifein, 2007), 89.

37. Story courtesy of Fr. Bishoy El-Antony. Used with permission.

CHAPTER 7. THE BEAUTY OF PARADISE

1. Irenaeus *Against Heresies* 1.19.2 (ANF 1:344).

2. Irenaeus *Against Heresies* 4.20.7 (ANF 1:489).

3. Father Tadros Malaty, *The Gospel According to St. John: Part One* (Alexandria, Egypt: St. George's Coptic Orthodox Church, 2003).

4. John Chrysostom *Homily XV on St. John* 1 (NPNF[1] 14:52).

5. Ibid., 1–2 (NPNF[1] 14:52).

6. Ibid., 2 (NPNF[1] 14:52).

7. Ibid. For more, see also John of Damascus *Exposition of the Orthodox Faith* 4.2 (NPNF[2] 9:74), and Hippolytus of Rome *On Daniel* 7:13 (ANF 5:189).

8. Theophilus of Antioch *Letter to Autolycus* 1.5, 7 (ANF 2:90–91).

9. Hilary of Poitiers *Commentaries on the Psalms: On Ps. 118 [119]*. In William

A. Jurgens, *The Faith of the Early Fathers* 1 (Collegeville, MN: The Liturgical Press, 1978), 386.

10. Cyprian of Carthage *Letter of Cyprian to the People of Thibar* 58[56].10. Ibid., 231.

11. Polycarp *The Epistle of Polycarp to the Philippians* 9 (ANF 1:35).

12. *Sayings of the Desert Fathers: The Alphabetical Collection*, Benidicta Ward, trans. (Trappist, KY: Cistercian Publications, 2006), 222–223.

13. This was translated, transcribed and adopted from an audio recording and also a video recording in my possession of two instances in which Mother Erene tells this same story. I was also assisted by the transcription of this account from the following source: "The Story of Repentance," *Abba Antony Magazine*, 17.5 (May 2007): 4, 6. Used with the much-appreciated permission of Fr. Anastasi St. Antony.

14. Nahed Mahmoud Metwalli, *Islam Encounters Christ: A Fanatical Muslim's Encounter with Christ in the Coptic Orthodox Church* (Edina, MN: Light & Life Publishing Company, 2002).

15. Fr. Seraphim Rose, *The Soul After Death* (Platina, CA: St. Herman of Alaska Brotherhood, 2009), 135–136, 144.

16. Ibid.

17. *The Letters of Saint Boniface,* Ephraim Emerton, trans. (New York, NY: Farrar, Strauss and Giroux, 1973), 28–29.

18. Gregory the Great *Dialogues* 4.16. In *The Fathers of the Church: A New Translation* 39, Odo John Zimmerman, trans. (Washington, DC: CUA Press, 2000), 209–210.

19. It appears that Mother Erene was speaking of herself, and that this was her experience. See The convent of the great martyr St. Philopater Mercurius, *Tamav Erene: A Monastic Life Kindled with Love at the Feet of Christ—Book 3* (Old Cairo, Egypt: The Convent of the Great Martyr St. Philopater Mercurius "Abi Seifein" for nuns, 2010), 46–50.

20. This story as written is derived from two sources. Primarily, the text here is taken from: "Our Mother Elyria," *Abba Antony Magazine* 17.2 (February 2007): 8. Used with the much-appreciated permission of Fr. Anastasi St. Antony. (Text edited to improve readability, and name spelling was changed.) Additional detail was derived from the following source and incorporated in part, with some minor revisions to maintain textual flow; this source also reveals that this nun was actually Mother Erene herself: The convent of the great martyr St. Philopater Mercurius, *Tamav Erene: A Monastic Life Kindled with Love at the Feet of Christ—Book 3* (Old Cairo, Egypt:

The Convent of the Great Martyr St. Philopater Mercurius "Abi Seifein" for nuns, 2010), 46–50.

21. Story courtesy of Fr. Bishoy El-Antony, as he told it to me himself. Used with permission.
22. Alexander I, archbishop of Alexandria *Epistles on the Arian Heresy and the Deposition of Arius* 6 (ANF 6:293).
23. Justin Martyr *Hortatory Address to the Greeks* 33 (ANF 1:287).
24. Augustine *Confessions* 11.13.15; 11.13.16; 11.14.17 (NPNF[1] 1:167–168).
25. Bercot, *DECB*, 246 (quoting Hippolytus of Rome *Against Plato, on the Cause of the Universe* 3 [ANF 5:223]).
26. Gregory Nazianzen *The Third Theological Oration on the Son* 3 (NPNF[2] 7:302).
27. "'One Body in Christ': Death and the Communion of Saints," *Sobornost/ ECR* 3.2 (1981): 182–183.
28. Coptic Orthodox Church Diocese of Qena, *Blessed Servant: Life & Miracles of the Thrice Blessed His Grace Late Bishop Makarios of Qena* (Qena, Egypt: Diocese of Qena, 2010), 62–63.
29. Bercot, *DECB*, 243 (quoting Irenaeus *Against Heresies* 4.28.2 [ANF 1:501]).
30. H.G. Bishop Youannis, *Heaven: An Orthodox Christian Perspective* (Los Angeles, CA: Saint Paul Brotherhood, 2007).
31. Bercot, *DECB*, 247 (quoting Origen *De Principiis* [*On First Principles*] 2.11.6–7 [ANF 4:299–300]).
32. Bercot, *DECB*, 249 (quoting Cyprian of Carthage *The Epistles of Cyprian* 55.10 [ANF 5.350]).
33. The convent of the great martyr St. Philopater Mercurius, *Tamav Erene: A Monastic Life Kindled with Love at the Feet of Christ—Book 3* (Old Cairo, Egypt: The Convent of the Great Martyr St. Philopater Mercurius "Abi Seifein" for nuns, 2010), 50–51, 54.
34. Ibid., 94–95.
35. It is quite possible that this story is actually the experience of Mother Erene as described previously. She may have told this on an occasion where she tried to mask her identity as the person who experienced this event, out of humility.
36. Coptic Orthodox Church Diocese of Qena, *Blessed Servant: Life & Miracles of the Thrice Blessed His Grace Late Bishop Makarios of Qena* (Qena, Egypt: Diocese of Qena, 2010), 62–63.

37. "The Reposed Anba Makarios," *Abba Antony Magazine* 17.3 (March 2007). Used with the much-appreciated permission of Fr. Anastasi St. Antony. (Note: the word "Anba" was replaced with "Abba.")

38. Origen *Homily 3 on Numbers*. In Thomas Scheck and Christopher Hall, *Ancient Christian Texts: Homilies on Numbers, Origen* (Downers Grove, IL: InterVarsity Press, 2009), 11.

39. Origen agrees with this understanding too, but further expounds upon this verse as just explained.

CHAPTER 8. VARYING DEGREES OF REWARD AND GLORY

1. Irenaeus *Against Heresies* 4.14.1 (ANF 1:478).
2. Ibid.
3. Augustine *Tractates on the Gospel According to St. John* 49.10 (NPNF[1] 7:273–274).
4. Aphraates the Persian *Treatises* 22.19. In William A. Jurgens, *The Faith of the Early Fathers* 1 (Collegeville, MN: The Liturgical Press, 1978), 305.
5. Jerome *Against Jovian* 2.32. In William A. Jurgens, *The Faith of the Early Fathers* 2 (Collegeville, MN: The Liturgical Press, 1979), 200.
6. Bercot, *DECB*, 242 (quoting *Fragments of Papias* 5 [ANF 1:154]).
7. A monastic discipline refers to the manner by which the spiritual lives of groups of monks or nuns are arranged. There are certain renowned monks whose rules are emulated, such as St. Pachomius, who established the first cenobitic or communal monastery.
8. When she saw St. Pachomius in Paradise, he told her that this monastic discipline was the safest way because it was moderate and "the middle way saves many." The convent of the great martyr St. Philopater Mercurius, *Tamav Erene: The Jewel of Heaven and the Beacon of Monasticism* (Old Cairo, Egypt: The Convent of the Great Martyr St. Philopater Mercurius Abi Seifein, 2007), 108–109. (Note: the word "Anba" was replaced with "Abba.")
9. Ibid., 53–54 (slight revisions made to improve readability).
10. Bercot, *DECB*, 245 (quoting Tertullian *Scorpiace* 6 [ANF 3.639]).
11. *Coptic Synaxarium* (20th of Babah), 1:59.
12. *On Wealth and Poverty*, Catharine Roth, trans. (Crestwood, NY: St. Vladimir's Seminary Press, 1999), 68.

13. Ibid., 73.
14. *Eusebius: The Church History*, Paul L. Maier, trans. (Grand Rapids, MI: Kregel Publications, 1999), 191–192 (see Book VI Chapter 5).
15. *Coptic Synaxarium* (23rd of Abib), 4:442.
16. Ibid., (24th of Baounah), 4:402.
17. Ibid., 4:402–403.
18. Ibid., (5th of Abib), 4:418.
19. Ibid., (13th of Baramhat), 3:257–258.
20. Present-day Wadi El Natrun, Egypt—also known as the Nitrian Desert or "Scetis" in Greek, and by a number of other names: Shiheet, Scete, Scythis, etc.
21. *Coptic Synaxarium* (26th of Tubah), 2:200.
22. Ibid., (15th of Hatour), 1:98–99.
23. Cyprian of Carthage *Treatises of Cyprian* 10.16. Adapted from two sources. Paul Middleton, *Martyrdom: A Guide for the Perplexed* (London, ENG: T&T Clark International, 2011), 85; (ANF 5:495).
24. *Coptic Synaxarium* (26th of Baramhat), 3:274–275.
25. Ibid., (19th of Abib), 433–436.
26. Ibid., (20th of Babah), 57.
27. Coptic Orthodox Church Diocese of Qena, *Blessed Servant: Life & Miracles of the Thrice Blessed His Grace Late Bishop Makarios of Qena* (Qena, Egypt: Diocese of Qena, 2010), 64–65.
28. The convent of the great martyr St. Philopater Mercurius, *Tamav Erene and Glorious Horizons in Monastic Life, Part II* (Old Cairo, Egypt: The Convent of the Great Martyr St. Philopater Mercurius "Abi Seifein" for nuns, 2009), 114–115.
29. Bercot, *DECB*, 245 (quoting Hippolytus of Rome *Against Plato, on the Cause of the Universe* 3 [ANF 5:223]).
30. H.G. Bishop Youannis, *Heaven: An Orthodox Christian Perspective* (Los Angeles, CA: Saint Paul Brotherhood, 2007).
31. "Our Mother Elyria," *Abba Antony Magazine* 17.2 (February 2007): 8.
32. Translated and transcribed from a video recording in my possession of Mother Erene telling this story to teach people about the benefits and glory that people receive for performing "works of mercy."

33. Please note that as Mother Erene retold the story, she was smiling and laughing, so that the tone she used was comical, not cynical, as it may appear was the case from the translation above. Those who are in Paradise are full of joy, warmth, and peace.
34. Clement of Alexandria *The Stromata* or *Miscellanies* 6.14 (ANF 2:506).
35. *Coptic Synaxarium* (13th of Amshir), 2:222.
36. Ibid., (23rd of Amshir), 2:232–233.
37. Ibid., 2:233.
38. Pope Kyrollos VI Sons, *St. Mary's Modern Miracles* (Maryut, Egypt: St. Mena Monastery, 2003), 10.
39. Fr. Seraphim Rose, *The Soul After Death* (Platina, CA: St. Herman of Alaska Brotherhood, 2009), 134.
40. St. Gregory the Theologian mentions this notion that we will reign with Christ (*Oration* 16.11), a sentiment which is echoed by St. John Chrysostom (*Homily XIV on Romans*), Andrew of Caesarea (Cappadocia) of the sixth century (*Commentary on the Apocalypse* 3.21–22), and also Father Tadros Malaty in *The Book of Revelation* (Alexandria, Egypt: St. George's Coptic Orthodox Church, 1996), 56.
41. The convent of the great martyr St. Philopater Mercurius, *Tamav Erene: The Jewel of Heaven and the Beacon of Monasticism* (Old Cairo, Egypt: The Convent of the Great Martyr St. Philopater Mercurius "Abi Seifein" for nuns, 2007), 113–114.
42. Ibid., 114.
43. Ibid.
44. Ibid., 127.
45. Athanasius *Life of Anthony*. In Paul Middleton, *Martyrdom: A Guide for the Perplexed* (London, ENG: T&T Clark International, 2011), 84–85.
46. John Chrysostom *Homilies on Hebrew* 11.6. Ibid.
47. Augustine *Sermon on Martyrdom*. Ibid.
48. Translated and transcribed from an audio recording in my possession of Mother Erene giving a talk while she was in Boston, Massachusetts to a Coptic congregation about various miracles. Exact date of recording unknown.
49. *On Wealth and Poverty*, Catharine Roth, trans. (Crestwood, NY: St. Vladimir's Seminary Press, 1999), 124.
50. Kyriacos Markides, *The Mountain of Silence* (New York, NY: Doubleday,

2001), 84–85.

51. *On Wealth and Poverty*, Catharine Roth, trans. (Crestwood, NY: St. Vladimir's Seminary Press, 1999), 66.

52. Ibid., 63.

53. Ibid., 69–70.

54. Most of the early Christians and Church Fathers I have surveyed who expounded on Isaiah Chapter 33 mostly reflect on this passage as referring to the first advent of Christ and/or being symbolic of the Church (e.g., Cyril of Alexandria *Commentary on Isaiah* 33.21-24; Gregory the Great *Morals on the Book of Job* 4.18.60; Clement of Alexandria *Christ the Educator* 1.12.100). However, Hippolytus of Rome allows for interpreting this passage as referring to Christ's second advent (cf. *On the Antichrist* 44), as does Venerable Bede (cf. *Homilies on the Gospels* 1.24), both of whom interpret Isaiah 33:17 ("Your eyes will see the King in His beauty") in this way; with this perspective, the previous and ensuing verses can therefore fairly be read to speak of God's judgment and the abode of the righteous in the afterlife.

55. *Book for Commemoration of the Living and the Dead*, Fr. Lawrence, trans. (Jordanville, NY: Holy Trinity Monastery, [date of publication unknown]), 77. The Coptic form of this prayer can be found in the prayers for the departed during the Divine Liturgy, where the clergy prays: "Graciously, O Lord, repose all their souls in the bosom of our holy fathers, Abraham, Isaac, and Jacob. Sustain them in a green pasture, by the water of rest in the Paradise of Joy, the place out of which grief, sorrow, and groaning have fled away in the light of your saints. *The Divine Liturgies of Saints Basil, Gregory, and Cyril* (Tallahassee, FL: St. Mary & St. George Coptic Orthodox Church, Coptic Orthodox Diocese of the Southern United States, 2001).

56. The convent of the great martyr St. Philopater Mercurius, *Tamav Erene and Glorious Horizons in Monastic Life, Part II* (Old Cairo, Egypt: The Convent of the Great Martyr St. Philopater Mercurius "Abi Seifein" for nuns, 2009), 97–98.

57. Gregory of Nyssa *On Infants' Early Deaths* (NPNF[2] 5:376).

58. Ibid., 378.

59. Ibid., 377.

60. Ibid., 376.

61. Athenagoras *On the Resurrection of the Dead* 14 (ANF 2:156).

62. The convent of the great martyr St. Philopater Mercurius, *Tamav Erene: A*

Monastic Life Kindled with Love at the Feet of Christ—Book 3 (Old Cairo, Egypt: The Convent of the Great Martyr St. Philopater Mercurius "Abi Seifein" for nuns, 2010), 44.

63. Ibid., 54–55.

CHAPTER 9. THE HIERARCHY OF GLORY IN PARADISE

1. *On Wealth and Poverty*, Catharine Roth, trans. (Crestwood, NY: St. Vladimir's Seminary Press, 1999), 119.

2. Ibid., 119–120.

3. Hilarion Alfeyev, *The Spiritual World of Isaac the Syrian* (Kalamazoo, MI: Cistercian Publications, 2009), 278; Also see *The Ascetical Homilies of St. Isaac the Syrian*, Dana Miller, trans. (Boston, MA: Holy Transfiguration Monastery, 1984) 56.

4. His place had a large space of green pasture. There was a structure with several rooms with a strong light radiating from each of them. He came out of one of the rooms dressed in a white tunic and his face was glowing brightly. He said that the reason he came to such a beautiful place is that he would forgive quickly and confessed and partook of communion weekly. He was always a very sympathetic person. The convent of the great martyr St. Philopater Mercurius, *Tamav Erene: A Monastic Life Kindled with Love at the Feet of Christ—Book 3* (Old Cairo, Egypt: The Convent of the Great Martyr St. Philopater Mercurius "Abi Seifein" for nuns, 2010), 78–79.

5. Ibid., 47.

6. Todd Burpo, *Heaven Is for Real* (Nashville, TN: Thomas Nelson, 2010).

7. Nahed Mahmoud Metwalli, *Islam Encounters Christ: A Fanatical Muslim's Encounter with Christ in the Coptic Orthodox Church* (Edina, MN: Light & Life Publishing Company, 2002).

8. In the month preceding the feast of the Nativity (Christmas) in which the Copts heighten their focus on St. Mary for her role as the Mother of God, there is a beautiful hymn known as "The Burning Bush," which includes the following refrain: "The burning bush seen by Moses, the prophet in the wilderness, the fire inside it was aflame, but never consumed or injured it. The same with the Theotokos Mary, carried the fire of the divinity, nine months in her holy body, without blemishing her virginity."

9. Cyril of Alexandria *Scholia on the Incarnation of the Only-Begotten*. In *A Library*

of Fathers of the Holy Catholic Church, Anterior to the Division of the East and West 47, E.B. Pusey, John Keble, and C. Marriott, eds. (London, ENG: Rivington, 1881), 194.

10. Francis Johnston, *When Millions Saw Mary* (Chulmleigh, Devon, ENG: Augustine Publishing Company, 1980), back cover. Much of the ensuing details regarding this miracle are derived from this source.

11. Ibid., 4.

12. Paul Perry, *Visions & Miracles* ([DVD], Vanguard Cinema, 2010).

13. This statement is extrapolated from the parable in which it can be understood that Christ speaks of His divine role exemplified in the person of the "landowner" (Mt 20:1).

CHAPTER 10. PARADISE AND THE GARDEN OF EDEN

1. "The term originated in Old Iranian languages, (e.g., Avestan *pairi-daeza*; from *pairi*, round, plus *diz*, form), in which it designated a park surrounded by a wall. This Iranian word entered Greek as paradeisos (park, pleasure grounds), then became the Latin *paradis(us)*, and the Old and Middle English *paradis*, or paradise." *Late Antiquity: A guide to the Postclassical World*, Glen Warren Bowersock, Peter Brown, and Oleg Grabar, eds. (Cambridge, MA: Harvard University Press, 1999), 635.

2. Paul Swarup, *The Self-Understanding of the Dead Sea Scrolls Community* (London, ENG: T&T Clark International, 2006), 185.

3. Irenaeus *Against Heresies* 2.30.8 (ANF 1:405–406); John Chrysostom *Homilies on Second Corinthians* 26.2 (NPNF[1] 12:399). St. Irenaeus also tells us that "men, if they do truly progress by faith towards better things, and receive the Spirit of God, and bring forth the fruit thereof, shall be spiritual, as being planted in the Paradise of God." Irenaeus *Against Heresies* 5.10.1. In Gerard Luttikhuizen, *Paradise Interpreted: Representations of Biblical Paradise in Judaism and Christianity* (Leiden, NL: Brill, 1999), 153–154.

4. Methodius *Symposium* (also known as the *Treatise on Chastity* or *Dialogue on Virginity*) 9.3. Ibid., 154.

5. Athanasius *Statement of Faith* 1 (NPNF[2] 4:84).

6. Gregory of Nyssa *On the Baptism of Christ* (NPNF[2] 5:524) (with minute revisions).

7. Cyril of Jerusalem *Catechetical Lecture* (also known as *Catechesis*) 19.9. In

Gerard Luttikhuizen, *Paradise Interpreted: Representations of Biblical Paradise in Judaism and Christianity* (Leiden, NL: Brill, 1999), 155.

8. Cyril of Jerusalem *Procatechesis* (also known as *Prologue to the Catechetical Lectures*) 15–16. Ibid., 154.

9. H.G. Bishop Youannis, *Heaven: An Orthodox Christian Perspective* (Los Angeles, CA: Saint Paul Brotherhood, 2007).

10. Ibid.

11. Theophilus of Antioch *Letter to Autolycus* 2.24 (ANF 2:103–104).

12. For example, many early Church Fathers, such as St. Augustine and St. John Chrysostom, were of the opinion that even the fiercest creatures were benign before the fall of Adam (John Chrysostom *Homilies on Genesis* 9.4; St. Augustine quoted and endorsed the same view, elaborating on it in his work *Against Julian* 5.25.) Before Adam's fall, the ground was welcoming and seemed self-sufficient, with God providing for its needs (Gen 2:15). Afterward, God pronounced as a punishment that the earth would be cursed (Gen 3:17–18). God eventually "drove out the man" and then "placed a cherubim at the east of the garden" (Gen 3:24). Thus, the status of earth's nature seems inextricably linked to the status of man. That mode of thought may help explain St. Paul's remarks in his Epistle to the Romans, where he says the creation of God awaits the redemption of man's nature (Rom 8:19–22).

13. Ignatius of Antioch (first century) writes in his epistle to the Magnesians that the Old Testament prophets waited for Christ so that He would come and raise them from the dead: "How shall we be able to live apart from Him, whose disciples the prophets themselves in the Spirit did wait for Him as their Teacher? And therefore He whom they rightly waited for, having come, raised them from the dead." *Epistle to the Magnesians* 9 (ANF 1:62).

CHAPTER 11. SECOND CHANCE

1. You can find his story in Chapters 5 and 7.

2. "The Story of Repentance," *Abba Antony Magazine* 17.5 (May 2007): 4, 6.

3. *Sayings of the Desert Fathers: The Alphabetical Collection*, Benedicta Ward, trans. (Trappist, KY: Cistercian Publications, 2006), 63–64.

4. Quoted from Good News Translation (Today's English Version, Second

Edition) Copyright © 1992 American Bible Society. All rights reserved.

5. "'One Body in Christ': Death and the Communion of Saints," *Sobornost/ECR* 3.2 (1981): 179.
6. Ibid., 180.
7. Ibid.
8. *Mystic Treatises by Isaac of Nineveh*, A.J. Wensinck, trans. (Amsterdam, Netherlands: Netherlands Academy of Arts and Sciences, 1923), 308–309.
9. Fr. Seraphim Rose, *The Soul After Death* (Platina, CA: St. Herman of Alaska Brotherhood, 2009), 171–172.
10. Ibid.
11. Bishop Ignatius Brianchaninov, *Collected Works* 3, Tuzov ed. (St. Petersburg, 1883), 129. In ibid., 171.
12. This is likely meant to refer to the basic meaning of this ancient word, as referring to a garden. So here, this sentence can be read to say: "There were many gardens."
13. *The Paradise of the Holy Fathers* 1, E.A. Wallis Budge, ed. (Putty, AU: St. Shenouda Monastery Press, 2009), 246–249.
14. *Orthodox Life* 26.4 (July–August 1976): 1–36. Typos and punctuation have been edited.
15. Ibid.
16. "The Reposed Anba Makarios," *Abba Antony Magazine* 17.3 (March 2007): 8.
17. The convent of the great martyr St. Philopater Mercurius, *Tamav Erene and Glorious Horizons in Monastic Life, Part II* (Old Cairo, Egypt: The Convent of the Great Martyr St. Philopater Mercurius Abi Seifein, 2009), 52–53. (Note: the name "Abu Sefein" was altered from its original spelling of "Abi Seifein" from the source text. Moreover, some capitalization and other minor adjustments have been made).
18. *On Wealth and Poverty*, Catharine Roth, trans. (Crestwood, NY: St. Vladimir's Seminary Press, 1999), 135.
19. Ibid., 45.
20. *To Demetrian* 25. In William A. Jurgens, *The Faith of the Early Fathers* 1 (Collegeville, MN: The Liturgical Press, 1978), 223.
21. Ibid., 96.
22. Story courtesy of Fr. Bishoy El-Antony, as he told it to me himself. Used

with permission.

23. Story courtesy of Fr. Bishoy El-Antony. Used with permission.

24. For more on how the early Church understood the concept of justification and how Christians needed to maintain a life of righteousness, see Clement of Rome *The First Epistle to the Corinthians* 32–33 (ANF 1:13).

25. Note: The translator of this passage here numbered this psalm according to the LXX. I have changed the psalm number to match the NKJV.

26. Athanasius *On the Incarnation* 26. In *On the Incarnation*, John Behr and Augustine Casiday, eds. (Yonkers, NY: St. Vladimir's Seminary Press, 2011), 105.

27. St. Nikodimus of the Holy Mountain and St. Makarios of Corinth, *The Philokalia: The Complete Text* 1, G.E.H. Palmer, Philip Sherrard, and Kallistos Ware, eds and trans. (New York, NY: Faber and Faber, Inc., 1979), 200–201.

28. Ibid., 124.

29. John Chrysostom *Homily 67 on John*. In Thomas Goggin, *The Fathers of the Church: Saint John Chrysostom, Commentary on Saint John the Apostle and Evangelist: Homilies 48–88, Volume 2* (Washington, DC: CUA Press, 2000), 226.

30. *The Way of a Pilgrim and The Pilgrim Continues His Way: A New Translation*, Helen Bacovcin, trans. (New York, NY: Doubleday Image Books, 1992), 28.

31. Bercot, *DECB*, 244 (quoting Clement of Alexandria *The Stromata* or *Miscellanies* 4.18 [ANF 2:430]).

32. His Holiness Pope Shenouda III, *Have You Seen The One I Love* (North Charleston, SC: BookSurge Publishing, 2008), 24–25.

33. Story taken from a sermon delivered October 16, 2012 by His Grace Bishop Bessada of Akhmim at St. Mary's Coptic Orthodox Church in Roswell, GA which I attended and recall to memory. The story, His Grace said, was derived from something he had recently read. The exact original source of the story is presently unknown.

34. Gregory the Great *Dialogues* 4.40. In *The Fathers of the Church: A New Translation* 39, Odo John Zimmerman, trans. (Washington, DC: CUA Press, 2000), 245-246.

35. *On Wealth and Poverty*, Catharine Roth, trans. (Crestwood, NY: St. Vladimir's Seminary Press, 1999), 139–140.

Notes

APPENDIX A: THE LIFE OF FATHER BOTROS AND HIS AFTERLIFE STORY

1. Anonymous Monk, *Biography of Love* (Cairo, Egypt: Dar Al-Quitar Lel Tabee-a, 2004).
2. Kamel also wrote this message on a piece of paper, and it was given to his family. In it he wrote: "The Lord Jesus Christ Himself, to Him be the glory, assured me about all of you, and I decided to stay in the monastery so He can take care of you."
3. Monks take the name of the monastery as their last name.
4. According to the ecclesiastical tradition of the Coptic Church, and in accordance with manuscripts from the 11th and 16th centuries in the library of the monastery of St. Macarius the Great, the crypts of St. John the Baptist and also Elisha the Prophet were discovered below the northern wall of the large church there during its restoration. A detailed account of this discovery and an assessment of the authenticity of the relics have been published by the monastery.
5. While there have been adjustments to this translation, it is very close to the original I worked on about 15 years ago.
6. Angels are neither male nor female, but are nonetheless consistently referred to in Scripture with male pronouns.
7. This word refers to the notion of subjugating the body and its passions and lusts by abstinence and ascetic discipline.
8. Father Botros later clarifies that we do not "pay the dues" of salvation ourselves; it is by the blood of Jesus that our debt to God is paid (Heb 10:19). To explain what he means here, he references Christ's parable found in Luke 19:11–24 of the nobleman (whose role symbolizes God's) who entrusted ten servants with money for the purpose of making profit (which symbolizes us being entrusted by God with our lives with which we are expected to make wise choices for God's glory). Father Botros points particularly to verse 15 where we find the nobleman, having returned from his journey, called his servants to him "that he might know how much every man had gained by trading." It is that moment that Father Botros is describing, where he is called upon by God to give an answer and an account for his life.
9. This can also be translated "evil company" (cf. 1 Cor 15:33).
10. This is reminiscent of the white robe worn by the newly baptized to signify their spiritual cleansing and new birth (1 Pet 3:21).

11. As will be understood later in this account, the companion in death is not a fellow monk or friend, but seems to be a random person who died and whose spirit he happened to have "encountered at the moment of crossing over."

12. This is the act of kneeling, bowing one's head to the ground, and rising again. It signifies repentance for one's sins and expresses submission to God, imploring God's favor and mercy.

13. Abba Youssef expresses his opinion regarding this notion that Father Botros says was expressed by the angel: "I have taken what no one else has taken and I have seen what has passed." His Grace is reluctant to read into this remark applying it broadly, signifying that no one else will die and, in their spirit, see the way people are reacting to their death. Maybe what was meant by the author was something more limited. Maybe he meant to say that few people are exposed to this.

14. The schema in the rite of Coptic monasticism usually refers to a leather belt given to a monk (or nun) after he (or she) has been initiated into the monastic order. There is also the "great schema" which is signified by another belt given to select monks or nuns who have reached an exemplary level of spirituality; in former times it was commonly given to bishops, abbots, and abbesses before being installed in their positions. Father Botros refers here to the former schema, also known as the "small schema." The belt given to him is worn around the waist under the outer garment, to remind the monk (or nun) of their symbolic death, because the leather is made of the flesh of an animal. Additionally, "the belt beneath the monastic garb is a symbol of purity and chastity. Its closeness to the body warns the monastic against bodily satisfactions (such as eating too much) and protects the bearer against attacks of the evil one who may 'arouse sexual desires and physical unrest.'" Pieternella van Doorn-Harder, *Contemporary Coptic Nuns* (Columbia, SC: University of South Carolina Press, 1995), 68, 100.

15. Abba Youssef points out, while "ordination" is the correct translation of the common phrase used to describe this rite in Arabic (*Taqs Risamet El Raheb*), yet it is not one of the mysteries of the Church and therefore it is not correct to call it an ordination; rather, it is better referred to as an appointment.

16. The head of the angels mentioned previously is here revealed to be his guardian angel.

17. See n. 8.

18. Father Botros here references 1 Corinthians 2:9, which reference I omitted

as it appears to have been made in error, because nothing in that verse seems even remotely applicable to this portion of his narrative.
19. Literally "tasted."
20. This is accomplished through the mystery of repentance and confession, as well as partaking of the body and blood of the Lord in the Eucharist.
21. This Arabic suffix designates the monastery where he lived as a monk. Thus, he is the monk named Botros of the St. Macarius Monastery.
22. This concluding statement appears to have been written by Father Botros himself, as evinced by the original document he left for us, and as made evident by analyzing the handwriting itself and its conformity with the rest of the document. This does not seem to be some later addition by some other writer. This serves as further evidence that he knew the day of his final departure from this life, as his life story indicates.

APPENDIX B: PHOTOS & IMAGES

1. Used with permission of Father Botros's sister, Samia.
2. Used with permission of Father Botros's family.
3. Ibid.
4. Ibid.
5. Photo provided by Rafik Abdelsayed. Used with permission.
6. Used with permission of Father Botros's family.
7. Ibid.
8. Ibid.
9. Photo by Wagih Rizk, photographer in Egypt.
10. Photo from the convent of Philopateer Mercurius in Old Cairo, Egypt. Used with permission, thanks to His Eminence Metropolitan Youssef.
11. Icon from the convent of Philopateer Mercurius in Old Cairo, Egypt.

APPENDIX C: GLOSSARY OF ORTHODOX CHRISTIAN PEOPLE AND
TERMINOLOGY USED IN THIS BOOK

1. Fr. Tadros Y. Malaty, *Dictionary of Church Terms* (Alexandria, Egypt: St. George's Coptic Orthodox Church, 1992), 6. *Encyclopedia of Ancient Christianity* 1, Angelo Berardino, ed. (Downers Grove, IL: IVP Academic, 2014), 4.

2. Pieternella Van Doorn-Harder, *Contemporary Coptic Nuns* (Columbia, SC: University of South Carolina Press, 1995), 61. *Encyclopedia of Ancient Christianity* 1, Angelo Berardino, ed. (Downers Grove, IL: IVP Academic, 2014), 4.

3. Richard J. Goodrich, *Contextualizing Cassian: Aristocrats, Asceticism, and Reformation in Fifth Century Gaul* (New York, NY: Oxford University Press, 2007), 136–137; John Cassian *Institutes* 2 (NPNF² 11:205–212).

4. *Coptic Synaxarium* (22nd of Tubah), 2:193–195.

5. There are variations in various early biblical manuscripts that indicate the number of the apostles mentioned in this verse to be either 70 or 72. This difference is inconsequential. Greek and Syriac manuscripts read "seventy," while the Vulgate prepared by St. Jerome in the fourth century translates this as "seventy-two." Origen enumerates 72, while Tertullian as well as St. Irenaeus speak of 70. Maybe the number is 72 but rounded off to show a perfect measure of seven multiplied tenfold, like the seventy elders accompanying Moses (Num 11). Even in that story, some think the number to be seventy-two instead (six from each tribe of Israel). John MacEvilly, *An exposition of the Gospel of St. Luke* (New York, NY: Benziger Brothers, 1898), 116; J. Elsley and James Slade, *Annotations on the Four Gospels and the Acts of the Apostles: Compiled and Abridged for the Use of Students* (London, ENG: C. & J. Rivington, 1824), 224; Louis Feldman and Gohei Hata, *Josephus, the Bible, and History* (Tokyo, JP: Yamamoto Shoten Publishing House, 1988), 22–24.

6. Ibid.

7. *Coptic Synaxarium* (7th of Bashans), 3:329–333. Also see *Coptic Synaxarium* (30th of Tute), 1:39. *Encyclopedia of Ancient Christianity* 1, Angelo Berardino, ed. (Downers Grove, IL: IVP Academic, 2014), 274–281.

8. Augustine, *The Confessions of St. Augustine*, Rosalie de Rosset, ed. (Chicago, IL: Moody Publishers, 2007); Henry Chadwick, *Augustine: A Very Short Introduction* (New York, NY: Oxford University Press, 2001), 1–2.

9. *The New Schaff-Herzog Encyclopedia of Religious Knowledge* 1, Samuel Macauley Jackson, ed. (New York, NY: Funk and Wagnalls Company, 1909), 1166–1167.

10. *Coptic Synaxarium* (8th of Abib), 4:420–421.

11. Augustine *On the Literal Interpretation of Genesis* 12.2 In *On the Literal Meaning of Genesis* 2, Johannes Quaster, Walter Burghardt, and Thomas Lawler, eds. (Mahwah, NJ: Paulist Press, 1982), 180–181.

12. Everett Ferguson, *Baptism in the Early Church: History, Theology, and Liturgy in the First Five Centuries* (Cambridge, UK: Wm. B. Eerdmans Publishing Co., 2009); Alfred Butler, *The Ancient Coptic Churches of Egypt* 2 (London, ENG: Clarendon Press, 1884).

13. Fr. Tadros Y. Malaty, *The School of Alexandria, Book One, Before Origen* (Jersey City, NJ: St. Mark's Coptic Orthodox Church, 1995); also see St. Jerome's *Lives of Illustrious Men*.

14. Bercot, *DECB*, xvi. Also, Jerome *Lives of Illustrious Men*; Irenaeus *Against Heresies* 3.3.3; Eusebius *Church History* 3.4.1. Matthew Bunson, *Our Sunday Visitor's Encyclopedia of Catholic History* (Huntington, IN: Our Sunday Visitor Publishing, 2004), 225.

15. John Dowling, *The History of Romanism: From the Earliest Corruptions of Christianity to the Present* (New York, NY: Edward Walker, 1845), 30–31; Marilyn Stokstad, *Medieval Art* (Boulder, CO: Westview Press, 2004), 11–12. Eusebius Pamphilus, *The Life of the Blessed Emperor Constantine* (Merchantville, NJ: Evolution Publishing). *Encyclopedia of Ancient Christianity* 1, Angelo Berardino, ed. (Downers Grove, IL: IVP Academic, 2014), 593–594.

16. Prior to the Arab invasion, nearly all Egyptians were Christian. While due to persecution and other forces many Egyptians left their faith and converted to Islam, hardly any Arab converted to Christianity. Amid all of that, throughout history the Orthodox Christian Egyptians maintained the biblically sound practice of restricting marriage only to other Orthodox Christians; thus, Coptic Christians remained the most ethnically linked to the Egyptians because they rarely added to their number any Arabs, and virtually always intermarried with other Egyptian Christians. In other words, of that core group of Egyptian Christians, people left, but hardly anyone was added to them. In this way, the Copts are most accurately distinguished from Arab Muslims as the truly indigenous people of Egypt. Although some Muslims refuse to abide by this notion, many agree with this sentiment, such as the published author Leila Muhammad who writes in her book *A Border Passage: From Cairo to America—A Woman's Journey* as follows: "Copts, for example, were not Arab. In fact they were Copts precisely because they had refused to convert to the religion of the Arabs and had refused, unlike us Muslims, to intermarry with Arabs. As a result Copts (members of the ancient Christian church of Egypt) were the only

truly indigenous inhabitants of Egypt and as such, in our home anyway and in the notion of Egypt with which I grew up, Copts had a very special place in the country."—(New York, NY: Penguin Books, 2000), 244.

17. Fr. Matta El-Maskeen (Matthew the Poor), *The Coptic Calendar* (Nitrian Desert, Egypt: The Monastery of St. Macarius, 1988), 3.

18. Ibid.

19. Bercot, *DECB*, xvi.

20. Otto Meinardus, *Two Thousand Years of Coptic Christianity* (Cairo, Egypt: The American University in Cairo Press, 2002), 78–79.

21. Bercot, *DECB*, xvii.

22. Ibid., 158 (quoting Ignatius *Epistle to the Trallians* 3 [ANF 1:67]).

23. H.G. Bishop Mettaous, *Sacramental Rites in the Coptic Orthodox Church* (El-Syrian Monastery, [year unclear—possibly 2000]).

24. *Coptic Synaxarium* (13th of Tubah and 12th of Bashans), 2:179–180 and 3:338–341.

25. Also see Ezekiel 28, which is often considered an allegorical reference to Satan.

26. *Coptic Synaxarium* (23rd of Baramoudah), 3:312–313; Edward Clapton, *The Life of St. George* (London, ENG: Swan Sonnenschein & Co. Limited, 1903). Alban Butler, *Butler's Lives of the Saints: Book 4 (April)* (Collegeville, MN: Liturgical Press, 1999), 162–163.

27. *Coptic Synaxarium* (23rd of Hatour), 1:106–107. *Encyclopedia of Ancient Christianity* 2, Angelo Berardino, ed. (Downers Grove, IL: IVP Academic, 2014), 187–189.

28. H.G. Bishop Youannis, *Heaven: An Orthodox Christian Perspective* (Los Angeles, CA: Saint Paul Brotherhood, 2007).

29. Bercot, *DECB*, xvii; *Coptic Synaxarium* (24th of Kiahk), 2:153.

30. Jerome *Against Vigilantius* 6 (NPNF[2] 6:419).

31. *On Wealth and Poverty*, Catharine Roth, trans. (Crestwood, NY: St. Vladimir's Seminary Press, 1999); *Coptic Synaxarium* (7th of Hatour), 1:101–102.

32. *Light from Light: Scientists and Theologians in Dialogue*, Gerald O'Collins, Mary Ann Meyers, eds. (Cambridge, UK: Wm. B. Eerdmans Publishing Co., 2012), 241–242.

33. *Coptic Synaxarium* (27th of Baramhat), 3:277–280.

34. "Pillars of Our Time—Ordinary People Serving in Extraordinary Ways:

Bishop Makarious," *Mighty Arrows Magazine* 10.2 (Spring 2011): 13.

35. *Coptic Synaxarium* (15th of Hatour), 1:98–100.

36. Otto Meinardus, *Two Thousand Years of Coptic Christianity* (Cairo, Egypt: The American University in Cairo Press, 2002), 157; also see *Coptic Synaxarium* (27th of Tubah), 2:159–160.

37. The convent of the great martyr St. Philopater Mercurius, *Tamav Erene: The Jewel of Heaven and the Beacon of Monasticism* (Old Cairo, Egypt: The Convent of the Great Martyr St. Philopater Mercurius "Abi Seifein" for nuns, 2007), 79–80.

38. Mehrdad Kia, *The Persian Empire: A Historical Encyclopedia* (Santa Barbara, CA: ABC-CLIO, 2016), 123.

39. Bercot, *DECB*, xix; Fr. Tadros Y. Malaty, *The School of Alexandria, Book Two: The Deans of the School of Alexandria, Origen* (Jersey City, NJ: St. Mark's Coptic Orthodox Church, 1995); Eusebius *Church History* 6.8.

40. Iris Habib el Masri, *The Story of the Copts: The True Story of Christianity in Egypt* 1 (Newberry Springs, CA: St. Anthony Coptic Orthodox Monastery of Southern California, [year unclear; possibly 1978]), 212–222; P. Rousseau, *Pachomius* (Berkeley, CA: University of California Press, 1985), 72; Susanna Elem, *Virgins of God* (Oxford, ENG: Oxford University Press, 2004).

41. *Coptic Synaxarium* (2nd of Amshir), 2:208–210. Peter Gorg, *The Desert Fathers: Saint Anthony and the Beginnings of Monasticism* (Collegeville, MN: Cistercian Publications, 2003), 77–78.

42. Bibliotheca Hagiographica Graeca (Greek collection of the lives of the saints); Michel Van Esbroeck, *The Coptic Encyclopedia* (New York, NY: Macmillan, 1991); Elizabeth Jeffreys, *The Chronicle of John Malalas* (Melbourne, AU: Australian Association for Byzantine Studies, 1986), 181–182; *Coptic Synaxarium* (7th of Bashans), 3:332; H.G. Bishop Youssef, "Abu-Seifein: Loyalty Perseveres," http://suscopts.org/resources/literature/298/abu-seifein-loyalty-perseveres/ (retrieved July 3, 2012).

43. Tertullian *Prescription Against Heretics* 32.

44. Stephen Davis, *The Popes of Egypt: The Early Coptic Papacy* (Cairo, Egypt: American University in Cairo Press, 2004), ix.

45. Gawdat Gabra, *The A to Z of the Coptic Church* (Plymouth, UK: Scarecrow Press, Inc., 2008), 229.

46. John Watson, *Among the Copts* (Portland, Oregon: Sussex Academic Press, 2002), 63–66.

47. Frank R. Trombley, *Hellenic Religion and Christianization* (Boston, MA: Brill Academic Publishers, Inc., 2001), 207; Gabra, *The A to Z of the Coptic Church* (Plymouth, UK: Scarecrow Press, Inc., 2008), 241; Otto Meinardus, *Two Thousand Years of Coptic Christianity* (Cairo, Egypt: The American University in Cairo Press, 2002), 229–230; *Coptic Synaxarium* (7th of Abib), 4:419.

48. Bercot, *DECB*; Christine Trevett, *Montanism: Gender, Authority, and the New Prophecy* (New York, NY: Cambridge University Press, 2002), 3–4; John Parker, *Tertullian: Apologetic and Practical Treatises* (London, ENG: J. G. F. and J. Rivington, 1842), i–ii.

49. Information derived from an interview conducted on January 12th, 2012 with my priest, Father Luke Wassif (of the St. Mary Coptic Orthodox Church in Roswell, GA) who was ordained by this bishop and served in Tanta, Egypt under the bishop's guidance before coming to the United States.

50. "His Grace Bishop Youssef," https://suscopts.org/diocese/bishop/ (retrieved July 3, 2012).]

Bibliography

Ancient Christian Texts: Greek Commentaries on Revelation (Oecumenius and Andrew of Caesarea). William C. Weinrich, trans., Thomas C. Oden, ed. Downers Grove, IL: IVP Academic, 2011.

Anonymous. "At Sunset." *Saint Antony Monastery Magazine* 19.6 (July 2009): 10.

———. *Biography of Love*. Cairo, Egypt: Dar Al-Quitar Lel Tabee-a, 2004.

———. "He Went Off," *Abba Antony Magazine* 9.19 (September 2009): 5, 6, 15.

———. "The Man with Galibiya and Takia." *Abba Antony Magazine*, 16.12 (December 2006): 9.

———. "The Meeting between Mother Irini and the Families of the Choir in 1999 AD." *Abba Antony Magazine* 16.12 (December 2006): 9.

———. "Our Mother Elyria." *Abba Antony Magazine* 17.2 (February 2007): 8.

———. "Pillars of Our Time—Ordinary People Serving in Extraordinary Ways: Bishop Makarious." *Mighty Arrows Magazine* 10.2 (Spring 2011): 13.

———. *Pope Kyrollos the Sixth—A Melody from Heaven*. Scarborough, Ontario: Mina Printing, 2001.

———. "The Reposed Anba Makarios." *Abba Antony Magazine* 17.3 (March 2007): 8.

———. "The Story of Repentance." *Abba Antony Magazine* 17.5 (May 2007): 4, 6.

Alexander servant of God. *Father Arseny, 1893-1973: priest, prisoner, spiritual father.* Crestwood, NY: St. Vladimir's Seminary Press, 1998.

Alfeyev, Archbishop Hilarion. *The Spiritual World of Isaac the Syrian*. Collegeville, MN: Cistercian Publications, 2009.

The Ante-Nicene Fathers: Translations of the Writings of the Fathers Down to A.D. 325. Alexander Roberts and James Donaldson, eds. Buffalo, NY: The Christian Literature Company, 1885-1896.

The Ascetical Homilies of St. Isaac the Syrian. Dana Miller, trans. Boston, MA: Holy Transfiguration Monastery, 1984.

Athanasius. *St. Athanasius: The Life of St. Antony*. Walter Burghardt and Robert Meyer, trans. New York, NY: The Newman Press, 1950.

Augustine. *The Confessions of St. Augustine*. Rosalie de Rosset, ed. Chicago, IL: Moody Publishers, 2007.

Baedeker, Karl. *Palestine and Syria, Handbook for Travellers*. London, ENG: Dulau and Co., 1876.

Basset, René. *Le Synaxaire Arabe Jacobite* in *Patrologia Orientalis* 11. Paris, France: Paris Firmin-Didot, 1915.

Bercot, David. *Dictionary of Early Christian Beliefs*. Peabody, MA: Hendrickson Publishers, Inc., 2010.

Book for Commemoration of the Living and the Dead. Fr. Lawrence, trans. Jordanville, NY: Holy Trinity Monastery, [date of publication unknown].

Brianchaninov, Bishop Ignatius Brianchaninov. *Collected Works*. Tuzov ed. St. Petersburg, 1883.

Bunson, Matthew. *Our Sunday Visitor's Encyclopedia of Catholic History*. Huntington, IN: Our Sunday Visitor Publishing, 2004.

Butler, Alban. *Butler's Lives of the Saints*, 12 vols. Collegeville, MN: Liturgical Press, 1995–2000.

Butler, Alfred. *The Ancient Coptic Churches of Egypt* 2. London, ENG: Clarendon Press, 1884.

Chadwick, Henry. *Augustine: A Very Short Introduction*. New York, NY: Oxford University Press, 2001.

Clapton, Edward. *The Life of St. George*. London, ENG: Swan Sonnenschein & Co. Limited, 1903.

Cobb, Sylvanus. *The New Testament of our Lord and Savior Jesus Christ with Explanatory Notes and Practical Observations*. Boston, MA: [self-published by Cobb] 1864.

The convent of the great martyr St. Philopater Mercurius. *Tamav Erene and Glorious Horizons in Monastic Life, Part II*. Old Cairo, Egypt: The Convent of the Great Martyr St. Philopater Mercurius "Abi Seifein" for nuns, 2009.

The convent of the great martyr St. Philopater Mercurius. *Tamav Erene: The Jewel of Heaven and the Beacon of Monasticism*. Old Cairo, Egypt: The Convent of the Great Martyr St. Philopater Mercurius "Abi Seifein" for nuns, 2007.

The convent of the great martyr St. Philopater Mercurius. *Tamav Erene: A Monastic Life Kindled with Love at the Feet of Christ—Book 3*. Old Cairo, Egypt: The Convent of the Great Martyr St. Philopater Mercurius "Abi Seifein" for nuns, 2010.

Coptic Orthodox Church Diocese of Qena. *Blessed Servant: Life & Miracles of the Thrice Blessed His Grace Late Bishop Makarios of Qena*. Qena, Egypt: Diocese of Qena, 2010.

Coptic Orthodox Church of Saint Mark. *The Holy Pascha According to the Rites of the Coptic Orthodox Church*. Jersey City, NJ: Coptic Orthodox Church of Saint Mark, 2008.

Coptic Synaxarium. 4 vols. Chicago, IL: St. George Coptic Orthodox Church, 1987–1995.

Davis, Stephen. *The Popes of Egypt: The Early Coptic Papacy*. Cairo, Egypt: American University in Cairo Press, 2004.

The Divine Liturgies of Saints Basil, Gregory, and Cyril. Tallahassee, FL: St. Mary & St. George Coptic Orthodox Church, Coptic Orthodox Diocese of the Southern United States, 2001.

Dowling, John. *The History of Romanism: from the Earliest Corruptions of Christianity to the Present*. New York, NY: Edward Walker, 1845.

El-Masri, Iris Habib. *The Story of the Copts: The True Story of Christianity in Egypt*. Newberry Springs, CA: St. Anthony Coptic Orthodox Monastery of Southern California, year unclear—possibly 1978.

Elem, Susanna. *Virgins of God*. Oxford, ENG: Oxford University Press, 2004.

Elsley, J. and James Slade. *Annotations on the Four Gospels and the Acts of the Apostles: Compiled and Abridged for the Use of Students*. London, ENG: C. & J. Rivington, 1824.

Encyclopedia of Ancient Christianity. 3 vols. Angelo Berardino, ed. Downers Grove, IL: IVP Academic, 2014.

Esbroeck, Michel Van. The Coptic Encyclopedia. New York, NY: Macmillan, 1991.

Eusebius: The Church History. Paul L. Maier, trans. Grand Rapids, MI: Kregel Publications, 1999.

Feldman, Louis and Gohei Hata. *Josephus, the Bible, and History*. Tokyo, JP: Yamamoto Shoten Publishing House, 1988.

Ferguson, Everett. *Baptism in the Early Church: History, Theology, and Liturgy in the First Five Centuries*. Cambridge, UK: Wm. B. Eerdmans Publishing Co., 2009.

Gabra, Gawdat. *The A to Z of the Coptic Church*. Plymouth, UK: Scarecrow Press, Inc., 2008.

Goggin, Thomas. *The Fathers of the Church: Saint John Chrysostom, Commentary on Saint John the Apostle and Evangelist: Homilies 48-88, Volume 2*. Washington, DC: CUA Press, 2000.

Goodrich, Richard J. *Contextualizing Cassian: Aristocrats, Asceticism, and*

Reformation in Fifth Century Gaul. New York, NY: Oxford University Press, 2007.

Hanna, Fr. Markos. *The Coptic Offices for the Coptic Orthodox Church, Part IV: Funeral Services.* Los Angeles, CA: St. Mark Coptic Orthodox Church, 1995.

Herzog, Johan and Philip Schaff. *A Religious Encyclopedia* 3. New York, NY: Christian Literature Co., 1889.

Johnston, Francis. *When Millions Saw Mary.* Chulmleigh, Devon, ENG: Augustine Publishing Company, 1980.

Jurgens, Williams A. *The Faith of the Early Fathers.* 3 vols. Collegeville, MN: The Liturgical Press, 1978-1979.

Kallistos, Metropolitan (Timothy Ware). *The Orthodox Church.* London, ENG: Penguin Books, 1997.

Kia, Mehrdad. *The Persian Empire: A Historical Encyclopedia.* 2 vols. Santa Barbara, CA: ABC-CLIO, 2016.

Kuhn, Karl Heinz. *A Panegyric on John the Baptist attributed to Theodosius Archbishop of Alexandria.* Louvain, Belgium: Secrétariat du CorpusSCO, 1966.

Late Antiquity: A guide to the Postclassical World. Glen Warren Bowersock, Peter Brown, and Oleg Grabar, eds. Cambridge, MA: Harvard University Press, 1999.

The Letters of Saint Boniface. Ephraim Emerton, trans. New York, NY: Farrar, Strauss and Giroux, 1973.

Light from Light: Scientists and Theologians in Dialogue. Gerald O'Collins, Mary Ann Meyers, eds. Cambridge, UK: Wm. B. Eerdmans Publishing Co., 2012.

Lives of Saints. Demetrius of Rostov ed. Moscow, Russia: Synodal Printshop, 1902.

Luttikhuizen, Gerard. *Paradise Interpreted: Representations of Biblical Paradise in Judaism and Christianity.* Leiden, NL: Brill, 1999.

MacEvilly, John. *An exposition of the Gospel of St. Luke.* New York, NY: Benziger Brothers, 1898.

Malaty, Father Tadros. *The Book of Revelation.* Alexandria, Egypt: St. George's Coptic Orthodox Church, 1996.

Malaty, Father Tadros. *Dictionary of Church Terms.* Alexandria, Egypt: St. George's Coptic Orthodox Church, 1992.

Malaty, Father Tadros. *The Gospel According to St. John: Part One.* Alexandria, Egypt: St. George's Coptic Orthodox Church, 2003.

Malaty, Father Tadros. *The School of Alexandria, Book One, Before Origen.* Jersey

City, NJ: St. Mark's Coptic Orthodox Church, 1995.

Malaty, Father Tadros. *The School of Alexandria, Book Two: The Deans of the School of Alexandria, Origen.* Jersey City, NJ: St. Mark's Coptic Orthodox Church, 1995.

Markides, Kyriacos C. *The Mountain of Silence.* New York, NY: Image Books | Doubleday, 2001.

Matta El-Maskeen (Matthew the Poor). *The Coptic Calendar.* Nitrian Desert, Egypt: The Monastery of St. Macarius, 1988.

Matthew the Poor. *Orthodox Prayer Life.* Crestwood, NY: St. Vladimir's Seminary Press, 2003.

Meinardus, Otto. *Two Thousand Years of Coptic Christianity.* Cairo, Egypt: The American University in Cairo Press, 2002.

Mettaous, H.G. Bishop. *Sacramental Rites in the Coptic Orthodox Church.* El-Syrian Monastery, year unclear—possibly 2000.

Metwalli, Nahed Mahmoud. *Islam Encounters Christ: A Fanatical Muslim's Encounter with Christ in the Coptic Orthodox Church.* Edina, MN: Light & Life Publishing Company, 2002.

Middleton, Paul. *Martyrdom: A Guide for the Perplexed.* London, ENG: T&T Clark International, 2011.

Mikhail, Albair Gamal. *The Essentials in the Deacon's Service.* Shobra, Egypt: Shikolani, 2002.

Mileant, Bishop Alexander. *Life After Death.* Pamphlet, Los Angeles, CA: Holy Protection Russian Orthodox Church, 1999.

Mystic Treatises by Isaac of Nineveh. A.J. Wensinck, trans. Amsterdam, Netherlands: Netherlands Academy of Arts and Sciences, 1923.

The New Schaff-Herzog Encyclopedia of Religious Knowledge 3-4. Samuel M. Jackson, ed. New York, NY: Funk and Wagnalls Company, 1909.

Nicene and Post-Nicene Fathers: First Series. Philip Schaff, ed. 1886-1889. Repr. New York, NY: Cosimo, Inc., 2007.

Nicene and Post-Nicene Fathers: Second Series. Philip Schaff and Henry Wallace, eds. 1890-1900.

On the Incarnation. John Behr and Augustine Casiday, eds. Yonkers, NY: St. Vladimir's Seminary Press, 2011.

On the Literal Meaning of Genesis 2. Johannes Quaster, Walter Burghardt, and Thomas Lawler, eds. Mahwah, NJ: Paulist Press, 1982.

On Wealth and Poverty. Catherine Ross, trans. Crestwood, NY: St. Vladimir's

Seminary Press, 1999.

Pamphilus, Eusebius. *The Life of the Blessed Emperor Constantine.* Merchantville, NJ: Evolution Publishing, 2009.

The Paradise of the Holy Fathers. 2 vols. E.A. Wallis Budge, ed. Putty, AU: St. Shenouda Monastery Press, 2009.

Parker, John. *Tertullian: Apologetic and Practical Treatises.* London, ENG: J. G. F. and J. Rivington, 1842.

Pelikan, Jaroslav. *Mary Through the Centuries.* New Haven, CT: Yale University Press, 1996.

Perry, Paul. *Visions & Miracles* ([DVD], Vanguard Cinema, 2010).

Pope Kyrollos VI Sons. *St. Mary's Modern Miracles.* Maryut, Egypt: St. Mena Monastery, 2003.

Rawlings, Maurice. *Beyond Death's Door.* Nashville, TN: Thomas Nelson, Inc., 1978.

Rose, Seraphim. *The Soul After Death.* Platina, CA: St. Herman of Alaska Brotherhood, 2009.

Rousseau, P. *Pachomius.* Berkeley, CA: University of California Press, 1985.

Rubenson, Samuel. *The Letters of St. Antony: Monasticism and the Making of a Saint.* London, ENG: A&C Black, 1995.

Russell, Jeffrey Burton. *Satan: The Early Christian Tradition.* New York, NY: Cornell University Press, 1981.

Sayings of the Desert Fathers: The Alphabetical Collection. Benedicta Ward, trans. Trappist, Kentucky: Cistercian Publications, 2006.

Scheck, Thomas and Christopher Hall. *Ancient Christian Texts: Homilies on Numbers, Origen.* Downers Grove, IL: InterVarsity Press, 2009.

Seyffert, Oskar. *A Dictionary of Classical Antiquities: Mythology, Religion, Literature and Art.* London, ENG: Swan Sonnenschein and Co.; New York: Macmillan and Co., 1895.

Shenouda III, His Holiness Pope. *Have You Seen The One I Love.* North Charleston, SC: BookSurge Publishing, 2008.

Shenouda III, His Holiness Pope. *Many Years with the People's Questions, Part I.* El Kawmia, Cairo: Dar El Tebaa, 1993.

Shenouda III, His Holiness Pope. *Many Years with the People's Questions, Part IV.* El Kawmia, Cairo, Egypt: Dar El Tebaa, 1993.

Shenouda III, His Holiness Pope. *The Seven Words of Our Lord on the Cross.* El

Kawmia, Cairo: Dar El Tebaa, 1991.

St. Adamnan. *Life of St. Columba.* Wentworth Huyshe, trans. London, ENG: George Routledge & Sons, Ltd., 1939.

St. Nikodimus of the Holy Mountain and St. Makarios of Corinth. *The Philokalia: The Complete Text* 1. G.E.H. Palmer, Philip Sherrard, and Kallistos Ware, eds and trans. New York, NY: Faber and Faber, Inc., 1979.

Stokstad, Marilyn. *Medieval Art.* Boulder, CO: Westview Press, 2004.

Swarup, Paul. *The Self-Understanding of the Dead Sea Scrolls Community.* London, ENG: T&T Clark International, 2006.

Thurston, Herbert. *The Catholic Encyclopedia.* New York, NY: Robert Appleton Company, 1910.

Tikhon, Archimandrite. *Everyday Saints and Other Stories.* Moscow, Russia: Pokrov Publications, 2012.

Trevett, Christine. *Montanism: Gender, Authority, and the New Prophecy.* New York, NY: Cambridge University Press, 2002.

Trombley, Frank. *Hellenic Religion and Christianization.* Boston, MA: Brill Academic Publishers, Inc., 2001.

Uekskuell, K. *Orthodox Life* 26.4 (July–August 1976): 1–36.

Van Doorn-Harder, Pieternella. *Contemporary Coptic Nuns.* Columbia, SC: University of South Carolina Press, 1995.

Ware, Kallistos. "'One Body in Christ': Death and the Communion of Saints," *Sobornost/ECR* 3.2 (1981): 179–191.

Watson, John. *Among the Copts.* Portland, OR: Sussex Academic Press, 2002.

The Way of a Pilgrim and The Pilgrim Continues His Way: A New Translation. Helen Bacovcin, trans. New York, NY: Doubleday Image Books, 1992.

Youannis, H.G. Bishop. *Heaven: An Orthodox Christian Perspective.* Los Angeles, CA: Saint Paul Brotherhood, 2007.

Youssef, H.G. Bishop. "Abu-Seifein: Loyalty Perseveres." http://suscopts.org/resources/literature/298/abu-seifein-loyalty-perseveres/. Retrieved July 3, 2012.

www.ingramcontent.com/pod-product-compliance
Lightning Source LLC
Chambersburg PA
CBHW031312160426
43196CB00007B/501